The Storyteller's Daughter

'This is an extraordinary book by a remarkable young woman. Afghan by descent, but brought up in England, she claims to have thought herself half Western liberal, half wild Afghan warrior. To try and resolve this conflict she went to Afghanistan at the time of the Soviet invasion and was propelled into the world of the mujahidin. She was twenty-one years old, and beautiful: dangerous some would think, but she spoke Farsi, knew all their traditions; they treated her as one of them. Her courage is such that even reading about some of her exploits is frightening. This book will speak not only to the many people who admire the Afghan people and pity their ordeals, but to those like Saira Shah who owe allegiance to two cultures . . . more and more of them now in the world.

This is such a good book. There is not likely to be a better one about Afghanistan.'

Doris Lessing

'This is a remarkable and essential book about Afghanistan which succeeds in describing the people of that country – men and also women – their identities, hopes, fears, generosity and cruelties, all of which have too long been buried under the rubble of endless geopolitical clashes. It is alive with detail, emotion, myth, fable, bleeding reality and those laughs and freedoms which arise defiantly out of the darkest of times to assert the human spirit. Saira Shah's descriptions of her relatives – Auntie Soraya with her folded painted face, for example – are written from the position of an intimate who is also an outsider with values which do not forgive the unforgivable. The murders, threats, violence of life in the Afghanistan she has previously only known in the stories fail to really disarm this brave woman with enviable verve and imagination.'

Yasmin Alibhai-Brown

'Saira Shah takes us on an extraordinary journey from an English childhood, laced with Afghan myths handed down from her forebears, to the terrors and complexities of present Afghanistan. The transport is her own lyrical and expressive telling of a tale that only an Afghan-born English-educated child could ever tell. She embraces an amazing breadth of history, family, and plain old East/West collision. At the end of it you are left with the truest sense of this magical country together with the recognition this exceptional English writer is still unmistakably Afghani.'

Jon Snow

'*The Storyteller's Daughter* is the deeply moving account of two daring journeys: one across the deadly front lines of wartime Afghanistan, and the other between the author's different selves: mild-mannered girl from rural England, and fiery daughter of Afghan nobility, fuelled by the untameable passion of her ancestry.

Few books successfully evoke the profound joys and pains of such adventure: this is one of them. As a personal memoir it is both poignant and incisive. It is also a timely and important book which sheds light on much that is misunderstood about the country and the complex bounty of its culture. Here is a book written with resolute grace, much humour, and underpinned by an unflinching spirit of enquiry. It is impossible not to admire the author for her bravery and penetrating honesty.'

Jason Elliot

The Storyteller's Daughter

SAIRA SHAH

MICHAEL JOSEPH
an imprint of
PENGUIN BOOKS

MICHAEL JOSEPH

Published by the Penguin Group
Penguin Books Ltd, 80 Strand, London WC2R ORL, England
Penguin Putnam Inc., 375 Hudson Street, New York, New York 10014, USA
Penguin Books Australia Ltd, 250 Camberwell Road, Camberwell, Victoria 3124, Australia
Penguin Books Canada Ltd, 10 Alcorn Avenue, Toronto, Ontario, Canada M4V 3B2
Penguin Books India (P) Ltd, 11 Community Centre,
Panchsheel Park, New Delhi – 110 017, India
Penguin Books (NZ) Ltd, Cnr Rosedale and Airborne Roads,
Albany, Auckland, New Zealand
Penguin Books (South Africa) (Pty) Ltd, 24 Sturdee Avenue,
Rosebank 2196, South Africa

Penguin Books Ltd, Registered Offices: 80 Strand, London WC2R ORL, England

www.penguin.com

First published 2003
1

Set in 12/14.75 pt Monotype Bembo
Typeset by Rowland Phototypesetting Ltd, Bury St Edmunds, Suffolk
Printed in England by Clays Ltd, St Ives plc

A CIP catalogue record for this book is available from the British Library

ISBN 0-718-14562-3

For James, in loving memory

Acknowledgements

The list of thanks is very long – and I apologize in advance to those I have forgotten.

First of all, I owe a huge debt to three companions along the way: James Miller for his extraordinary talent and toughness during *Beneath the Veil* and *Unholy War*, and for his unstinting generosity, friendship and support during the writing of this book; Cassian Harrison for being a brilliant producer, director and friend on *Beneath the Veil*; and Beat Kraettli, with whom I shared so many adventures.

I'd also like to thank the many people who helped me in Pakistan and Afghanistan, some of whom I can't name, and many whose names I don't know, but who include: the brave women of RAWA; Homaira Usman; Usman Najand; John Weaver; Samiullah; Kamal and Jamal Hyder; and all at UNOCHA.

Special thanks are due to David Henshaw of Hard-cash Productions, executive producer of *Beneath the Veil* and *Unholy War*, who gave me the opportunity to go to Afghanistan in 2000 and 2001; to Dorothy Byrne of Channel Four Television who took a risk with me on *Beneath the Veil*, and who sent me back again to make *Unholy War* after 11 September; to David Lloyd, also at Channel Four Television, who has supported me so often and for so long; to Jennifer Hyde of CNN, who championed *Beneath the Veil* before 11 September and to all else at CNN, particularly Vivien Schiller; and to Rebecca Carter, for her good advice.

I'm deeply grateful to my editors, Louise Moore and Sonny Mehta – who have nerves of steel – and to my wonderful agent, Patrick Walsh, who persuaded me I should write about Afghanistan, and who envisaged this book even before I did.

Finally, I owe both thanks and apologies to my family: my mother, who has spent years of her life worrying about me; my brother and sister, who have spent years of theirs covering for me; all my relatives in Peshawar, India and Afghanistan, whom I hope will one day forgive me. However, my biggest debt is to the storytellers: my aunt Amina, my grandfather Sirdar Ikbal Ali Shah and, above all, my late father, who taught me that you only truly own what cannot be lost in a shipwreck. To them, I owe everything, and without them this book could not have been written.

Permissions

All material from the works of Idries Shah reproduced, quoted or retold with permission from the Estate of Idries Shah.

Quotations from the *Gulistan* of Sa'adi adapted from the translation by Edward Eastwick (with permission of the Sufi Trust) or from manuscript translations by Idries Shah (with permission of the Estate of Idries Shah).

Quotations from Rumi's *Masnavi i Ma'anavi* adapted from the translation of E. H. Whinfield (with permission of the Sufi Trust), or from published and unpublished translations by Idries Shah (by permission of the Estate of Idries Shah). Quotations from other works of Jalaluddin Rumi from published or unpublished translations by Idries Shah (with permission of the Estate of Idries Shah).

Quotations by Bobo taken from her pseudonymous and lightly fictionalized memoirs: *My Khyber Marriage* and *Valley of the Giant Buddhas* by Morag Murray Abdullah. With permission of the Octagon Press Ltd.

For security, I have changed names (even code names) and minor details that might prejudice the safety of RAWA's operatives and operations.

The names of some of the characters in this book have been changed.

BOOK ONE
The Garden

Wherever there is a spring of fresh water, men and bees and ants will gather.

Jalaluddin Rumi

I

I am three years old. I am sitting on my father's knee. He is telling me of a magical place: the fairytale landscape you enter in dreams. Fountains fling diamond droplets into mosaic pools. Coloured birds sing in the fruit-laden orchards. The pomegranates burst and their insides are rubies. Fruit is so abundant that even the goats are fed on melons. The water has magical properties: you can fill to bursting with fragrant *pilau*, then step to the brook and drink – and you will be ready to eat another meal.

On three sides of the plateau majestic mountains tower, capped with snow. The fourth side overlooks a sunny valley where, gleaming far below, sprawls a city of villas and minarets. And here is the best part of the story: it is true.

The garden is in Paghman, where my family had its seat for nine hundred years. The jewel-like city it overlooks is the Afghan capital, Kabul. The people of Paghman call the capital Kabul *jan*: beloved Kabul. We call it that too, for this is where we belong.

'Whatever outside appearances may be, no matter who tells you otherwise, this garden, this country, these are your origin. This is where you are truly from. Keep it in your heart, Saira *jan*. Never forget.'

★

Any Western adult might have told me that this was an exile's tale of a lost Eden: the place you dream about, to which you can never return. But even then, I wasn't going to accept that. Even then, I had absorbed enough of the East to feel I belonged there. And too much of the West not to try to nail down dreams.

My father understood the value of stories: he was a writer. My parents had picked Kent as an idyllic place to bring up their children, but we were never allowed to forget our Afghan background.

Periodically during my childhood, my father would come upon the kitchen like a storm. Western systematic method quickly melted before the inspiration of the East. Spice jars tumbled down from their neat beech-wood rack and disgorged heaps of coloured powder on to the melamine sideboard. Every pan was pressed into service and extra ones were borrowed from friends and neighbours. The staid old Aga wheezed exotic vapours – *saffran*, *zeera*, *gashneesh*; their scents to this day are as familiar to me as my own breath.

In the midst of this mayhem presided my father, the alchemist. Like so many expatriates, when it came to maintaining the traditions, customs and food of his own country he was *plus royaliste que le roi*. Rather than converting lead into gold, my father's alchemical art transported our English country kitchen to the furthest reaches of the Hindu Kush.

We children were the sorcerer's apprentices: we chopped onions and split cardamom pods, nibbling the fragrant black seeds as we worked. We crushed garlic and we peeled tomatoes. He showed us how to steep

4

saffron, to strain yoghurt and to cook the rice until it was *dana-dar*, possessing grains — that is, to the point where it crumbles into three or four perfect round seeds if you rub it between your fingers.

In the kitchen, my father's essential *Afghaniyat*, Afghan-ness, was most apparent. The Afghan love of *pilau* is as fundamental to the national character as the Italian fondness for spaghetti. The Amir Habibullah, a former ruler of Afghanistan, would demolish a vast meal of *pilau*, meatballs and sauce for lunch, then turn to his courtiers and ask: 'Now, noblemen and friends, what shall we cook tonight?'

We knew to produce at least three times more *pilau* than anyone could ever be expected to eat. Less would have been an insult to our name and contrary to the Afghan character. As my great-great-great-grandfather famously roared: 'How dare you ask me for a *small* favour?'

If, at any point, my father found himself with an unexpected disaster — rice that went soggy or an over-boiling pan that turned the Aga's hotplate into a sticky mess — he would exclaim: 'Back in Afghanistan, we had cooks to do this work!'

He would tell us, with Afghan hyperbole: 'We are making a *Shahi pilau*, a *pilau* fit for kings. This recipe has been handed down through our family since it was prepared for up to four thousand guests at the court of your ancestors. It is far better than the *pilau* you will find when you visit homes in Afghanistan today.'

On one notable occasion, my father discovered the artificial food colouring, tartrazine. A *pilau*-making session was instantly convened. Like a conjurer pulling off a particularly effective trick, he showed us how just one tiny teaspoon could transform a gigantic cauldron of *pilau* to a virulent shade of yellow. We were suitably impressed. From that moment on, traditional saffron was discarded for this intoxicating substance.

Years later, I learned that all of the Afghan dishes my father had taught me diverged subtly from their originals. His method of finishing off the parboiled rice in the oven, for example, was an innovation of his own. Straining yoghurt through cheesecloth turned out to be merely the first stage in an elaborate process. In Kent, rancid sheep's fat was hard to come by, so he substituted butter. Cumin was an Indian contamination. And so it went on.

Yet although his methods and even his ingredients were different, my father's finished dishes tasted indistinguishable from the originals. He had conveyed their essential quality; the minutiae had been swept away.

During these cookery sessions, we played a wonderful game. We planned the family trip to Afghanistan that always seemed to be just round the corner. How we would go back to Paghman, stroll in the gardens, visit our old family home and greet the relatives we had never met. When we arrived in the Paghman mountains, the men would fire their guns in the air – we shouldn't worry, that was the Afghan way of welcome and celebration. They would carry us on their shoulders, whooping and cheering, and in the evening we would eat a *pilau* that eclipsed even the great feasts of the court of our ancestors.

My mother's family background, which is Parsee from India, rarely got a look in. As far as my father was concerned, his offspring were pure Afghan. For years, the mere mention of the Return was enough to stoke us children into fits of excitement. It was so much more alluring than our mundane Kentish lives, which revolved round the family's decrepit Land Rover and our pet labrador, Honey.

'Can we take the Land Rover?' asked my brother Tahir.

'We shall take a fleet of Land Rovers,' said my father grandly.

My sister Safia piped up: 'Can we take Honey?'

There was an uncomfortable pause. Even my father's flight of fantasy balked at introducing to Afghans as a beloved member of our family that unclean animal, the dog.

When I was fifteen, the Soviet Union invaded and occupied Afghanistan. During a *pilau*-making session quite soon after that, I voiced an anxiety that had been growing for some time now. How could my father expect us to be truly Afghan when we had grown up outside an Afghan community? When we went back home, wouldn't we children be strangers, foreigners in our own land? I expected, and possibly hoped for, the soothing account of our triumphant and immi-nent return to Paghman. It didn't come. My father looked tired and sad. His answer startled me: 'I've given you stories to replace a community. They are your community.'

'But surely stories can't replace experience.'

He picked up a packet of dehydrated onion. 'Stories are like these onions – like dried experience. They aren't the original experience but they are more than nothing at all. You think about a story, you turn it over in your mind, and it becomes something else.' He added hot water to the onion. 'It's not fresh onion – fresh experience – but it is something that can help you to recognize experience when you come across it. Experiences follow patterns, which repeat themselves again and again. In our tradition, stories can help you recognize the shape of an experience, to make sense of and to deal with it. So, you see, what you may take for mere snippets of myth and legend encapsulate what you need to know to guide you on your way anywhere among Afghans.'

'Well, as soon as I'm eighteen I'm going to go to see for myself,' I said, adding craftily: 'Then perhaps I'll have fresh experiences that will help me grow up.'

My father had been swept along on the tide of his analogy. Now, he suddenly became a parent whose daughter was at an impressionable age and whose country was embroiled in a murderous war.

'If you would only grow up a little in the first place,' he snapped, 'then you would realize that you don't need to go at all.'

April 2001

At thirty-six years old, I have never seen Afghanistan at peace. I am choking under the *burqa*, the pale blue veil, which begins in a cap upon my head. It covers my face, my body, my arms and my legs, and is long enough

8

to trip me up in my muddy plastic shoes. A crocheted grille obscures my vision. A grid of black shadows intersects trees, fields and the white road outside. It is like looking out through prison bars.

I have not had enough air for four hours now and we have eight more to go before we reach Kabul. I have an almost irresistible urge to do whatever it takes to breathe, simply breathe. How can I describe it? I want to rip off the *burqa* in the way that a drowning man will grapple his rescuer in his urge to reach the air above. But I cannot: it is all that protects me from the Taliban. Even lifting the front flap of my *burqa* is a crime, punishable by a beating.

In the front of the car, the taxi driver fumbles in a secret compartment and produces a cassette. It is a good sign: music is banned. I was told that we would have a safe car with a driver we knew, but when it came down to it, we jumped into a taxi at random. If he is willing to play music in front of us, perhaps the taxi driver and we may trust each other. We are fellow conspirators. Perhaps he will not give us away.

Afghan popular music blares out, singing of lover and beloved. The Taliban detest this kind of language. The refrain goes, '*Jan, jan . . .*' and I feel a sudden flash of happiness. It's crazy: in ten minutes, I could be dead. But I can't help myself. We are heading for Kabul – beloved Kabul.

On the face of it, I am a journalist, filming a documentary for Channel Four Television, called *Beneath the Veil* about the Taliban's Afghanistan. Now I have left my crew behind, to travel in disguise with

9

the Revolutionary Association of the Women of Afghanistan.

We have just crossed the border illegally into Taliban-controlled Afghanistan. As a Westerner, if I am caught, I may be imprisoned and accused of espionage. If the Taliban discover my family history and decide I am an Afghan, then I share the same risks as the Afghan women who are helping me: torture, a bullet in the head or simply disappearing in Pul i Charki, Kabul's notorious political prison. The women are willing to take this risk because they belong to an organization that opposes the Taliban. Their activities – secret schools and clinics for women – are already politically subversive enough to get them killed.

Beside me, my female companion is being sick. She holds a plastic bag, and vomits without lifting her *burqa*.

I don't need to ask her what she is doing here: I need to ask myself.

For many years, in the secret cubbyhole where precious things were stored, my father kept a dusty file containing two pieces of paper. The first was the crumbling title deed to our estate in Paghman. The other was our family tree, stretching back before the Prophet Muhammad, two thousand years back, to the time before my family had even heard of Afghanistan.

The title deed was no longer worth the paper it was written on. In Afghanistan, if you are not present to defend your property, you had better be prepared to take it back by the gun. As for our family tree, we didn't need a piece of paper to tell us who we were.

My father, and his father before him, saw to it that our lineage was etched on our hearts.

Our family traces its descent through Fatima, the daughter of the Prophet Muhammad. The man who, during his lifetime, founded one of the world's great monotheistic religions, who united the feuding tribes of Arabia, and who could have accumulated wealth beyond compare, died in poverty. On his deathbed he left this bequest: 'I have nothing to leave you, except my family.' Since then, his descendants have been revered throughout the Muslim world. They are entitled to use the honorific Sayed.

My grandfather maintained that ancestry was something to try to live up to, not to boast about. As an old man, his hooded, faintly Mongolian eyes, his hooked nose and his tall *karakul* lambskin hat made him look like an inscrutable sage from a Mughal miniature. I remember this venerable figure telling me a joke: 'They asked a mule: "What kind of creature are you?" He replied: "Well, my mother was a horse!"'

The old man laughed, enjoying the punch-line, and so did I, though I barely understood it. 'Do you understand? He was only a mule, but he boasted of the horse, his ancestor! So, you see, Saira *jan*, it is less important who your forebears were than what you yourself become.'

Islam, as I absorbed it, was a tolerant philosophy, which encouraged one to adopt a certain attitude to life. The Qur'an we studied taught: 'There is no compulsion in religion.' The Prophet we followed said: 'The holy warrior is he who struggles with himself.'

Many of the sayings of the Prophet that I was raised on are from a compilation by the Afghan authority Baghawi of Herat. In the orthodox Muslim world it is eclipsed by the monumental collection of Imam Bokhari. Bokhari set out to preserve the literal words and traditions of the Prophet as an act of pious scholasticism. He investigated six hundred thousand sayings, passing only around five thousand as incontestably authentic.

The purpose of Baghawi's collection, on the other hand, is instrumental, rather than scholastic. It was revered by the classical Persian poets, and is widely used in dervish mystical communities to this day. Sayings are included for content. The distinction between these two great Islamic figures is a matter of emphasis: the literal or the spiritual.

Probably because Afghans were thin on the ground in Tunbridge Wells, my father hired an Iranian Qur'an teacher for us. We didn't like him. He felt that, when it came to the Holy Word of God, rote learning was more important than understanding. He slapped my six-year-old sister for failing to memorize in Arabic the mystical verse from the Qur'an known as the Niche for Lights:

Allah is the light of the heavens and of the earth.
His light is like a niche, wherein there is a lamp:
The lamp within a glass, the glass like unto a pearly star.
It is lit from a blessed olive tree
Neither of the East, nor of the West
The oil of which itself shines, although fire has touched
    it not:
Light upon light!

Outside our sealed bubble of tolerant Muslim culture, the Islamic world was changing. Some years before the Iranian revolution, our Qur'an teacher became fascinated by the ideas of Ayatollah Khomeini. He was hurriedly dismissed, and he eventually returned to Iran to study in a religious seminary. When the thirst for Islamic revolution had stirred his heart sufficiently, he decided he had been brought to our household for a purpose: to witness the depravity and error into which our branch of the family of the Prophet had sunk. For a while, we children were hurried past the thick laurel bushes in the driveway, in case our erstwhile Qur'an instructor was lurking there, ready to attack us.

What unacceptable religious ideas had he encountered in our home? What teachings did he find so detrimental to the hearts of the faithful? Perhaps Baghawi of Herat's sayings of the Prophet, which adjured one to think for oneself rather than conform to externals without question:

'One hour's teaching is better than a whole night of prayer.'
'Trust in God, but tie your camel first.'
'The ink of the learned is holier than the blood of the martyr.'
'You ask me to curse unbelievers, but I was not sent to curse.'
'I order you to help any oppressed person, whether they are Muslim or not.'
'Women are the twin halves of men.'

These were the values I grew up with. This was the Islam I bought into.

April 2001

Now I have entered a world where I am forbidden to show my face, paint my nails or fly a kite. Nothing is too trivial for the scholars of Islamic law to prohibit. Even paper bags are banned – just in case the paper they are composed of should chance to have written upon it the Holy Name of Allah, which might consequently run the risk of defilement. Allah really cares about getting the details right. There is a serious debate raging as to whether the acceptable Islamic way to punish homosexuality is by tipping a wall over the offender, or by throwing him off the highest minaret.

Nothing is permitted unless the Holy Qur'an specifically sanctions it, or unless it is an authenticated practice of the Prophet. Everything else must undergo examination by the religious scholars. They use a rigorous process of analogy and theological debate to determine what is permitted and what is prohibited. The Ministry for the Prevention of Vice and the Promotion of Virtue, the feared religious police, enforces their edicts.

The twenty-first century throws up constant challenges to faith. Television and video are banned, but cassette tape might contain Qur'anic recitations. It should only be destroyed if there is music on it. Instrumental music is not permitted, but simple religious chants are allowed.

Cigarettes are permitted, but some cigarette packets

have pictures of women on them. These are banned. The strictest care must be taken not to allow images of the human form. Passport photographs present a dilemma. It has been determined that the heads and shoulders of males may be shown, for the purpose of identification. Top-to-toe shots are unlawful.

The stakes are high: this is the prototype for a perfect Islamic state. Morals must be above reproach. Women must be protected, and the best way to do that is to keep them indoors. They are prohibited from going outside without a male relative as an escort. Even then, they must be entirely covered in the *burqa*, to prevent them leading men into temptation. Girls over nine are barred from school. Females are banned from almost all jobs.

Sufism, the philosophical tradition of my forebears, has been pushed underground. The Taliban deplore its assertion that spiritual essentials are more important than external practices.

My ancestors maintained that the Qur'an was revealed in seven layers, with an outer, literal meaning, and successive deeper levels of mystical value. Their suggestion that, while it is possible to rise by the Shariah, the religious law, the Prophet also had an inner circle of disciples to whom he taught an esoteric path, is now regarded as heresy.

The border post at the mouth of the Khyber Pass is controlled by Taliban guards. Through the *burqa*'s grille I see them patrolling. They wear the trademark black turbans of Kandahar, the hometown of their movement. We will have to cross the frontier on foot, under their gaze. Wearing the *burqa* is an art that I haven't had time to acquire, and I trip trying to clamber out of the car. I am aware that I walk too confidently: like a Westerner – or a man. I try to look suitably submissive. I hunch my shoulders and attempt to efface even my thoughts.

There are three of us. A man and a woman alone might excite suspicion: the Taliban might demand proof that we are married or related. But one man with two veiled women, following a few footsteps behind, is too common a sight to arouse suspicion.

I have rehearsed my cover story and learned off pat the answers I will give if I am stopped and questioned. My name is Fatima. I come from the southern town of Ghazni. I am an Afghan refugee, returning to visit my family in Kabul for my sister's wedding. I am Persian-speaking. I do not speak Pushtu, the language of the Taliban.

But nobody stops me. The Taliban guards neither smile nor scowl as we pass. They do not even look at me. I require no documents. I am merely a notation on the papers of my male escort. As a woman, I have ceased to exist. The *burqa* is my passport, my cloak of invisibility.

It occurs to me that I have been doing this all my life: using the raw materials of a culture to subvert it. Although I have spent my adult life chasing the dream of a national identity, my allegiance is not to a country, or even to a tribe. It is to a set of values.

Two people live inside me. Like a couple who rarely speak, they are not compatible. My Western side is a sensitive, liberal, middle-class pacifist. My Afghan side I can only describe as a rapacious robber baron. It revels in bloodshed, glories in risk and will not be afraid.

In 1842, nearly five thousand fighting men – the whole Kabul force of the British army – were hacked to pieces by an Afghan horde. Twelve thousand camp followers – unarmed and innocent civilians – were also butchered. Only one man made it to safety. The exhausted Dr Brydon, humiliatingly mounted on a donkey, was the sole surviving representative of Afghanistan's British occupiers. His arrival brought tidings to a stunned world that an entire British army had been wiped out. This human catastrophe inspired a gloating Afghan battle song:

> Doktor brydon, khar-i lang-ash
> Ham quwad dar khak-i mast
>
> Doctor Brydon, on his lame donkey,
> All his troops are in our soil.

I grew up applauding a massacre that, if it happened today, I would surely condemn as an atrocity. The song has a catchy tune and I used to hum it during netball practice at my grammar school. I didn't mean anything by it politically: I was oblivious to the irony of my situation. However, if British identity can be judged by which team you support, I suppose I failed the test.

My own identity was shaped more by myths and legends than by my passport or birth certificate. Most of them enshrined lessons from history.

The disparate features of the people of Afghanistan bear the traces of countless invading armies: the fair skin of the Turkic hordes, the slant eyes of the Mongols, the blond hair of Alexander's men, the hawk-noses of Arabs. Few invaders cared for this desolate crossroads of Asia where, the Afghans say, when God finished making the world, he laughed and threw down his rubbish. Most of them were heading south, dreaming of the boundless treasures, the warm waters and the alluring, soft underbelly of India.

Rather than growing weary of war, the Afghans themselves raised armies and went to conquer and pillage. The great Afghan ruler Mahmud of Ghazna invaded India more than seventeen times. The Afghan king Babur (himself a descendant of the Mongol invaders of Afghanistan) conquered Delhi in 1526 and ruled India as the first Mughal emperor. Two centuries later, the Afghan Durrani Empire included modern Afghanistan, much of Pakistan and parts of Iran.

Running through this turbulent history was a theme: nurturing the Afghan reputation for unpredictability might help you survive.

In preparation for a British visit to his court, the late-nineteenth-century king Abdurrahman Khan ransacked the jails and dressed condemned prisoners as courtiers. Feigning a fit of pique during the audience, the king snapped his fingers. Without turning a hair, the captain of the guard gave an order, his men aimed and fired; a dozen richly dressed figures collapsed to the ground, dead.

'You are a cruel man,' gasped a horrified British officer.

'I rule, alas, a strong people,' replied the king.

How fitted that attitude is for surviving in the wild reaches of the Hindu Kush; and how particularly unsuitable for life in leafy Tunbridge Wells. I can see now that, in many ways, my family had simply refused to adapt to local conditions. It has taken me years to fling off the conviction that seafood is a poison that will kill me instantly (Afghanistan is a landlocked country, with poor roads and no refrigeration). Similarly, I grew up unable to admit to feeling fear.

You can't afford fear in a place where centuries of war mean courage is not a luxury. Above all, do not fear death: in the mountains death comes too suddenly and too often to live in dread of it. When I was a child, I was afraid of the dark. My father told me this story.

'Once upon a time there was a lion. One day, he went to the side of the water to drink. Staring back at him from the water, he saw another lion. The lion growled, but he was met by a growl of such ferocity that he jumped back. For a whole day he stayed by the pool, getting thirstier and thirstier, more and more frightened. Finally the lion's thirst overcame his fear and in desperation he bent his head deep into the water. In a trice, the other lion – which had merely been his own reflected self – disappeared and the real lion was free to take a long drink of the cool, clear water.

'Which goes to show – never, ever fear what you don't understand. Afghans do not fear, Saira *jan*. Never be afraid.'

April 2001

I have been living with fear for days now. Not the exhilarating fear of my ancestors: the roar of battle, the shot of adrenaline that spurs you on for the fight. I have never known fear quite like this before: slow and seeping fear, like cold in your bones; like toothache. I have a tremor in my core. My voice quavers. When I move, I fumble. This fear wears me down. It is as low-grade and debilitating as being chilled, damp, undernourished and weary all the time. It dwells inside me and never goes away.

I look into the faces of my companions and know that I am not alone. Fear has sunk into the fabric of Kabul life. The people who live in the ruins of the capital gave up fighting years ago, even fighting to survive. Nobody eats well. The children have huge sores. When I ask about them, people shrug: all children get them, they last for a year. They do not have a name.

We are heading for a secret school for girls. The way is muddy, and we are afraid. I despise myself for it. We arrive at an ordinary, once middle-class home. The teacher impresses me. She has pride in her eyes and smouldering anger. She used to teach in a high school. When the Taliban came to power, they dismissed her because she was a woman.

The teacher draws the net curtains in her parlour. She wears a chiffon scarf and defiant red lipstick. She smiles but the anger never leaves her eyes. It is closer to her than her jugular vein. Her anger at what is happening has become part of her soul.

Her pupils arrive in twos and threes. That way they

won't draw attention to themselves. Even the youngest girls wear the *burqa*. In the Taliban's Kabul, conceal-ment is a blessing. They enter silently and let their veils slip to the floor. After a spell in this city, it is a shock to see so many uncovered female faces. They look like flowers, in a row, upturned to the light.

I had not intended to do an interview but the teacher wants to talk. She wants the world to know what is going on here.

Do I know that seventy per cent of teachers in Kabul used to be women? Not only girls are denied education, boys are deprived of it too. If the Taliban find this class everyone in the room – children included – will be beaten and sent to jail.

I ask myself: Would I send my daughter to school if she ran the risk of ending up in jail? Ninety per cent of Afghan women are illiterate. How do you choose between jail in the present or a future without hope?

A couple of weeks ago, we drove through these streets with a Taliban chief of intelligence. I was travel-ling as part of a television documentary crew, equipped with an official journalist's visa. In his district of the city alone, he has three hundred informants. Neighbour spies on neighbour. You never know your friend from your enemy. His main task, he told me, was rooting out and rounding up members of the political oppo-sition. That means the teacher and my escorts from RAWA. That means me.

Inside me, smouldering through the coldness of my fear, I can feel the fire of anger getting stronger. The Taliban aren't just oppressive. They have corrupted all the qualities I grew up believing to be quintessentially Afghan: generosity of spirit, courage, boundless self-confidence and, above all, a sense of humour.

2

If ever, as a child, I wanted reminding of the qualities that epitomized the Afghan people, I didn't need to look further than the example of my illustrious ancestor, the mystic and warlord Jan Fishan Khan.

To this day, I can visualize the portrait of him that dominated our living room. In it he carries his famous bird-headed sword, but he is not wearing the diamond-encrusted armour he was reputed to sport upon the battlefield. He has a full black beard and splendid turban, and his hooded eyes and hooked nose are reflected in the features of members of my family to this day.

His real name was Sayed Muhammad Khan, son of Sayed Qutubuddin Khan of Paghman. His appellation – Jan Fishan – combined two concepts, the mystical and the temporal. Jan Fishan means 'scatterer of souls'. As a warlord, the Khan often had occasion to scatter the souls of his enemies. However, the name originated in a couplet of Sufi poetry, referring to the supplicant's devotion to God:

> Gar dast dehad hazar jan-am
> Dar pai mubarakat fishan-am
>
> If I had a thousand lives
> I would scatter them all at your blessed feet.

While he would have put to the sword anyone who impugned his honour, the soul-scattering Khan often displayed unexpected humility. One of his aphorisms was: 'I am so often treated better than I deserve without complaining, why should I always protest when I am treated worse?'

Jan Fishan was the last of our family to hold the title *shah-saz*, kingmaker. He was an independent warlord who held court and maintained his own standing army. Since Paghman commanded a strategic position on the heights overlooking the capital, his forces could sweep down and raid the city whenever they pleased. On the lips of the men of Paghman, the endearment Kabul *jan* – beloved Kabul – thereby acquired a certain sinister connotation.

Some years before their ill-starred invasion of Afghanistan in 1839, the British tried to intimidate Jan Fishan into becoming their ally. They invited him to India to watch a military display. To emphasize the impressive performance of their heavy guns, the British officer escorting the Khan exclaimed every time a shell was fired: 'Oh, I say! Jolly good shot! Did you see that? It hit the target.'

In reciprocation, Jan Fishan invited the British back to his fortress in Paghman to view his legendary horses. At the time, no one in Afghanistan had stables to match his.

'How remarkable! They are eating grass,' exclaimed Jan Fishan, as they approached a group of horses standing in their field. The British were nonplussed, but they politely affirmed that this was, indeed, the case.

'Look at the groom! He is combing the horse's mane!' cried the Khan. Another horse passed them, and the feared warlord shouted: 'By Allah – it can walk! It can actually walk!' The British began to wonder whether their host was mad.

As they were leaving, Jan Fishan turned to them with a smile and said: 'You have seen, gentlemen, that if you have guns that hit the target exactly as they were designed to do, I too am surrounded by things that appear to be fulfilling their function quite adequately. What I have learned from you is to get excited about it.'

The circumstances under which our family had abandoned the magical gardens of Paghman and the citadel our ancestors had loved for so many generations were shrouded in mystery. It was years before I dared to ask about them. I'd always suspected there was some skeleton hidden in our closet, that some terrible family original sin had cast us out of Paradise, to become for ever wanderers.

'It is a long story,' said my father, but if he'd hoped to put me off, that was the wrong way to go about it. I loved long stories. 'It took generations,' he said, but that was all right too. I had plenty of time. 'Well,' he said, at last, 'I suppose you're old enough to hear about it.'

Now, legends are legends. I believe the story he told me contains the spirit of what happened but, if the tawdry facts are wrong, don't blame me. This is the tale as it was handed down to me.

Many years ago, our illustrious ancestor Jan Fishan Khan set us off on the course we have followed ever since. He was faced with a choice between his country's interests and his sense of personal duty. It happened like this.

Jan Fishan, as we know, was a kingmaker. He was allied by marriage to a former king of Afghanistan, Shah Shujah. The fellow was weak-willed, vain and heedless, but what could be done? Family allegiance was inviolable. Shah Shujah had been exiled in British India for years. He even collected a pension from the Raj.

When there is no threat from outside Afghanistan, national interests dissolve before tribal ambitions. Afghan history took its usual turbulent course. One king deposed another, while the country's rival warlords backed various candidates for the throne. Things often got bloody. A common, and relatively merciful, method of eliminating a pretender was to put out his eyes: the law stipulated that a blind man could not rule.

Until 1839 Shah Shujah was all but forgotten. Then the British, looking for an excuse to invade Afghanistan, began flattering the impressionable former king. Their army was invincible. Why did he not allow them to help him regain his throne?

The British had been trying for years to win Jan Fishan to their side. But all to no avail: he had outwitted them time and again. However, in Shah Shujah, they had found his Achilles heel. When the former king determined to accept the help of a British force, Jan Fishan's sense of family honour would not allow him to attack the occupying infidel army from his eyrie in Paghman.

British troops accompanied Shah Shujah to Kabul.

Their presence ensured that he would never be more than a hated puppet. The wild tribes of the frontier lands co-operated only because they were promised enormous bribes. The British foolishly neglected to pay up and the resulting rebellion soon became a general uprising. *Afghaniyat*, the sense of Afghan national identity, rose and swallowed up tribal differences. When Jan Fishan still refused to side against his kinsman, Shah Shujah, he was regarded as a traitor.

At the end of 1842, the British army began one of the most disastrous episodes of its history: the retreat from Kabul. Pathetically, the British commander General Elphinstone continued to believe the Afghan promises of a truce even as, day after day, the frontier tribesmen picked off his forces in the mountain passes. Wolves and human predators tore apart the dead and wounded, who had been simply abandoned in the snow. The army's camp followers – including thousands of women and children from British India – starved, froze or were cut into pieces.

On the fifth day of the British retreat, Akbar Khan, the bloodthirsty and treacherous leader of their Afghan tormentors, suddenly offered to take the handful of surviving English women and children into protective custody. My family's legend has it that Jan Fishan Khan had used the last shreds of his prestige to help bring about and maintain this small act of mercy. He was rewarded by a brief footnote in the diary of one of the women whose life was saved: Lady Sale.

Jan Fishan paid dearly for sacrificing Afghan patriotism to personal honour. For the rest of his life he was seen as someone who had collaborated with the hated force of infidel occupation. So, after all these years, I had discovered that my family's secret shame was this: rather than take part in the massacre and rout of the British, my ancestor had tried to save the lives of women and children.

That I had never heard this story before was surely a sign that, even after a century and a half, the wounds were still raw. Then, my father shocked me by saying: 'Of course, that was how we escaped. We needed that disgrace to help us break out of the nation state.'

Jan Fishan found it expedient to leave Afghanistan for a time – although he was too powerful a figure to be banished permanently. He took his army with him. They marched south, deep into British India. Here, they felt sure, they would find fighting and plunder enough to satisfy warriors who were not afraid to die.

Some years later, the British made the Khan an offer that possibly only a group of Afghans would take seriously. The Red Fort in Delhi was in the hands of Indian mutineers. If he and his men could breach its fortifications and capture Delhi, then Jan Fishan Khan would win the city as his prize.

This was a lure the soul-scattering Khan could not resist. Jan Fishan vowed that he would storm the fort, whatever it cost him. He led his men to the base of its formidable Mughal ramparts. They were considered impossible to breach. But, craning up, the Khan found one tiny flaw in their defences. If a single brave man succeeded in scaling the sheer walls at a certain point, victory could be theirs. This honour Jan Fishan gave to his eldest son.

The lad was barely half-way up when the fort's defenders spotted him. They fired, and Jan Fishan watched, expressionless, as his firstborn's body plunged down into the dust. Then the warlord gave his second son his blessing, and sent him up. Minutes later, the boy's body joined his brother's. All through the gore-drenched day this continued: one by one Jan Fishan Khan sent his six sons to scale the walls. One by one, he sent them to their deaths. When he had no sons left, the old warlord said his prayers, slung his sword on his back and clambered up the wall himself. At the seventh attempt, Allah smiled on our family and allowed the Khan to break the fort's defences.

When he told this story, as he did quite frequently, my father never expressed anything but the greatest admiration for the Khan's conduct. My brother, sister and I, however, grappled with a mixture of emotions. Our British upbringing had made us soft. We could never entirely forgive Jan Fishan Khan for sending his sons up before him.

I suppose we had failed a crucial test of *Afghaniyat*. Our values were too Western. The Khan and his sons, of course, regarded death as just another stage of the way. Each would die only at his appointed hour, and none could be successful without the aid of Allah. Jan Fishan Khan had staked his honour on taking the fort. For the sake of this same honour, he had already sacrificed his good name. There are more important things than family or possessions, even than life.

As we children – or any Westerner – might have guessed, the British reneged on their promise to place Delhi in the hands of an uncouth Afghan warlord.

Jan Fishan Khan sat down with his army at the gates of Delhi, the city whose red dust had soaked up the blood of his sons and over which he had hoped to rule. He did not attack, nor did he give way. He and his men simply refused to move until they were given a kingdom.

They caused, for a short time, a minor political incident. Furious dispatches flew among the Raj authorities, until a compromise was found. Jan Fishan Khan was made the Nawab of Sardhana, a province in North India. He married a young wife and had another set of sons, from whom we are descended.

I have inherited a memory of my father's, which has nagged at me for years. He told it to me when I was very young and in my mind, as I believe it was in his, it is a vivid snapshot: isolated and inexplicable, drenched in the over-saturated colour of early memory.

My father is a very small child – about two or three years old. He is sitting on the back of a gorgeously caparisoned elephant on our land in India. Beneath the elephant's lumbering tread, and as far as the eye can see, lush fields of sugar-cane stretch across the plain. Stooped figures – stunted and deformed by generations of under-nourishment – are cutting the cane in the glare of the sun. As he watches them, the child becomes aware for the first time that these, too, are human beings. His grandfather is with him on the elephant's back. The old man reads the boy's thought and answers his unspoken question: 'Yes, we are oppressing these people. And mark my words: although they may seem to you now to be as weak and helpless as twigs, one day they will rise up and destroy us utterly.'

I assumed this was a literal memory. Then, years later, I found almost the same remark in the works of one of the great classical Persian poets, Sheikh Sa'adi of Shiraz. So now I can never be sure that my father really did sit on the back of that elephant, gazing across those endless plains. But because of that image, I will never forget Sa'adi's words. The myths we choose to tell reflect the message we wish to preserve.

'Beware the sigh of the wounded heart,' said Sa'adi. 'The smoke from the hearts of the oppressed can overturn a world.'

Year after year, we planted sugar-cane on the estate the British had given us in Sardhana. This crop sucks the fertility out of the soil, but nobody seemed to care that the land would soon be exhausted. This was not our country. These were not our people. The Afghan robber barons had not lost their old ways.

For three generations we maintained estates in both India and Afghanistan. As the world was settling down into nations, we found ourselves traversing borders. We have been nomads ever since.

April 2001
Time has caught up at last with my family. I am no longer alone. Four million Afghan refugees have been exiled from their homes for two decades. A whole generation has grown up outside Afghanistan. They

have never lost their Afghan identity, because they have never been offered another in its place. They have learned, through bitter experience, the value of a myth.

If you have a myth, you can be proud of where you come from. You cannot be proud of a shred of a tent in the dustbowl that is a refugee camp in Pakistan. If you have a myth, you can hold your head high when the lowliest locals call you a dirty Afghani and accuse you of trying to take their jobs. If you have a myth, you can quote back at them the great Afghan poet Jalaluddin Rumi: 'A royal falcon landed among owls. They hooted at him in anger. He replied: "Oh, foolish ones – you think I am trying to usurp your homes, but my true place is on the wrist of a king!"'

I am visiting an Afghan refugee camp in Pakistan with a documentary crew, a few days before my undercover trip to Kabul with RAWA. Vast brick kilns spew their toxic fumes into the air. The refugees were here first. The brick kilns sprang from the prospect of trapped slave labour. Now no one who enters this place can ever escape them; there is no choice but to breathe the rank, polluted air.

It reminds me of Sheikh Sa'adi's words: 'The foundation of tyranny in the world was trifling at first. Everyone added to it until it attained its present magnitude.' Over the past twenty years, everyone has added just a little to the tyranny here, until this place has become a living hell.

Everyone exploits these people's misery – even me. I am with a camera crew, and we stop to talk to a little boy who is mixing water with dust to make clay. He pours it into moulds, which he stacks up to be baked. He is too young for such heavy work. His bones are still pliant. The lifting and carrying is warping his frame, laying the ground for a lifetime of disability.

He works to feed his family: twelve hours' grind each day for pennies. His parents have written him off. As long as he works, his younger brothers can attend school and maybe, one day, they at least will get out of this hell. I am talking to a living human sacrifice.

The boy and his family have only just arrived from Afghanistan. Before I know it, he is telling me a long and convoluted story about how the Taliban came to his village. The men rampaged through the vines where they spotted the daughter of his neighbour. For their amusement, they fired a rocket-propelled grenade at her. He saw her guts spewing out.

It is obvious that the child has witnessed some atrocity or other. But the details are inconsistent. The director wants it again. The second time, the boy forgets to mention the guts spewing out. The director needs those. The third time, it all comes out in a nervous rush – too quick. So it goes on. I cannot bear it any longer, but I am cowardly – I don't complain. I promise myself I will put my foot down next time. But I don't, I carry on asking.

Finally, the boy says: 'The Taliban were in the vines, they shot the young girl. Her mother came up, crying and saying: "Oh, my daughter – by Allah, may you not be dead." She washed the body and dressed her in her finest clothes. All the time she prayed to Allah. Then the girl opened her eyes and she was alive. Her mother kissed her again and again. The girl was wed that day and there was a joyful celebration.'

I have tears in my eyes when the boy finishes, because this story tells me all I need to know about the power of myth – and that I have added too much to his burden of tyranny.

A few feet away from this victim of the Taliban is the house of one of their local commanders. He has black circles of kohl around his dilated eyes and when I meet him he is giggling with feral excitement at the thought of battle. His chestnut hair is long, wavy and, since he is on holiday from the front, startlingly clean. He looks like some deranged shampoo advertisement.

The commander is twenty-four years old. He has been fighting since he was eleven. His job is the war in Afghanistan but here, this dusty camp in Pakistan, is home. He is from Afghanistan's lost generation – the adults who have never in their lives known peace.

It is the holy month of Ramadan so his band of men has come down from the hills for rest and recreation. This particular group of Allah's militia is flouting Islamic law by spending the fasting month smoking pot. If his men don't observe even basic Muslim strictures, why fight for purists like the Taliban? The commander shrugs: he used to oppose the Taliban as part of Ahmad Shah Massoud's force. The Taliban offered him newer weapons if he would fight for them instead, so he switched sides. It didn't change anything. They attack the commander over on the next hill. They always have done. Someone or other has always supplied them with the money and weapons to do it.

The commander has souvenirs: photographs, in which he and his men stand posing with their weapons before an attack. They are all smiling, as if they are on holiday. His own family was killed when he was a child. These men are his family now. He points to a lad of ten or eleven years old – about the same age as the little boy making bricks who saw his neighbour shot in the vines. This boy is about to join them. It is time. At the end of Ramadan he will go with the men up to the hills to learn how to wage war.

I look around the bare room, trying to make sense of what seems like pure insanity. There is a ghetto-blaster in the corner. The commander puts in a tape and the sound of heavy artillery fire fills the air. He says: 'I always record my battles, so that I can play them later for relaxation and so that my name will live for ever.'

Between explosions, the cries of the wounded are audible on the tape. He points to the child who will soon be joining the fray. This is the commander's favourite battle because during it the child's father was martyred. The tape reminds him that his friend is now in Paradise. I ask him what he would do if there were peace. He looks confused: the thought of peace has never occurred to him. If peace came, they would all be unemployed.

Is this the culture I was brought up to admire? Were the tales of battles I adored merely the atrocities of another age, dressed up as historic victories? As I grapple with this disturbing thought, the men pass round the communal hash pipe, listening to the music of battle and smiling at the thought of martyrdom.

Later, that same day, I speak to a group of orphans. The smoke from their hearts rises and mingles with the fumes of the kilns.

'. . . I am nine years old. I hid in the bread oven when the Taliban came. I could see them but they couldn't see me. They went to my father and said: "Give us money, or we will kill you." He said: "I am a poor shopkeeper, however would I find that much money?" So the Taliban shot him. I heard them say: "We can take his watch and waistcoat and sell them for some cash." Our boots were standing in the corridor, and they talked among themselves saying: "We can get a few pennies for those as well . . ."'

'. . . I am five years old. My name is Shams. My father was watching the sheep, and the Taliban came and he went to sleep. The Taliban killed him because he was a Hazara . . .'

'. . . I came across a group of Taliban. They didn't like my haircut – they thought it was too Western. They had dogs, so they chased me with them. I ran into my uncle's house and he took his gun and shot the dogs. Then the Taliban were angry and they shot my uncle . . .'

'. . . My friend and I were out walking. The Taliban said to her: "You are wearing white shoes and white is the colour of our flag. That means you have insulted our flag." They gave her a beating . . .'

Once, the Prophet promised that the prayers of three types of people would be answered: those of a parent, a wayfarer and a person who is oppressed.

The air is black with oppression. I think: Who will teach these children what to pray for? What vengeance will they seek when they grow up? This place will erupt some day. One way or another, it will erupt.

3

When I look at Maryam, my guide in Kabul, my own youthful self stares back. She is educated and cosmopolitan and, like me, she was born and raised outside Afghanistan.

Like me at her age, Maryam loves the myth of her homeland so much she has to know that the real Afghanistan lives up to its impossible ideals. She also wants to prove that she can live up to the myth. So Maryam has joined an underground organization, the Revolutionary Association of the Women of Afghanistan. It has sent her from the safety of her refugee camp in Pakistan to work clandestinely in Taliban-occupied Kabul. Maryam longs to risk everything for her cause. 'Let me be tested,' she says. 'I am ready for martyrdom.' Unconsciously she is echoing the sentiments of her sworn enemies, those other teenage Afghan idealists: the Islamic radicals.

Her bravery is humbling. For the last four months, this shy, nicely brought-up girl has hidden a video camera under her *burqa* to record life in the occupied city.

Now that I have joined her, we are about to try our most ambitious project yet: secretly filming inside the Taliban-controlled women's hospitals. We have tried to persuade a friendly doctor to let us in. No luck.

Everyone is too scared. There is nothing for it but to march through the Taliban checkpoint on the gate and pretend we are visiting a patient.

I have the camera in a bag. The lens shines like a jewel, a burning eye. The Taliban guards stare accusingly straight into it. I let my guilty thoughts get smaller and disappear like the little black point on a television when you turn it off. The guards will pick up nothing suspicious from me. I am thinking: Through.

The wards are filthy. Most female doctors have fled and the Taliban do not allow male doctors to treat female patients. The sick women here have no medicines and little medical care. If their relatives do not bring them food every day, they starve.

In the women-only area, we have to take off our *burqa*s. We are exposed. We have been told there are Taliban spies everywhere. I film and Maryam does the talking. It is a terrifying disaster. She exudes guilt. Her voice is a high-pitched babble. We scud nervously through the wards. There is no time to get a steady shot.

Slowly I realize that, over the years, I have acquired a skill I've never thought about, and have certainly never articulated before. I take Maryam aside into a dark part of the corridor, and in three minutes teach her everything I've learned in my life about becoming invisible. How you retract, shrink even your thoughts into a tiny speck, then find a spot beyond where you are now and vanish into it. And there is another way: you can disappear by emerging as something else, by being so bold that nobody imagines you are doing wrong.

We do the latter. We stop at every bed to talk. We are over-the-top. We exclaim about the absence of our fictitious relative: it would be just like her not to tell us she has recovered! Look at the fruit we've brought her – will you have some? Allah rewards the generous! We radiate confidence; we have a perfect right to be here. The confidence comes from within. We insist on being accepted on our own terms. The possibility of getting caught does not exist in our universe.

Maryam is spectacular. She has got it in one. I'm flushed with pleasure because I know I have shown her something that she will be able to use for the rest of her life. It was, after all, being a woman in the East that taught me the advantages of invisibility.

Under my *burqa*, it is easy for me to move about in Kabul. The streets teem with ghosts: the shrouded blue figures of women. All that is visible are their outstretched hands. They cannot go to work to earn a living but, with sick irony, they are permitted to beg.

I come to a street where merchants are selling scraps of mouldy bread for animal feed. A woman runs some through her hand, slowly and painstakingly. She picks out the scraps with the least mould. When she has bought a handful, she invites my guide from RAWA and me to visit her home. As we walk behind her, I build a picture of her in my mind: young and fragile – her hands are long and her walk is graceful. But when she takes off her veil I see that I was wrong. There is no beauty about her. She is old, haggard and resigned. She lives under a tarpaulin strung between two ruined walls. Rain plops down on her seven large-eyed children, on their one urine-sodden mattress, and on us.

She blows the worst of the mould off the bread and begins to pound it. Her children watch from the driest corner. They are uninterested in my video camera: the rhythmic movement of their mother pounding their food transfixes them.

As she works, she speaks. Her voice is a monotonous whine, almost bored. It is a beggar's spiel. Her husband is sick and cannot work to support them. She used to be a cleaner in the hospital but the Taliban sent the cleaners home. Now she has to beg. It is not enough to survive on. She has started sending her eldest daughter out on to the streets as well. The girl is ten years old. For the first time in our conversation, fire enters her voice: 'Imagine how it feels as a mother, to ask your own daughter to beg.'

When you meddle with the foundations of society, the whole structure tumbles down. The women were the bricks at the bottom of the pile. No wonder the city is just a pile of rubble.

In coming to Kabul, I am following in the footsteps of my Scottish grandmother, Bobo. When she was just sixteen she fell desperately in love with the romance of the East. At an Edinburgh University reception, she met a young medical student. He was the Sirdar Ikbal Ali Shah, the son of an Afghan chieftain. When she offered this impossibly glamorous figure a plate of cream cakes, he shot back a haughty look and declared: 'We men of the hills have no time for sugar buns!'

Bobo was smitten on the spot. A Highlander herself, she talked to him of her own mountains and glens in Scotland. The pair eloped before she was seventeen.

Bobo's father never spoke to her again. The Sirdar's father sent a telegram enquiring whether she was prepared to become a Muslim and whether she would be able to defend a fortress, if required. On hearing that the answer to both questions was yes, the old man gave his blessing to the match.

Fortunately for my grandmother, her friends' predictions that she would find herself locked in the harem of an Arabian sheikh turned out to be unfounded. I have a book of her memoirs and, more than half a century later, the Kabul she describes is as fresh and enchanting as first love.

In Paghman, up on the heights, 'In summer the gardens were a mass of flowers, making a little paradise of each house. There were no encircling walls and passers-by had the benefit of a flower show in every garden.'

Kabul itself was a boomtown, continually expanding, with smart new villas being built all the time. In spring, 'with startling suddenness, every garden sprang into life and, as if by magic, roses of all kinds and colours dripped over the walls'. The workmen were never too busy to pluck the blooms as they passed, and often put them behind their ears. Tulips, their petals as thin as tissue paper, and a deliciously scented mauve flower were sold in the bazaars at about three *afghanis* – sixpence – for a large bunch.

Before the Second World War Afghanistan was in a

flurry of modernization. Both America and the Soviet Union had come a-wooing and both sides were generously dispensing financial and technological support to further their suits. The newspapers chattered excitedly of five-year plans, industrialization, exports of *karakul* lamb and apricots; and of women's emancipation. But Bobo had no time for such vulgar hustle and bustle. A cream rambling rose made a fairyland of her garden. 'White and coloured irises were everywhere, and surely Kabul might have been called the home of roses. Hollyhocks, nasturtiums, sweet peas and most of the flowers we knew well in Europe grew well and plentifully.'

Kabul's moderate climate suited her and was not too different from her native Edinburgh. At a Scottish friend's request, she sent back some seeds of typical Kabul flowers. 'She was intensely betrayed when the result was a riot of nasturtiums and some impossibly English-looking hollyhocks.'

Bobo died before I was born but I've always felt as though I knew her. She seems close by: an old friend whom I have neglected, whose features have become misted through my negligence. One sunny day, I came across my own full name – Saira Elizabeth Luiza Shah – staring back at me from a mossy tombstone. No one had ever mentioned her Scottish name, and my parents had forgotten to tell me that I am her namesake.

Now I look for the villas that Bobo wrote about. But all rubble looks alike. There are no flowers in Kabul. Half of the buildings in the capital have been destroyed, so people live among the ruins. This is a place that has ceased to function; even the sewerage system has collapsed. Lumps of human faeces bob in the puddles in the streets.

The genteel net curtains of the Kabul safe-house in which I am staying must stay closed, in case the neighbours are informers. I am the guest of the family whose prison this has been for years. The mother, Halima, looks like what she is: pure gold hidden in a ruin – honest, down-to-earth and cheerful. Her open face is pop-eyed with a thyroid deficiency. Her husband is much older, or war has made him old. Children ferry dishes in the gloom. Dusk is falling, and there is no light.

The *pilau* is accompanied by every kind of delicacy: radishes, cheese, even meat and vegetables. These items are almost unobtainable in Kabul. At table, the family sits in a formal little row opposite me. It is like a panel interview, except no one speaks. Gradually I become aware that, in the semi-darkness, they are only pretending to eat.

Their furtive generosity brings a lump to my throat. Every mouthful of my own food is purgatory. But Halima is distraught that I'm not eating: 'Does the food not please you? We could get something else. Take a little more meat, so that you may remain strong.'

With the air of one opening an important conversational topic, Halima's husband asks: 'Tell us, what are ordinary people in the West saying about our lives?'

At this time, in spring 2001, people are saying nothing whatsoever about Afghanistan. They've barely even heard of Kabul. Days before I came out here, a very old friend of mine asked me to stop talking about it, adding: 'I just don't see why we should care.' Now, sitting here in the gloom – feeling, rather than seeing, this family's expectant faces – I cannot bear to tell them any of this. So I take a coward's way out. I quote them lines of the poet Sa'adi of Shiraz:

The people of the world are limbs from one body,
     sharing one essence.
When a single limb is oppressed, all the others suffer
     agony.

To the family, this concept is so familiar it is self-evident. They wait for me to make my point, because they already assume people in the West believe oppression anywhere in the world concerns us all. But they are wrong: they have been abandoned. Sitting here in the darkness, they are quite alone. I can't carry on lying to them, even to give them hope.

To cover the silence, and perhaps to spare his guest the burden of the West's embarrassment, Halima's husband gathers his children around him, as my father used to do. He says that, since I like Sheikh Sa'adi, he'll tell us all a story from the poet's masterpiece, the *Gulistan*.

A king had a terrible malady. Physicians said that only the blood of a child with certain qualities would save his life. A search was made, and a peasant boy with the right attributes was found. His father and mother were given rich presents and agreed to hand him over. The judge ruled it was lawful to kill a subject to save the life of a king.

As the executioner raised his axe, the boy looked up to

heaven and smiled. The king asked him, 'What reason do you have to laugh?'

The boy replied: 'Children depend on their parents for safety, and people seek mercy from judges and justice from kings. Now, my mother and father have sold me, the judge has condemned me, and the Sultan hopes my death will be his cure. Except for God most high, I have none to protect me.'

At these words, the king decided he would prefer to die rather than shed the blood of this boy. He recovered that same week.

The story is well worn and comforting. Like every Afghan child, I was raised on the *Gulistan*. At last we have found a shared experience, a point of connection. We fall to discussing a thirteenth-century poet as if we are gossiping about a friend, smiling at centuries-old reminiscences.

Now the ice has been broken, Halima tells me about the time in 1992, when she heard the Communists had been defeated; that the mujahidin had taken Kabul. She thought: Thank God. They have saved Afghanistan – it's over. At last, this misery is over.

But all their new rulers wanted was power and money. They looted the city. They weren't holy warriors, they were thugs, simple as that. They picked young girls and boys off the street, raped them and threw their bodies into wells. You didn't dare to go outside. But then they came into your home, and took whatever they wanted anyway.

It was mayhem, chaos. Rival commanders fired from

street to street, fighting each other for territory, like gangsters. She can't describe it. Nobody stopped them. There wasn't a government. The mujahidin's political leaders were fighting each other too. Then the Prime Minister began shelling his own capital. Imagine! Where else could a thing like that happen? For months, shells fell dozens of times a day. Nobody's family escaped. They all lost people they loved. And the West did nothing. It just sat and watched the men it had supported destroy this country.

One day, a shell fell very close by. There was a crash, and then the ceiling was falling on top of them. Halima's eldest daughter threw herself to the ground. She lay there, buried and terrified. They dug her out, but her mother thinks that a rock must have hit her because, from that moment, she could neither speak nor hear.

By now Halima is weeping. I must see why she's been telling me all this. She needs to find a foreign doctor who can help her daughter, who is sitting next to her on the shabby sofa. She reaches out and mutely touches her mother's hand. The girl is a beauty. At eighteen years old, she has the kind of grace that transcends war, poverty, culture and language.

'Look at her,' sobs Halima, clutching her daughter's hand. 'She is intelligent. She has taught herself to lip-read. She embroiders wonderfully. But what will become of her? No one will marry her now, no one.'

At three in the morning, a mechanical roar wakes me. I leap out of bed because never, in this country, have I heard the sound of any machinery that was not connected to war. The entire family is sitting round a

47

collection of ancient electric sewing-machines. Electricity is sporadic: when it comes on, they must use it. They are embarrassed that, nowadays, they survive by tailoring. The father is an engineer. But no one in Afghanistan wants to rebuild, only to destroy.

During the Second World War, Afghanistan experienced a rare interval of peace. Like the little old lady who was so stubborn she even floated up-river, the country remained strictly neutral as the rest of the world went up in flames.

My grandparents were visiting Bobo's friends in Scotland when hostilities broke out, and it became hard to return to Afghanistan. There was a ban on civilian travel.

The family decided to sit tight and hope that it would all blow over. My grandfather chafed at the restrictions of wartime Britain. There were strict regulations to ensure that the civilian population was prepared for the onslaught from the air. Everyone, without exception, was advised to keep a stirrup pump in their house to put out small fires from incendiary bombs.

A warden demanded to see my grandfather's stirrup pump. As a citizen of a neutral country, the Sirdar had not equipped himself with this item. 'If you don't have a stirrup pump,' said the official, 'what are you going to do if your house catches fire?'

My grandfather rarely lost his cool. On this occasion he looked at the warden and said, in his precise English: 'Sir, I will have you know that Allah is my stirrup pump.'

Some time during the war, news came from Afghanistan that the Sirdar's father, my great-grandfather, had died. It was essential that my grandfather, as his father's heir, return to claim our estate in Paghman. But now the Sirdar found himself well and truly trapped. Foreigners in wartime Britain were often treated as spies. Try as he might, my grandfather could not cut through the red tape required to visit a country that some officials seemed to believe might ally itself to Germany at any moment.

Message after agonized message came from Paghman, saying that our lands were to be appropriated by the Afghan Crown or that they would be divided up, or fall into the hands of rival groups of relatives. Always the plea was the same: the Sirdar must return immediately. But he could not.

Months or years later, when he was finally able to go back to Paghman, it was too late. Our lands had been divided and swallowed up. To this day, I can't say exactly by whom: the name of the usurper was not considered important enough to pass into the myth. The estate in India, which by then was bankrupt anyway, also slipped out of our hands.

My grandfather had lost all his worldly possessions, but not his sense of humour. Soon after the full extent of these misfortunes became clear, he happened to rebuke my father for leaving his shoes lying around the house. My father retorted that he'd learned the habit from the Sirdar himself.

The Sirdar roared back at him: 'I may leave my shoes anywhere I please, because *I* am the son of a Nawab. *You*, however, are only the son of a professor!'

For many years, this great-grandson of a *shah-saz*, a kingmaker, travelled the globe. Although he was often penniless, the blood of the Prophet was his passport to the courts of the Middle East. Until the end of his days, when he was asked if he was going abroad for his holidays, he would reply: 'I *am* abroad.'

My grandfather's faithful entourage of Pushtun retainers never lost their freebooting ways. Once, while visiting a maharaja, the Afghan hillsmen were unable to eat the hotly spiced foods of their host. My grandfather's cook conjured fish *pilau* out of thin air. They left in a hurry when a hue and cry informed them that the maharaja's late grandmother, reincarnated into a carp, had gone missing from her ornamental pool in the palace grounds.

Or so the legend went. The stories gained a little embellishment with every telling. As a small child I loved and believed in all my grandfather's adventures as unquestioningly as I believed in the sky and the stars. As I got older, though, I found myself having to suppress uncomfortable doubts. It was like pulling at a thread from the fabric of my world. I was too Western to accept legends unchallenged. If my grandfather's tales were invented or exaggerated, then neither could I rely upon the greater myth that was Afghanistan.

My grandfather never minded overriding the literal: a devout Muslim, he threshed the kernel of religion from its chaff. When he was going on the pilgrimage, his relatives beseeched him for impossible quantities of water from the holy spring of Zamzam near the Ka'aba in Mecca. On his return, he satisfied everyone by diluting the original water with nine parts from the tap. 'The holy essence of Zamzam will sanctify the tap water it touches,' he explained.

Periodically he would offer to bestow the hand of his daughter Amina upon those he deemed worthy of the honour. Sometimes she was thrown into the bargain as part of a grandiose Afghan-style plan he was hatching: restoring a monarch to his throne, say, or starting a pan-Islamic movement. Invariably, these forays into the polluted realm of world affairs would end in disaster. Then he would retreat back into the clearer air of philosophy and letters.

He never did succeed in arranging a marriage for my aunt Amina, although he tried from her adolescence until she was well into middle age. By that time, she had formed an armour of eccentricity so formidable that even he admitted she was quite beyond his powers.

Sometimes in his wanderings he found echoes of his lost Afghanistan: in the Highland clans of his wife's dear Scotland or in the Wild West of America. He wrote over seventy books. To me, the title of one, *Westwards to Mecca*, is a clue that, wherever his physical body might have been, his spirit resided still in his ancestral home, Paghman.

When his wife, my grandmother Bobo, died, he stopped his wanderings and settled in Morocco. He could not bear to visit any of the countries where they had lived together. After his death, I found the diary he wrote in the last year of his life. I read entry after entry: he kept it meticulously every day. At first I couldn't work out what was so curious about it. Then it struck me. He was perfectly content – an old man, waiting quietly for his call to Allah. He rarely had any money, and if he came by some, he used it to buy presents for people or gave it away. His mind was already fixed on the next stage of the way.

I remember a kindly old man, who told me stories, wonderful ones, which tug at the edges of my memory like forgotten dreams. He may have told me this one, or perhaps somebody else did, but I always associate it with him.

Once upon a time there was a man of great wisdom who had a foolish apprentice. After a while, the boy felt that all he had learned was that there would be a golden age in a few hundred years' time. Gradually, he became obsessed with it. He begged his master to put him to sleep for seven hundred years. When he woke up, he was lying in the ruins of magnificent palaces and gardens. In his master's old wooden shack sat the sage's great-great-great-great-great-grandson, and by now he, too, was a very old man. He said: 'Too bad, my child, you have missed the golden age by three hundred years.'

My grandfather did not have to wait long for the Call. He died when I was six. He was buried beside the body of his beloved Bobo. On his grave, except for his name, was nothing except the appellation 'Al Mutawakkil' – the one who resigns himself to the will of the Almighty. Of nation, of identity, of lands, of blood, of achievements – even of honour – there was no mention.

★

After just five days it is time for me to leave Kabul. I do not dare to stay: the city is full of informers; it is only a matter of time before I am betrayed.

I wish that, like my grandfather, my own identity was so transparent to me that I could afford to ignore it. But I need to know what is fact and what is fairytale more than I need the reassurance of the myth. Only truth can answer the questions that for years I haven't even dared to ask my own heart. Does the Afghanistan of our myths really exist? Are we still Afghans? And if I am not an Afghan, what am I?

There is one last place to visit. As I climb the steep mountainside to the Paghman plateau, I am gripped with fear. If the magical gardens my father told me of never existed, then part of me will be a lie as well.

I am standing upon a desolate plateau. No birds sing. The fruit trees have been cut down for firewood. The irrigation channels are bombed and the once-fertile soil is dry. All my life, I have carried a picture of this place in my heart. All my life, this is where I have most longed to be.

The ground is seeded with mines and strewn with the debris of its former splendour: the blue mosaic tiles, the broken watercourses and the dried-out fountains. This myth, at least, was true: in my mind's eye, I can reconstruct what once must have been a magical garden.

Sa'adi once gazed on the full bloom of a garden such as this. His poet's vision saw that its beauty would fade. 'The rose of the garden has no continuance,' he said. 'Do not become attached to what will not endure.' He decided to create a garden that time could not destroy. He built his rose garden – his great work, the *Gulistan* – out of stories. It has survived for eight hundred years. 'Roses,' he said, 'live but for a few days. My Rose Garden will never die.'

Towering above me, unchanging, eternal, are the mountains. Down in the valley, a city of towers and minarets sparkles in the late-afternoon sun. Kabul *jan* – beloved Kabul – lies like a jewel at my feet. I know by now that its beauty is an illusion: close up, the city is in ruins, as shattered and broken as this garden. I have missed the golden age. I have come too late.

My journey here has taken me over twenty years. While I was making my way towards it, the place that inspired the myth has been destroyed. But only because of the myth – the map of tales my family drew for me all those years ago – can I recognize the beauty in this ruin.

BOOK TWO

The Map of Tales

Deep in the sea are riches beyond compare.
But, if you seek safety, it is on the shore.

'The Rose Garden,'
from *Gulistan*, Sheikh Sa'adi of Shiraz

4. An Offer of Marriage

If a Shirazi Turkish maid would take my heart into her
    hand,
I'd give Bukhara for the mole upon her cheek – or
    Samarkand.

Hafiz of Shiraz

I was seventeen before I met my extended family. It was
my first proof that my heritage wasn't just a chimera, a
story my father had invented to stem the terrible loneliness of being for ever outsiders. For the first time in my
life I was *nufus-dar*, the Afghan term that means literally
'having people' – but which conveys a sense of safety
and belonging. I had found my tribe.

'If I was not this day marrying my son to some other
woman,' said my uncle Mirza, taking a thoughtful
mouthful of *pan*, betel leaf, 'I would have given him to
you.' He sighed and slightly puckered his mouth and
forehead, as if to mourn the impotence of the individual
in the face of higher powers.

'It's too bad. We've already fixed it with the bride's
family. There'd be a scandal. No, it's been left too late
. . . Zulfikar must go to her, and she isn't even a
relative.' There was a pause, and then an expression of

unworldly sweetness came into the old man's watery grey eyes, as the pleasant kick of betel, a mild stimulant, struck. 'And do you know why I would offer my son to you, in place of this girl, even though her family is rich?'

'No, Uncle,' I said dutifully.

He straightened his already poker-straight back. His green *chapan*, the splendid Afghan silk robe, and his incongruously English hat added to his immense dignity. 'Because,' he said, 'you are family. *Az khude ma hasten.* You belong to us.'

My brother and sister, Tahir and Safia, my elderly aunt Amina and I were all attending the wedding of Uncle Mirza's son. On seeing two unmarried daughters in the company of a female chaperone, he had obviously concluded that we had been sent here to be married off.

I was taken aback by the visceral longing I felt to be part of this world. I had never realized that I had been starved of anything. Now I discovered that, like a princess in a fairytale, I had been cut off from my origins. This was the point in the tale where, simply by walking through a magical door, I could recover my gardens and palaces. If I allowed my uncle to arrange a marriage for me, I would belong.

Uncle Mirza was continuing: 'In the sight of Allah, the most blessed form of marriage is one between first cousins. Now, you are Zulfikar's second or third cousin, so that would have been the second or third most blessed form of marriage. But don't worry, you have plenty of other cousins. Only when there is no cousin available should we consider a marriage outside the family. This is because the purity of the blood of the Prophet – peace be upon him – flows in our veins. That blood is a sacred trust.'

This was the first hint that there were subtle differences between my uncle's branch of the family and my own. I had never heard of trying to marry within our own family to keep our blood pure. If that was what Allah preferred, then both my grandfather and my father had risked His ire by marrying not only out of their families but also out of their communities.

'I've got to finish my education before I think about marriage, Uncle,' I stalled.

Uncle Mirza beamed approvingly. 'Of course,' he said, spitting the blood-red betel juice into the stainless-steel spittoon by his elbow. 'You will make a much better match if you are educated. But that is no reason why we should not think of it now.'

Although Uncle Mirza's home was closer than I had ever been, I was not yet inside Afghanistan. This branch of my family lived in Peshawar, in Pakistan's North West Frontier Province. Like most Afghans, however, we regarded the border as a technicality imposed by the British to divide the territory of the free tribes of the area. As far as we were concerned, Peshawar ought to have been an Afghan city.

Peshawar lived up to its reputation as a wild frontier town, a melting pot whose inhabitants were armed to the teeth, and where anything could happen at any time. It was just thirty miles from Afghanistan where, in 1979, Red Army tanks had helped install a puppet ruler the Soviets felt would be more pliable than the previous Communist dictator. In the conflict that ensued, one million Afghans had been killed. That was five per cent of the population, mostly civilians. Another five million people had fled their homes.

Now Peshawar's population – mostly the unruly Pushtun tribesmen whose clans straddle the border with Afghanistan – was swollen with Afghan refugees from different ethnic groups. Huge Pushtuns strode along, blankets thrown over their shoulders and the mountains in their grey eyes. Hazaras, the Asiatic Shi'ites of Central Afghanistan, hawked their wares. Rosy-cheeked northerners – Uzbeks and Turkomans – gaped with open mouths at this one-horse town that was, to them, a hub of civilization.

Just beyond the city limits lay the forbidding Hindu Kush mountain range. Every now and then Peshawar's thick smog lifted, unveiling it briefly: mysterious, beautiful and stern. The road that led out of the city wound through the fabled Khyber Pass, the gateway to Afghanistan. The mountains beckoned me to a forbidden country, and I longed to cross them.

I'd only been in Peshawar for a short time, but I already knew I adored Uncle Mirza. He was a kindly old man, with a proud military career behind him; an Afghan who – having been caught on the wrong side of the artificial border – was swept into service in the Imperial British Army during the Second World War.

The bane of Uncle's life was his wife – the product, I longed to remind him, of a marriage arranged by his parents. Possibly to speed my own thoughts towards matrimony, he told me about his courtship.

'When I was a young lieutenant, the match was

arranged. In those days, of course, the groom was strictly forbidden to see his bride before the wedding day. But I thought that I could not pledge to spend the rest of my life with a woman I had not even glimpsed. So, one night, another officer and I crept outside her bedroom to peep at her through the keyhole. At the last moment, my nerve failed. I said to my friend: "You look for me and tell me if she is all right." He had a peek and said: "It's all right – you can go ahead."''

In Uncle Mirza's home, as in most traditional Muslim households, Auntie Soraya was the undisputed boss, presiding over every detail of family life. Like many intelligent but socially frustrated women, she was devoutly religious, although her adherence to Islam – a faith whose name means submission to the will of Allah – didn't prevent her flying into rages that bordered on insanity. It was often difficult to tell where the prayers left off and the scolding began.

'May Allah be my witness! You have been giving all our money away again,' she would shout, when my uncle made donations to the Afghan mujahidin resistance, or journeyed out in the heat of the day to run errands for impoverished refugees. 'How are we supposed to live? You should look after your own family first. Do you call yourself a Muslim? You've even missed the evening prayer! God defend me from you – you're no better than an infidel!'

Once, in a fit of temper, she sold my uncle's vegetable patch to a developer. Every now and then Uncle was reminded of this depredation and his eyes would mist over in sadness. 'My lovely vegetable garden. She sold it. Such wonderful melons. Beautiful cucumbers. All gone.' He would sigh, and take another munch of betel nut.

The day he disclosed his matrimonial ambitions for me, Uncle Mirza sat me at his right hand during lunch. This was a sign of special favour, as it allowed him to feed me choice titbits from his own plate. It was by no means an unadulterated pleasure. He would often generously withdraw a half-chewed delicacy from his mouth and lovingly cram it into mine: an Afghan habit with which I have since attempted to come to terms. It was his way of telling me I was valued, part of the family.

I'd never met anyone like my own nuclear family before – and suddenly here, in our extended tribe, were dozens of people who were just like us. It was like discovering the missing part of a jigsaw; I suddenly understood many of the quirks and customs I had assumed were mere eccentricities of my own parents. The Eastern side of my brain knew that, in an arranged match, I wouldn't be marrying an individual but a family, a tribe, a way of life; somewhere to belong to. It was a seductive feeling.

A huge cast of relatives had assembled for the wedding. Privacy was non-existent. My brother, who was initially given his own room in recognition of his superior male status, awoke one morning to find a middle-aged, but still voluptuous woman he'd never seen before snoring in his bed.

'Who are you?' he demanded, in fifteen-year-old horror.

'I am your auntie, of course,' she snapped back.

My favourite auntie was the old woman who had journeyed for five days on her own by bus from India. She had two lank grey plaits, and a once-fine sari. Her teeth were all gone, but it didn't stop her shovelling enormous quantities of wedding *pilau* into her mouth. When she saw me for the first time, she grabbed my scarf, kissed it, then quickly wound it round her own neck. Then she moved on to the other guests. She was a professional wedding freeloader.

I was also especially fond of Raj Bibi. She was a pretty, timid little creature, whose status was difficult to work out. Her clothes were dowdier than my cousins', but she was always clean and neat and cheerful. She seemed to be given an immense amount of fetching and carrying to do. She was very pale, with huge black eyes, and I was told she came from the mountainous regions of Chitral, in Pakistan's northern territories.

'Raj Bibi is *not* a servant,' my cousin Aisha told me, as poor Raj Bibi was sent away from the table on yet another errand.

'How did she come to join the family?' I asked.

'She is the wife of the Ikramullah *jan*, the cook,' said Aisha. 'My father Mirza went all the way to Chitral to buy her in the marriage market there. It was extremely difficult. In the spring in Chitral there are terrible winds, in the summer blazing heat, and in the autumn there are scorpions so deadly that if you don't carry antidote round with you they'll kill you in just twelve minutes.'

'What about the winter?' I asked, momentarily distracted.

'In the winter the snows make it impassable. It was

very kind of Mirza to travel all that way. So you see, Raj Bibi is a member of our family.'

Over the next few days, the man my family wished me to marry was introduced into the inner sanctum. I was informed that he was a distant cousin, affectionately nicknamed Jimmy. His luxuriant black moustache was generally considered to compensate for his lack of height. I was told breathlessly that he was a fighter pilot in the Pakistani air force.

I began to see the uses the extended family system can have for matchmaking. As an outsider, Jimmy would not have been permitted to meet an unmarried girl. But as a member of the family he had free run of the house. And because the rules stated that this was an area for family only, the women would cheerfully suckle babies or dash about in a state of undress.

Whenever I appeared, one of my female cousins would fling a young child into Jimmy's arms. He would pose with it, whiskers twitching slightly, while the women cooed their admiration. Jimmy's thirty-eight years and respectable military job made him a desirable catch, even if he was a little on the short, fat and bandy-legged side. Disconcertingly, he spoke with a kind of subcontinental twenties slang. 'Oh, my God, how spiffing!' he exclaimed, as yet another child was hurled into his lap. It had a hare-lip – the unsurprising conse-quence of my family's obsession with keeping its genes to itself.

It was all very confusing. Far away in Britain, the child and grandchild of mixed marriages, I had kept the faith: I still stalwartly clung to the belief that I was an Afghan.

But, after one generation of living just thirty miles from the Afghan border, Jimmy had become Pakistani.

As Jimmy held the infant, my female cousins cast meaningful glances at me. It made me feel warm and happy. They wanted me to stay here as much as I did. They wanted me to become their sister.

Over dinner, Uncle Mirza was holding forth: 'Nobody except the Afghans dared to scorn the might of the Imperial British Army. Afghans have never been afraid to attempt the impossible. Why, in 1919, King Amanullah Khan didn't bother to wait for Britain to invade Afghanistan. He sent his famous general Nadir Khan across the Hindu Kush, through terrain believed to be impassable, to invade the British Empire! That kind of spirit is why the British never succeeded in colonizing us.'

Now there was another war raging, across the border in Afghanistan. Peshawar was the town from which the mujahidin resistance was organized, but in those Cold War days, the world assumed that no 'Sovietized' country would ever escape the fold. The mujahidin were regarded by the West as brave and rather quaint.

Uncle Mirza helped me to a cup of sweet black tea from the urn that a servant carried round. It was mixed with evaporated milk, always referred to as Carnation Milk; another oblique reminder of the British Raj. He continued his history lesson. 'It wasn't until the Second World War that the colonized peoples slowly understood what the Afghans had known all along: the British were fallible. When I was in Burma, the Japanese would hide in the trees and shoot down at us. Terrible carnage.

We looked round for our British officers, and we discovered they had put the native troops in front. That was an important moment: that was when we realized that the British were afraid.' I knew that his account of the humiliation and cowardice of the British, the superpower of his day, had a purpose. He was trying to tell us – and perhaps himself – that the current Afghan struggle against the Soviet Union was worth pursuing. That the war across the border should not be seen with the pessimistic eye of world opinion. That it was part of a constantly revolving wheel of history and that other battles had seemed at least as impossible in their time.

'Eventually,' said my uncle, 'we learned to fire volleys into the branches ahead of us. And down fell the Japs. Plop! Plop! Plop!'

'Plop! Plop! Plop!' my uncle repeated, as if savouring some invisible and rather delightful vision of his own. He took another slurp of cloying, sticky tea. 'I love war,' he said benignly. 'Terrific.'

'Jamil Haidar!' announced a servant.

We all trooped out on to the veranda where, on the nice wickerwork garden furniture, was sitting what looked like a brigand-king of old. He wore an immense black silk turban and a matching waistcoat. His beard bristled fiercely, but his eyes were the dreamy green of a poet. His chest was strung with cartridges for his one concession to modernity – the AK-47 he held carelessly in one hand. He was surrounded by around fifteen men similarly attired. But there was something about Jamil Haidar that instantly told me he was the commander of a group of Afghan mujahidin.

A servant was despatched to bring delicate green tea, flavoured with cardamoms and served in my uncle's best teacups. The men sat around, Kalashnikovs dangling on their knees, delicately sipping tea from the finest bone china. Jamil Haidar had picked a deep pink Bukhara rose from the garden, and was thoughtfully inhaling its heavy perfume.

'My dear boy!' said Uncle. 'What news from Paghman, our homeland?'

In the soft Persian of the mountains, Jamil Haidar said: 'Two weeks ago, there was a great battle in Paghman. Many of our men were slain but, thanks be to Allah, we succeeded in repelling the enemy. There has been heavy bombardment there and I am sorry to report that your own family's seat, the citadel of the princes, has been damaged beyond repair.'

I listened enraptured. This kind of talk was irresistible to a seventeen-year-old. These wild men seemed to belong to a world that was both impossibly romantic and astonishingly immediate. They had walked across the Hindu Kush range with no more ado than if they were going for a stroll. They had fought terrible battles against the Soviet Union, an enemy which so outgunned them that the outside world assumed only their naïvety had led them even to attempt the task. And yet, here they were, in my uncle's sunny garden, smelling the flowers and sipping their tea. They had brought the war to me, promising a whole world of excitement just beyond the gates of Uncle's villa. I yearned to break out. Family life no longer seemed enough.

Preparations for the wedding were under way.

67

Zulfikar, the groom, sat in the storm whipped up by his numerous female relatives. His shot silk wedding *shilwar kamis* drooped on his slender frame. His gold *pagri*, the ceremonial turban, was too grand a garment to be worn with such an air of resignation.

Zulfikar seemed unconcerned at the mayhem all around him, as though it was some external manifestation of nature he could do nothing about. I wondered what he would say, or even if he would care, if he knew that his father had been flirting with the idea of switching me at the last minute for the rightful bride.

Square in the eye of the hurricane, resplendently attired in her emerald and gold wedding suit, was my aunt Soraya. As mother of the groom, the festivities belonged to her. To underline the importance of the occasion, she had lifted her usual religious objections to makeup. Her ravaged face now sported the mascara-smudged lashes of a *houri* and the Cupid's bow of a Hollywood nymph. For hours on end, she sat beside her son feeding him delicacies with her own plump fingers and occasionally muffling a sob. She paused only to hurl imprecations at the battalions of women darting around doing her bidding.

The wedding itself was to last for at least fourteen days and nights. During that time some three or four hundred guests would have to be lavishly fed. In the kitchens, Raj Bibi's husband, the cook Ikramullah *jan*, assisted by scores of minions, laboured to prepare mounds of special wedding rice. Everyone agreed that the traditional pink, green and orange hues of this dish had been enormously improved since the invention of synthetic food dyes. Ikramullah *jan* would have been appalled at the concept of *nouvelle cuisine*. He piled up the *pilau* on golden platters and scattered it with coconut and orange peel. The emphasis was on abundance; the aim was to impress.

In the evenings, there were parties. One night we relatives of the groom carried candles to the home of the bride. There was more *pilau*, this time supplied by her family. Because they were particularly liberal, they also laid on disco dancing – at least, for the men. We women sat in all our gaudy finery, slurping bottles of Sprite lemonade through straws, and pretending not to watch the males gyrating with each other. It was like participating in the mating ritual of some weird species of bird.

The bride was a quiet, well-educated girl of about eighteen. Like many Afghans, she had fair hair and pale skin. Her well-to-do family had fled from the war across the border and her eyes were full of sadness. The women of the groom's family spent hours decorating her hands and feet with intricate designs in henna paste. She had been content to marry Zulfikar, but now she endured the ritual patiently, without either a smile or a sigh. Perhaps she was mourning the lost mountains of her beloved Kabul.

The wedding celebrations culminated in a reception. The bride and groom sat on an elevated stage to receive the greetings of their relatives. While the groom was permitted to laugh and chat, the bride was required to sit perfectly still, her eyes demurely lowered. I did not see her move for four hours. She appeared to have slipped into a hypnotic trance. In her gold-embroidered *shilwar kamis*, her neck strung with gold, her face heavily painted, her hands and feet decorated with henna, she looked hunched and defeated, like a broken-winged bird.

Watching this *tableau vivant* of a submissive Afghan bride, I knew that marriage would never be my easy route to the East. My father's mythological homeland was a realm where I could live through the eyes of the storyteller. In my desire to experience the fairytale for myself, I had overlooked the staggeringly obvious: the storyteller was a man. Here, in the real world, the enchantment was at an end. I had assumed my own woman's body. If I wanted freedom, I would have to cut a path of my own.

The next day the weaker-willed relatives began to drift away. I was growing more and more fretful. This place of belonging could also be a prison for a woman. Until I visited Uncle Mirza's family, I had never been denied freedom, education or status because of my sex. Now, as a young unmarried girl, I wasn't even allowed to leave the villa without an escort. My brother roared in and out whenever he chose. He was having a wonderful time. His male cousins had shown him the gun factories and the opium market, and he had spent hours playing backgammon in the insalubrious tea-houses of the storytellers' bazaar. None of these places was considered suitable for a girl.

I began to understand why Aunt Soraya – intelligent and capable though she was – had resorted to using religion as a means of regaining some measure of control. Her piety gave her licence to impose her will on others. It was a pattern of behaviour that my aunt Amina recognized immediately. She and Soraya were, at this moment, locked in a tussle about whether nail varnish was permitted in Islam. At stake, both women knew, was the battle for supremacy within the household. Amina had taken to quoting the sayings of her ancestors, who happened to trace their lineage rather more directly to the Prophet than Soraya's. Soraya, however, was still clinging to the lead, thanks to a stringent programme of voluntary extra devotions. During the hours of daylight, and well into the night, she rarely left her raised prayer platform. I watched this contest of titans with interest, but I knew it wasn't a game I could play. It took years to get to the top of the pecking order. Seniority counted.

For the first time in my life, I found myself wishing I'd been born a boy. I decided it was time to take matters into my own hands. I would bend the rules so outrageously that my family would either have to throw me out or play along. My hair was already cut short, and at seventeen I was boyish. Dressed in a *shilwar kamis* of my brother's, I slouched down to breakfast as though nothing was up. I hoped to cash in on my uncle's notorious absentmindedness. Aunt Soraya gave a snarl of horror when she saw me. She thought it highly indecorous for a young girl to wear men's clothes. However, I was a guest. She couldn't order me to change. So far, so good. My uncle seemed oblivious of my appearance.

All morning, I listened to Uncle Mirza's stories about

war. By eleven o'clock, we were looking at his collection of medals. Over lunch, he began calling me 'splendid boy', which, of course, was exactly what he wanted me to be.

That afternoon, I asked whether it would be possible to tour some of the Afghan refugee camps nearby. Uncle beamed. 'Of course, dear boy. As a matter of fact, I was meaning to go and distribute some funds in Nasirbagh, one of the biggest camps. We'll leave at once.'

Uncle put on his hat, we got into his battered Toyota and set off. His villa was in the Cantonment, the old British military area of Peshawar. After Independence, the Pakistani official classes had simply moved into the neat white bungalows of their former British masters. Ornamental cannons still guarded the driveways. The wide avenues were lined with trees, their trunks lime-washed to just above the height where delinquent goats might gnaw.

The Cantonment seemed quintessentially British. But every now and then I noticed something subtly wrong. A water-buffalo would lumber past, driven by a ragged herder. Or we would suddenly pass a gun shop: 'Abdul Qadir, Modern Arms Store'. What was modern about an arms store? Why do you need modern arms?

Every few metres, Uncle pointed out a landmark. 'Residence, corps commander, North West Frontier Province . . . governor's house . . . cadet training college . . . military hospital.'

Outside the Cantonment, the chaos that had been merely hinted at took over. Spluttering rickshaws veered past bullock carts, herds of goats and women shrouded from head to foot in the *burqa*. Afghan lorries pounded along, decorated with gaudy pictures: *houris* of Paradise and the occasional multiple-barrelled rocket launcher. Their panelled sides boasted of their origins: Kabul, Jalalabad, Kandahar, and Herat. In keeping with the free Pushtun spirit, the trucks rarely stuck to just one side of the road. They had, after all, already ignored both a national border and the front line of the super-power conflict.

As my uncle and I pottered along in his battered Toyota Corolla, I asked him something I had been wondering about. After all these years, would he say he was Pakistani or Afghan? He smiled. 'I have faithfully served Pakistan from the day of its creation. I have saluted its flag. I have defended it in war and I have helped to build a nation during peace. There is no doubt that I am a Pakistani. But being an Afghan – that is a state of mind. The Afghans are quite unmanageable.'

We were, by then, on a straight stretch of road. A lumbering Bedford truck was heading towards us on the wrong side. Instead of swerving out of its path, Uncle Mirza held his ground. 'A piece of paper may make you a Pakistani,' he said, 'but you have to keep your hand in at being Afghan.'

The approaching truck was laden with wild-looking Pushtun tribesmen, who seemed to have no intention of giving way. Uncle said: 'I am an officer in the Pakistan army. Let them stop for me.'

'But, Uncle, you're wearing civilian clothes. How will they know?'

73

'Whatever Allah wills.'

The truck carried on, its horn blaring wildly. What frightened me most was that the Pushtuns on board loved every minute of it. A moment or two before impact, I heard them cheering. The unstoppable force had met the immovable object. I closed my eyes. There was a terrific crash and, to my surprise, I discovered I was still alive. The truck had given way, but so late that it had grazed the corner of the Toyota's bonnet.

The friendly Pushtuns scrambled out. In their dialect, expressions of concern sounded like boulders rolling down the mountainside. Accustomed to shouting to each other from peak to peak, they used no volume below a roar. They clapped Uncle on the back: he had sustained the most damage, but he had held his nerve. In this uneven contest, he was the undisputed winner.

Some time after the crash, my uncle told me a joke about what it means to be an Afghan. I never did work out if the two were connected.

An Iranian merchant was going on a dangerous journey. He disguised himself as an Afghan, because nobody dares to meddle with the unpredictable men of the frontier. On the way, he met a real Afghan. The latter drew out his curved knife and said: 'I am going to kill you – are you afraid?' The merchant said he was. 'And will you give me all the money you have if I spare your life?' The merchant agreed that he would. 'Well, then, you are no Afghan. You fear death, and you will trade your life for money. A true Afghan is not swayed by such things.'

By 1982, there were already two and a half million

Afghan refugees in Pakistan. More were arriving every day. Nasirbagh was one of the better camps. Among the tents, baked-clay shanties were springing up from the red earth. I thought: Dust upon dust.

The refugees were mountain people. In their eyes was blank astonishment at finding themselves here, in this dustbowl. The sun glared on them all day long. The gurgling brooks of Afghanistan had been replaced by a stagnant canal, in which the little boys insisted on swimming. The children had eye disorders and respiratory ailments, caused by the foul water and the unaccustomed dust.

The refugees were given no hope of jobs, permanency, housing or ever escaping the camps and making a fresh start. The international community wished to maintain the fiction that they would soon be returning home. Every day they queued for rations of flour and cooking oil. Every day they listened for news from the front, where their relatives were fighting. Every moment of every day, rumours swept through the camp.

There was a particular camp atmosphere, which I will never forget, and which I have experienced again and again. The whole place trembled on the edge of unnamed hysteria. Every eye followed me. As I passed, arms stretched towards me, as if to a magnetic pole.

An old woman, still dressed in the finery she had put on to flee Afghanistan, beckoned to me from her tent. Packed inside were her three daughters and many grandchildren. A baby was laid out on a pile of rags. Its breathing was laboured and feverish. The family

75

possessed a blackened kettle, suspended on two sticks over a cooking fire. Apart from a sack of flour, that was all.

Miming bombs and guns, they told me they came from Kunar province. One day helicopters had attacked their village. Everything, their crops and animals, was destroyed. They left for Pakistan that same day and ended up walking for weeks across the mountains. On the way, there was an attack. One woman was holding her baby in her arms. It was killed by a piece of shrapnel as she held it. The top of its head came off. The baby's mother, a pretty, delicate-featured girl, was dragged forward to confirm the story.

I reeled out of their tent, but when I got to another, I heard the same story about the baby again, from people who swore it had happened to them.

I thought: I am witnessing the birth of a myth. It was a kind of emotional howl-back; as if everyone's gruesome experiences, everyone's trauma, everyone's hopes and fears had been fed into a gigantic loop and allowed to bounce round and round until they became both distorted and magnified. Until they had acquired an unstoppable force of their own and now belonged to everyone.

Uncle Mirza did not appear to notice the misery and squalor of Nasirbagh camp. When skinny children ran up to him, he handed out a boiled sweet or two, chuckling benignly at the resulting scrum. He held a brief parley with the Pakistani camp administrator; a thin pen-pusher, whose look of weary resignation showed that he knew all too well what was in store.

'Hello, my boy. This lad and I have come to distribute a little cash to these unfortunate women and children.'

'Oh, no, Colonel. You know that regulations forbid it. Why not make your donations through the proper channels? The UN, perhaps . . .'

Uncle clapped him so heartily on the back that the little man's spectacles were propelled off his nose. 'Since when has the giving of *zakat*, alms for the poor – as you know, an obligation upon every Muslim – been forbidden in a Muslim country? Bring me a trestle table!'

It was set up in the least dusty section of the camp. Within seconds, an enormous queue had formed. 'I beg you, for your own safety . . .' The little bureaucrat was silenced by a look from my uncle.

It was a routine that was repeated regularly. Since his compatriots had begun pouring across the border, Uncle had taken to withdrawing a portion of his life savings every now and then and handing it out to any refugee who asked for it. This practice infuriated Auntie Soraya, but Uncle was undaunted by either her rebukes or the apparent futility of his gesture in this immense sea of need.

The refugees knew the procedure. One by one, the head of the family – often a child – stepped up to my uncle's table. These were people who had never before needed to beg. An elaborate ritual of salutations began. Each person told him the family's story: where they had come from, how they had suffered and who had died on the way. My uncle might have been the chief of their tribe, matter-of-factly dispensing what he could to whoever needed it.

By the time of the afternoon prayer, we had disbursed all we had: about eight hundred pounds, a fortune to my uncle. But the line of refugees was longer than ever. I read dismay, disappointment, then fury on the crush of faces around the table.

I began to get worried. The Pakistani bureaucrat had long since slunk away. There was going to be a riot. Imperturbably, Uncle packed up his few things and we began to pick our way through the throng. Women grabbed the hem of our clothes, in the traditional eastern gesture of solicitation. The intensity of their need was like a physical blow. There was nothing we could ever do to assuage this. I was close to tears – of anger, at this destruction of a whole people, and of fear, for us both.

Then the crowd parted. Coming towards us, mounted on a beautiful white horse, was Jamil Haidar. I felt as though we had been transported back to some earlier age of chivalry. He greeted us quickly in the traditional way. 'May you never be tired, esteemed Colonel.'

'May you never be unhappy,' replied Uncle, as though deliverance by an Afghan freedom-fighter on a horse was an everyday occurrence.

'I have been seeking you everywhere. They told me you would be here. There is a person desperately ill, who needs your help.'

To the good colonel, an appeal for help was as nectar to a bee. We leaped into his wrecked Toyota. With

Jamil Haidar leading us on his horse, we clopped and trundled through the shantytown that had grown up next to the camp.

Beside the canal, we came upon an even stranger procession. Six men, whose rifles and bandoliers proclaimed them to be mujahidin, were carrying a covered *charpoy*, a bed, converted into a makeshift stretcher.

Jamil Haidar came to a sudden stop and dismounted. The stretcher-bearers laid down their load in the shade of a mango tree. Gently, Jamil Haidar pulled back the cover.

A woman lay under the sheet. Her breathing was rough and fast. She seemed not to recognize anything that was happening. Everything about her – from her delicate hands, limp on the sheets, to her straight Afghan nose, to her high cheeks and half-open eyes, unseeing in the blaze of fever – was bright yellow.

'Jaundice,' murmured my uncle.

The commander looked fiercely at him. 'No man outside my family has ever looked upon the face of my wife,' he said. 'Now I am in a strange country, a refugee, and I have no kinsmen to turn to except you – my *ham-watan*, my fellow-Paghmani. Please, take my wife to the hospital, where she can be cured.'

My uncle snapped into action. There was no way we could fit the *charpoy* into the car so he calmly stepped into the road and flagged down a passing Pakistani police Land Rover.

'For God's sake, it is just a damned Afghani refugee,' said the policeman.

'I am a colonel in the Pakistan army, and this is army business,' replied my uncle.

We drove in convoy to the military hospital, where Uncle Mirza breezed in with utter authority, despite his civilian clothes and English hat. By the look on the face of the duty officer, he was a familiar sight. 'This is an army hospital,' the medic tried. 'You know very well that it is only for military personnel and their families.'

My uncle assumed his most benign expression. 'This woman is from my homeland. She is under my protection and therefore she is of my family,' he said. 'Now, remember that Allah rewards the righteous, and behave accordingly.'

Why did I need fairytales? I had stepped into a world where young warriors really did ride around on white horses, and where my own uncle had rescued a damsel in distress. There was no doubt in my mind: the mujahidin were proud and noble. The romantic Afghan struggle was just what it said on the can. The myth was true, and I was living it.

However, I still had the matter of my purported marriage with Jimmy to straighten out. He had returned to his airbase in Quetta, from where he sent a constant flow of lavish gifts: rich Baluchi embroideries, scarves and delicate slippers.

I was busy examining my hoard, when Auntie Soraya announced that my putative fiancé was on the telephone. Jimmy was a huge favourite of hers, and a much closer blood relative to her than he was to my uncle's side of the family. She had taken it upon herself to promote the match.

As she handed me the receiver, Jimmy delivered a line obviously culled straight from a Hindi movie: 'We shall have a love-match, *ach-cha*?'

Enough was enough. I slammed down the phone and went to find Aunt Amina. When she'd heard me out, she said: 'Well, I'm glad that finally you've stopped this silly wild-goose chase for your roots. I suppose I shall just have to extricate you from this mess. Wait here while I put on something a little more impressive.' With that, she swept into her room, only to emerge three minutes later wearing a splendid kaftan. As a piece of Islamic one-upmanship she wore not one but three headscarves, of different sizes and colours. In preparation for the fray, she had pencilled on eyebrows of quite frightening blackness and hauteur. She looked every bit the part of the domineering Islamic battle-axe.

Soraya was sitting on her prayer platform, telling her prayer beads and muttering imprecations against Uncle. Amina stormed into the room, scattering servants before her like chaff. I watched through the keyhole of the bedroom door. Within seconds, there was a knocking at my window. Little Raj Bibi had fled the impending storm, and was now eager to share the excitement at a safe distance. I helped her to clamber into my room and made space for her at my keyhole. I felt an odd sense of affinity with this forlorn creature, as though we were two maidens in a Victorian novel, reduced to listening at bedroom doors while others decided our fate.

In the drawing room, Amina was advancing like a ship in full sail. It was like watching two galleons circling for battle.

'Your relative Jimmy . . .' was Amina's opening salvo '. . . has been making obscene remarks to my niece.' Soraya's mouth opened, but before she could find her voice, Amina fired her heaviest guns: 'Over the *telephone!*'

'How dare you?' began Soraya.

It gave Amina exactly the opportunity she needed to move in for the kill. 'What? Do you support this lewd conduct? Are we living in an American movie? Are we residing, perhaps, in a Hollywood film? Since when have young people of mixed sexes been permitted to speak to each other *on the telephone*? Let alone to talk – as I regret to inform you your nephew did – of love! Since when has love had anything to do with marriage? What an absurd and dangerous concept! Who passed the telephone call of this rapacious male to my niece?'

Soraya looked as though she was floundering for air. 'I never thought –'

'You never thought? One of your age and position? Someone I had until now believed to possess a regard for decency and religion?' Amina drew herself up to her full height. Her scarves, ruffled by the ceiling fans, fluttered like triumphant banners. Soraya was not only outclassed, she was out-Islamed too.

It was time for the *coup de grâce*. 'My niece is a rose that has not been plucked,' thundered Amina. 'It is my task as her aunt and chaperone to ensure that this happy state of affairs continues. I know I am speaking for this girl's father in saying that a match under such circumstances – whatever the family connection – is quite out of the question. The engagement is off. I bid you good evening.'

A rough, inhuman sound came from Auntie Soraya. She had lost her battle for moral supremacy and, it seemed, her fight for sanity as well. In a gruff, slack-jawed way that I found particularly unappealing, she had begun to bark like a dog.

Back in the bedroom Aunt Amina, Raj Bibi and I did high-fives. 'You were inspired,' I said. 'You've beaten her at her own game.'

Amina gave me a withering look. 'This is nothing to the time my father promised me to the pretender to the Albanian throne. It took me a whole week to get out of *that*. And even then, things might have been different if he hadn't been eighteen while I was forty-three.'

The next day, Jimmy was summoned to Peshawar by the enraged Soraya. He was told to expect terrible news and rushed back early next morning to my uncle's villa. I lay in bed, listening to the satisfying sounds of his arrival. As he raised his head at the threshold, to kiss the Qur'an, which, according to tradition, is presented to a returning traveller, his forehead connected with a heavy iron frying-pan, wielded by my deranged auntie Soraya.

On careful reflection, I decided to keep his gifts. The matter was never referred to again.

That afternoon, after Jimmy had been painfully

despatched back to his military duties, Jamil Haidar came to call again on his white horse. Uncle and I were sitting quietly together on the veranda. Auntie Soraya was locked in her room in a fit of black fury, mercifully neither seen nor heard. Jamil Haidar dismounted, and handed my uncle an apple. 'It is from your orchard in Paghman,' he said. 'It is all I have with which to thank you. My wife is much better and – with the will of Allah – she will be spared.'

Uncle handed it to me. 'You had better take it, my boy. If you do, you will come back,' he said. '*Az khude ma hasten*: you are one of us.'

I smiled as I pocketed the apple. I knew in my heart he was right.

5. The Elephant in the Dark

Some Hindus were exhibiting an elephant in a tent, and many people collected to view this wonder. But, as the place was too dark to see the elephant, they had to feel it with their hands to get an idea of what it was like.

One felt its trunk, and declared that the beast was like a hose. Another felt its ear, and said it must be a large fan. Another touched its leg, and believed it was a pillar. Yet another felt its back, and proclaimed: 'You are all mistaken, my brothers, this creature is nothing but a great throne.'

> Your outward eye is like the palm of a hand:
> The palm cannot grasp the whole of the object . . .
> Ah, you who are asleep in this boat of your body,
> You see only the water; behold the water of waters!

Masnavi, Jalaluddin Rumi

Zahir Shah shared a name with the exiled king of Afghanistan, but there could be no doubt about who was the prouder. While the former king had lost his kingdom and was obliged to hold court in Rome, Zahir Shah was undisputed ruler of a mountain fortress in the foothills of the Hindu Kush. While the king was almost completely bald, Zahir Shah had a splendid beard and whiskers. He also had a lot of sophisticated weaponry, mostly supplied by the Americans. And here, in the tribal area that straddles Pakistan and Afghanistan, serious arms count. To this day, no central government dares administer this region: the AK-47 and the ancient tribal code of honour of the Pathans – *Pushtunwali* – hold sway.

Zahir Shah finished his immense plate of *pilau* flavoured with rancid sheep dripping, and transferred the grease from his hands to his luxuriant beard. He caught my eye, and his smile revealed a startling absence of some key teeth. 'My beard is the symbol of my manhood,' he said. 'Why should it not eat too?'

He reached for the pocket of the waistcoat hidden behind impressive strings of ammunition belts and grenades slung across his broad chest. From its depths appeared a pink plastic mirror and comb. He began to groom his whiskers, unashamedly admiring his own craggy and fearsome reflection, with barely contained murmurs of satisfaction.

Around us, watching in respectful silence, sat Zahir Shah's men. None had a beard as fine as his, or a chest as broad. That was why he was boss.

They were a pretty motley bunch. One at least bore the sunken cheeks, feverish eyes and abundance of phlegm that suggested an advanced stage of tuberculosis. The youngest member of the mob was a lad of no more than twelve or thirteen. He was being treated with special favour by Zahir Shah, which I found disturbing.

'*Gandom*,' said the commander, pinching the lad's cheek. 'This boy has skin the colour of wheat. It is very beautiful.' He leered suddenly at me. 'Your skin is also the colour of wheat.'

I noticed that his mirror and comb were a matched pair. They belonged in a little cardboard box that proudly proclaimed: 'Fancy comb set, Afridi gents goods, Kohat'.

We were in the territory of the Afridis, one of the tribes that straddle the border between Pakistan and Afghanistan. The tribal area, euphemistically called the tribally administered zone, is strictly forbidden to foreigners, as well as being extremely dangerous.

Not for the first time I wondered what on earth I was doing in a fortress somewhere in this lawless area chatting to a Pushtun commander with whom I hoped to enter Afghanistan illegally.

At twenty-one years old, I had fulfilled my uncle's prophecy and returned to the region in 1986. But this time, I had rebelled. I was not content with the Afghanistan of our myths and legends. I wanted the facts – and I was determined to find out the truth for myself.

I had spent years preparing for this trip. At university I read Persian and Arabic. I took lessons in martial arts. To fortify my nerve, I went on a series of parachute jumps. Above all, I devoured any scrap of news about Afghanistan. Gradually the gardens and fountains of my childhood gave way to a Communist dictatorship and a noble resistance army fighting a war it could never hope to win. I never stopped to think that I might just have been replacing one mythical world with another.

Because Afghanistan was at war, I decided to become

a journalist. I began my quest for truth peddling lies in the offices of Fleet Street editors. I spoke fluent Persian; I was personally known to most of the mujahidin leaders; I was an experienced reporter, hardened to combat. Even as I uttered these outrageous falsehoods, I marvelled that anyone could believe them.

I didn't realize it then but, unconsciously, I was following in the footsteps of the very myths I was trying to put behind me. Once there was a cobbler called Maruf who borrowed money from various rich merchants, claiming that a sumptuous caravan was on its way to him. But he began to believe the story he had created. Instead of investing the money, he gave it away. As his debts got bigger and bigger so – in his mind and the minds of everyone in the town – did the wondrous treasures of his mythical caravan.

Like Maruf, I too began to believe my own lies. I liked this intrepid version of myself better than the truth. My confidence was contagious. When I asked for letters of accreditation, nobody refused.

Maruf's story has an unexpected ending. Just as he was preparing to flee in disgrace, a sumptuous train of camels loaded with jewels marched into town. The myth that he believed in – and of which he had convinced all around him – had actually taken shape and become real.

And that, in a nutshell, is the difficulty I have always faced. The more my Western side sets out to discover the facts about Afghanistan, the more I find myself turning to myth.

When I finally made it to Peshawar in September

1986, the beetle-browed mujahidin elders scratched their beards and looked from this scrap of a girl to the pile of impressive papers I had slammed down on the table. Then they agreed to take me to the front line.

To smuggle me past the Pakistani checkpoint at the edge of the tribal area, Zahir Shah dressed me in a *burqa*. 'We can travel in my car. Everyone will think we are husband and wife,' he said suggestively.

Smothered under the *burqa*, my senses were stretched so taut they ached. I was afraid of missing something. I peered at the forbidden road rushing to meet us out of the darkness. My years of preparation seemed futile, absurd. How do you prepare for stepping into a fairytale?

Zahir Shah and I communicated in Persian, a foreign language for both of us. As I gasped for air beneath the folds of my *burqa*, he kept up a non-stop stream of talk. His conversational gambits were unusual. 'In this village there used to live an Englishman. He was a very good person. He grew his beard and wore *shilwar kamis* and learned Pushtu. If it was not for the fact that his eyes were yellow, you would not have known that he was an Englishman at all.'

'What was he doing there?'

'I don't know. I never asked him.'

As dusk fell, he stopped the car. 'I'm going to get luggage,' he said, and set off at a run across a field. He soon disappeared from view. Within seconds, little boys encircled the car finding it in the silent dusk as mysteriously as ants find honey. After ten minutes, Zahir Shah reappeared and banished them with a flick of the hand. 'Luggage' turned out to be a vicious hunting knife and six or seven Kalashnikov magazines.

We resumed our journey. Finally the road ended. It didn't peter out into a track: it just ended. We were suddenly driving along a riverbed littered with boulders the size of footballs. Mountains heaved up on both sides of us. Sometimes we drove through water. At last we came to a wall, almost invisible, mud against mud. There was a door in it.

We entered a sprawling fortress, built around two courtyards. We were not yet in Afghanistan. This was Zahir Shah's stronghold in the free territory of the Pushtuns, technically inside Pakistan.

I was ushered into a room that was clearly a bridal suite. Tinsel drooped from the ceiling, pennants gleamed over the bed. The plaster walls were sky blue, and were incongruously adorned with pictures of Switzerland. Their only other decoration was an intricate pattern of electric wiring.

The family gathered round: countless children and a shocked-looking wife. She vanished quickly, to re-appear with a bundled tablecloth. It had four pieces of ancient unleavened bread inside it. She distributed them as place mats.

Zahir Shah looked smug. 'I didn't tell my wife we would have a guest.'

After supper she asked me if I would have green or black tea. I said green. I heard a flurry of Pushtu among the family and thought I picked out the word 'sugar' repeated several times. Finally Zahir Shah's wife brought the tea and an enormous sugar bowl with a lid on it. We both stared at it for a moment. Then she boldly took a teaspoon and, keeping the lid tightly shut, asked in a firm voice: 'Sugar?'

'No, thanks. I prefer it bitter,' I said in Persian.

There was an almost imperceptible sigh around the room. Without a flicker, Zahir Shah's wife handed me my tea. Zahir took his without sugar too. His wife's mother arrived and they told her in Pushtu that there was no sugar. We finished the teapot; the sugar bowl was never opened. The tea tasted alive; the water had a warm, living flavour, like a swamp.

Next morning, I woke early. Breakfast entailed the same tablecloth and the same four pieces of bread.

'Shall we have them make more bread?' enquired Zahir Shah grandly. 'This has lost its oil.'

By now I was learning the ropes. 'No, thanks. This is delicious,' I said.

We ate cheese and biscuits. With a show of bravado, Zahir Shah tried to break off a piece of bread, failed, and left it. Like the sugar bowl, it had acquired a symbolic quality.

Later that day, the mujahidin arrived. They spent the evening filling cartridges with black gunpowder. Little children sucked the bullets, and helped pile them up. According to custom, the men from outside the family were confined to the guest room. I slipped away to the women's quarters, where Zahir Shah's harassed-looking wife was feverishly assembling slices of melon on a platter.

'*Mande nabash*,' she said. 'May you never be tired.'

91

'*Jor bash*, may you be well. Can I do anything to help you?'

'No! No!' she almost shouted. 'You are a guest. Just stay and talk to us.'

For the first time I noticed that there were two other women in the room. 'My mother and sister,' said my hostess. I sat down cross-legged, as the women scrambled to shove cushions under me. I liked the women's quarters – more properly in Afghan houses the shared quarters. I'd soon learned that when visiting segregated houses it really paid to be female. Men are left in the formal but remote visitors' room, condemned to make polite conversation, but the women's quarters are the engine room of the house: the blackened cooking pot on the fire; the mess of children running about; the chickens pottering in and out.

Zahir Shah put in an appearance, to chuck his children under the chin, and to smile blissfully at his womenfolk. Here he lost the self-important, rather boastful air he was obliged to maintain in front of his men. He dissolved into soppiness as his five-year-old daughter scrambled up to hug him.

'I have ten children,' he proclaimed, allowing his daughter to tweak the ends of his carefully combed moustaches. 'Every one is a blessing from Allah. And, if Allah wills, this one will bear me twenty more.' With that, he swept off back to the world of men.

'Humph,' muttered his wife. Her mother poked her in the ribs and whispered something. She reddened.

'What is it?' I asked.

'Go on, ask her,' prompted the old woman.

Zahir Shah's wife took a deep breath, then blurted: 'I have heard that in the West there is a magic pill that stops you having children.'

Both mother and sister now giggled openly at this ridiculous rumour. Zahir Shah's young wife leaned forward and seized my hand with surprising intensity. 'Do not tell my husband, but how may I get such a pill?'

'Er . . . why do you want it? Aren't children a blessing from Allah?'

She looked around bitterly. 'I love my children – but I am tired of having them. I have enough. I don't want any more. Can you get me this pill?'

I thought furiously. I was never likely to come back here. There was no doctor or dispensary for miles. If she did find one, she would face her husband's extreme wrath. If he discovered what she was doing, she would be shamed, divorced; possibly even – in this place of reputation, honour and tribal law – killed. There was nothing I could do. 'I'm really not sure that such a thing exists,' I murmured.

'You see?' shouted her mother. 'We told you it was simply impossible. Now that you have heard it for yourself, perhaps you will stop dreaming foolish dreams, and realize that what Allah has ordained for women is to remain at home, bear many sons, and not fill their heads with useless fancies.'

One person's reality is another person's wild legend. Zahir Shah's wife lived just a few kilometres from the thing she sought, yet for her it might as well have been on the moon.

There was an imperceptible barrier, too that pre-vented us leaving for Afghanistan. Day after day, as I waited in Zahir Shah's guestroom for my journey to begin, my own perceptions adjusted to my surround-ings. I realized that the elaborate patterns of wiring on the blue plaster walls were decorative, rather than functional: electricity had not yet arrived in this region. The longer I stared at the idealized Alpine scenes on the walls, the more ludicrous the concept of Switzerland became. What made me so sure that it existed at all?

Zahir Shah kept making excuses to delay our trip. Whenever I asked him when we were leaving, he would say haughtily: 'I have still some preparations to complete.'

I didn't know what was the matter, but I had the impression that my attire was to blame. In order not to appear too conspicuous, I had picked up a man's *shilwar kamis* and a waistcoat. I also had a pair of canvas boots of local manufacture – they were dark blue, with white go-faster stripes. Although I'd never done any moun-tain-climbing before, I had a vague notion that boots were considered important.

From the first, Zahir Shah had glared at this footwear with disfavour. Now he had descended into a terrible, black depression, which deepened whenever he looked at my boots.

One day he announced abruptly that we would be paying a visit to the local black-market. Here, on the Pakistani side of their territory, the tribesmen had made use of their special status to establish a free-trade zone beyond the reach of taxes or the law. It was a Mecca for all that was illicit, immoral or downright deadly. Russian air-conditioners and refrigerators – liberated from the homes of high-ranking Soviet officers and smuggled in Bedford trucks across the Afghan border – jostled with Japanese merchandise schlepped up from Karachi. Squelchy black opium tar of local provenance sat coyly beside bottles of Silvikrin shampoo from Europe. Stud chewing-gum ('delays ejaculation!') seemed a particular favourite – although I was puzzled as to whether the grizzly grey-eyed tribesmen peering at it from under their turbans had any idea of the lurid claim, in English, on the packet.

I even saw a mug with a cartoon of a pig on it. 'What is that animal?' I asked, to tease the shopkeeper.

He avoided my eye. 'It's a funny kind of elephant,' he said.

The cattle in this area wore a glazed expression: the rubbish dumps they grazed on were piled high with the rotting stems of opium poppies. In one corner of the market stood a row of hijacked aid-workers' vehicles, awaiting ransom by their owners. In another corner, small boys were refilling brass cartridge cases with homemade gunpowder. A seven-year-old child offered to devise a launcher for any large-calibre shell I happened to have lying around.

The tribal area is a can-do kind of place. Like Harrods, the market seemed to boast that it could supply you with anything, given enough time and the right money. It did the trick for Zahir Shah. He rejoined me a few minutes later, a little smile hovering round his mouth, his whiskers twitching with pleasure.

Wordlessly, he pointed to his enormous feet. They bore a brand new pair of boots in exactly the same style and colour as mine. No longer could it be said that the commander of the group had lesser footwear than a mere woman.

'My preparations are complete.' He beamed. 'Tomorrow we can go to Afghanistan.'

I trembled on the brink of the first real journey of my life: the long-awaited return to the homeland I had never seen. The night before we left for Afghanistan, I stood in Zahir Shah's courtyard, gazing up at the unheeding stars in a state of exaltation. 'At last I'm here,' I told them. 'I've come, just as I always promised.'

For my secret agenda was this: even as I chafed against the storyteller's version of reality, it was the fairytale I sought. Even as I demanded truth, I was chasing a myth.

In particular, I hoped that the myth of the romantic Afghan resistance would stand up to the rigours of my journalistic enquiry. I hoped my family's map of tales might be my guide without my having to sacrifice Western method. And above all I hoped that, by resolving these contradictions, I could reconcile my incompatible worlds of East and West.

6. The Valley of Song

Although a domestic fowl may have taken thee,
Who art a duckling, and nurtured thee,
Thy mother was a duck of the water . . .
Thy longing for water comes from thy mother.
Thy longing for dry land comes from thy nurse.
Quit thy nurse, for she will lead thee astray . . .
Do thou fear not, but make haste to the water.

Masnavi, Jalaluddin Rumi

Deep in the mountains of north-eastern Afghanistan lives a blacksmith who loves to sing. He sings of distant kingdoms, lost princesses, unimagined treasures. But best of all he sings of a marvellous valley across the mountains. The song is strange and haunting, and it tugs at the heart. Everyone who listens feels that some part of them knows the Valley of Song. Everyone who hears the song yearns for the valley.

The blacksmith is sure that the valley is real – more real, perhaps, than the world of our own senses – but he believes that it would be wrong to try to go there. However, he is in love with a maiden called Fawzia. She is the most beautiful girl in the village and he has many rivals for her hand. She says that she will only marry him if he proves his love by travelling to the valley of which he sings.

So, the blacksmith sets out to find the Valley of Song. He climbs and he climbs. Beyond every mountain range he finds another, higher and steeper than the one he has left behind. Finally, he reaches a range that looks just like his own. Beneath it is a village that seems familiar.

When he stumbles back into his own village, many months have passed, and the blacksmith has turned into a frail old man. The people rush out to greet him and, haltingly, as if the words themselves are poison, he spills out the terrible truth. The village in the Valley of Song is not just like their village: it *is* their village. Every one of them here in their village has a counterpart living a parallel life in the Valley of Song. 'But there is worse to come,' says the blacksmith. 'For they are not our shadows, we are theirs. We are merely reflections, *they* are the real people.' Soon afterwards, the blacksmith loses heart and dies, just as all who hear the story from his own lips, unable to bear the truth he has revealed, fade and die too.

As a child, I used to beg to hear this Afghan folk tale again and again. I never grew tired of it. Something in it eluded me. I would not find out what it was, I thought, unless I found the Valley of Song for myself.

Now, as I climbed into the back of the Toyota Hi-Lux pickup truck with Zahir Shah's men, I was finally on my way.

There was a tangible sense of pleasure in the Hi-Lux. I felt my Westernness melt away and my Afghan side become stronger with every turn of the wheels. I was involved, a part of this. It was a course set centuries ago by my ancestors. Even now I get homesick for Afghanistan if I don't go for a while. Even then I was homesick for something I didn't know.

As we roared over the border, the Pakistani frontier guards shouted farewell – and we were across. And it felt as though a lifetime of restrictions and rules had melted away; that we were in the last free country on earth.

After a while, we got out and started to march up the side of the mountain. How vividly I still remember the turquoise mountain ahead of me. How fresh the air smelt. There were bushes that looked like holly, but upon which acorns grew. There were boulders and mountain streams. I soon forgot my iodine-cleansed water bottle and slurped from them along with the others. I was greedy for experience, and I couldn't care less what it cost.

We left the dried-out riverbed at the bottom of the valley and rose through a green belt of pines and firs round the mountain's stomach. The air was thinning and I felt the first dizziness.

We broke through the tree-line, to a desolate stretch of stones and snow. By now I was suffering a raging thirst. Still we carried on up. I forgot everything I had read in books and munched on snow. Zahir Shah gave me resin from a pine tree for my altitude sickness. But I still had to stop every few minutes, thinking I was about to vomit. Strangely, after sitting still for even half a minute, I would feel fine again – but the second I got up, the dizziness, nausea and thirst began again.

After what seemed like hours, we reached the summit, a thin-aired but wonderful point. Nothing existed but mountains stretching in every direction, sprinkled with glistening snow, the sky above. The odd tinkle of a donkey harness far across the valley carried for miles in the still air – and there was nowhere to go but down. Fatigue melted away.

With whoops, the whole gang slid down the snowy mountain on their bottoms – a dozen hardened, battle-worn soldiers with huge shoulders and thick beards, laughing like children and holding their Kalashnikovs above their heads as they scooted through the snow. Then, when the snow ended, we half ran the rest of the way down, stumbling on boulders, tumbling and laughing.

Then, suddenly, we were in the gloomy forest, then in the valley, and – with a lurch – I realized the whole process was about to begin again. The shark-tooth peaks I'd seen stretching in all directions were where we were headed: there was no other way than on foot. I didn't know it then, but it was a journey that would take weeks.

An almost unbearable loneliness came over us. On the rare occasions we saw people on the lower slopes we shouted greetings across the valley. Local children, herding goats, scampered down their mountainside and up ours just to say hello.

'*Tzingay*? How are you?'

'*Kheim*! I'm fine.'

'*Be-kher rawla*! You have come well.'

The Pushtu greetings rang out like the thunder of avalanches. At noon, we saw a man selling AA batteries, glitter nail varnish, boiled sweets and a cheap imitation of Nivea – the clumsily stencilled lettering read 'Vinea'. Prompted by a sudden consumer lust, I bought some of everything, including one of each shade of glitter nail polish.

I'd gone on to autopilot. Although I was quite fit, my thigh joints swelled, making it agony to walk, let alone climb. Somehow the routine of climbing and descending helped me to detach from the pain. By the time I was two-thirds up a mountain, where the air was really thin, I'd entered a sort of trance. Once, as I marched through the snow a good five thousand metres above sea level, I felt a tiny prick – and saw a wasp stinging my hand. The pain seemed remote and far away.

I could appreciate why this spectacular range had earned the sobriquet 'Hindu Kush' – the Hindu-killer; it had been named after the Hindu money-lenders who had made the perilous journey through them. They risked life and limb in the hope of luring whole Pushtun villages into debt at thirty per cent interest a month. According to legend, the wild men of these hills would wait until the money-lenders were returning to Peshawar, laden with the gold jewellery they'd extracted from them, before applying a rusty knife to the jugular and leaving another body to freeze in the snow.

Towards each summit, the water in my canvas boots froze, and I felt shards of ice crunching between my toes.

For lunch, we stopped for a few minutes beside a stream in the saturated sunlight. Zahir Shah untied a *pattu* – the porridge-coloured blanket that every

Pushtun man carries – to reveal a feast of flat bread and cold goat. The *pattu* became our tablecloth. The bread was hard – Pushtuns have a cavalier attitude to bread: their favoured variety is known as 'elephant's ear' because of its shape, texture and, as far as I could tell, its flavour. They nail it to the dung walls of their huts, allow it to harden and serve it months later. The goat, too, was tangy, and covered with fluff. We washed this repast down with great draughts of mountain spring water, and I still remember how wonderful it tasted.

Then we picked up our pace. The only respite I got was whenever Zahir Shah passed a particularly scenic piece of rock. Then he insisted on striking a heroic pose and having his photograph taken. With the pettiness that comes from being trapped in any repetitive situation, I began to grudge him his harmless conceit. I'd brought a limited number of films and, at this rate, they would all be filled up with pictures of Zahir Shah.

He had also evidently forbidden his men to talk to me – I was sure some of them understood Persian, although their native tongue was Pushtu, of which I could understand little. Whenever I tried to talk to them, they averted their eyes and strode on in silence. But Zahir Shah was eager for attention and I found myself crossly refusing his offers of a hand as I scrambled down the steepest inclines.

The first night we stopped at a *chai-khana*, tea-house, with a rumbling black stove and endless glasses of sweet black and green tea. It was no more than a wooden shack, set above a stream. The mountains veered up in every direction.

I sat down gratefully on a *bist-o-band* – a comfortable pile of rags – and joined the men in enthusiastically drying my socks over the stove in the centre of the room.

After half an hour or so, I glanced upwards, and something caught my eye. A squat, fat-bellied, unexploded shell was protruding through the roof. It was around four feet long and a foot in diameter. Its nose peered down at us as we sipped our tea below. As far as I could tell, little except a wedge of wood and straw held it up.

It seemed a bad idea to stay there for the night, but the temperature outside was freezing. I decided to pretend I'd not noticed it.

Our meat finished, we ate *yakhnee* – a dish I became all too used to. It consists of the grease of a fat-tailed sheep, suitably rancid, melted down with water. Into this slimy concoction, the men mashed hard elephant's-ear bread, loudly licking their lips and fingers before dipping their blackened fists happily into the communal bowl. The delight of *yakhnee* was that its raw ingredients could be carried for days or weeks in a bundled *pattu* and would never go off any more than they arguably had already.

Yakhnee also had a lot of nice grease to rub into one's splendid black beard and whiskers. As the entire room settled down to do this for their evening's entertainment, I fumbled with my contact lenses. Within seconds, I was the centre of attention. A dozen fascinated pairs of eyes gathered round for a really close look. I overheard snippets of hushed conversation:

'See? She can take her eyes out. That is a truly wondrous thing.'

The next morning, I awoke at dawn as the group gathered for prayer. The smell of woodsmoke bit into the chill air, and water was soon warming for green tea. As they waited for it to boil, the thirteen-year-old boy, whom I'd nicknamed Gandom, and the man with TB, cheerfully examined a second unexploded shell, longer and thinner than the one in the roof. This one was impaled in the stony ground outside the hut.

Zahir Shah, who could never be out of the centre of things for long, rushed forward equipped with an impressive penknife, and began to use the attachment intended for taking stones out of horses' hoofs to try to prise off its nasty-looking cone.

This was evidently a manifestation of what we used to call at home the Afghan School of Engineering. It combines just the right degree of enthusiasm and hor- ribly misdirected ingenuity. Ahmad Shah, the first king of modern Afghanistan, was the first documented pro- ponent of its theories when, in 1751, he ordered his engineers to devise a massive cannon capable of firing a ball weighing five hundred pounds. As soon as it was cast, and without bothering to test it, Ahmad Shah took this formidable weapon to the city of Nishapur, which he happened to be besieging. On hearing its report, the citizens were so terrified that they immediately surrendered – which was lucky for Ahmad Shah, because on its first firing the gun had burst.

Fortunately for us all, by the time Zahir Shah had reached some tricky wiring, the water for tea came to the boil, and the mujahidin could leave their task with honour intact.

The days slipped into a rhythm of climbing and descending. I lost track of time. We were walking through Kunar province, in north-eastern Afghanistan. There had recently been heavy fighting in this area. I told myself I was going to assess the organization and capacity of the local mujahidin groups. Inside me, a nagging voice whispered that I knew little about journalism, war or life in the real world. What I was really here for was to learn about myself.

We travelled for days on end without seeing a dwelling of any kind. Occasionally we came across the ruins of what had been villages. All were bombed out, their terraces smashed, their crops destroyed.

The occasional flatter land we passed shocked me utterly: it looked like the surface of the moon. Huge craters gashed a uniformly grey surface. I was told to watch out for anti-personnel mines. They were dropped from the sky, or planted to booby-trap abandoned villages. It was an onslaught without maps – no records were kept. To this day, Afghanistan is still struggling with countless untraceable mines.

The mines were a deliberate strategy aimed at depopulating areas that were supporting the mujahidin. I began to understand what the refugees I had seen in Pakistan had fled from – and what dangers they had faced on the way. The villagers – women and children – had staggered across the same mountains that I'd been struggling against. Mostly their animals had died. In Pakistan they waited, hopelessly, in the parched dust, as the children succumbed to malnutrition and respiratory infections, dreaming of farms and villages that had been long destroyed.

Days passed. Further into the Kunar valley, we came across the remains of a Soviet convoy. Rusted metal, the skeletal anatomy of a long-forgotten battle. I counted the twisted remains of a dozen tanks.

We sat on the biggest and ate some bread. The sun shone quite warmly. The sight of destroyed tanks all along the road clearly made the mujahidin feel good – as if the reminder of this local victory vindicated their mad expectation that they would win the war. I had to pinch myself to remember that this was the front line of a super-power conflict. The Red Army – perhaps the world's mightiest fighting force – was committed to holding Afghanistan. Half-way across the world, sharp-suited CIA men were working overtime, funnelling weapons to the mujahidin, sponsoring people like this: a shaggy bunch of men, giggling like children in the sunshine.

At the time, one could read very little in the Western press about the mujahidin that was not tinged with politics of one shade or another. They were described either as valiant heroes of the free world, or reactionary bandits. Both views were Western constructs. These men neither loathed Communists (except as infidels) nor admired America.

The days of walking were taking their toll on me. My joints were agony, and I felt permanently bilious. I could no longer bear the sickly, heavy smell of *yakhnee*. Zahir Shah had indigestion too. But he refused to admit it. Along with all his other foibles, he was a great hypochondriac. 'My heart!' he cried dramatically, slapping his great chest so hard that his ammunition cases rattled. 'My heart is very weak.'

Now, at last, to our relief we could spot houses here and there. They clung in layers like wasps' nests on the intractable mountainsides, and reminded me a little of Swiss chalets. We were approaching the borders of Nuristan, a province of Afghanistan whose name literally means 'the land of light'.

I noticed a group of men coming towards me and thought: It must be a Western camera crew. There was something intangibly European about them. Perhaps it was their fairness: they were blond or red-haired to a man. Perhaps it was their determined gait – very different from the measured amble of the Pushtuns. Perhaps it was that they'd carefully knotted their *pattus* round their waists instead of draping them in the untidy manner of the Pushtuns. Or maybe it was the way they wore their *pukkal* – woollen hats – unrolled, and loosely rerolled, as though they were odd, foreign garments. But when they drew close I was amazed to hear them speak Pushtu.

The history and origins of the Nuristanis are buried in the mists of time, but they alone in the region sit on chairs at tables, carve wooden spoons, live in chalets and observe myriad other customs that seem to belong in a different hemisphere. They are reputed to be descended from the remnants of Alexander the Great's army. Until 1896 they were infidel. Then Amir Abdurrahman Khan, as a pious duty, conquered them and forcibly converted them to Islam.

Zahir Shah borrowed some traditional knee-bindings from them, primitive wrap-around socks that covered the legs from ankle to knee. Above his knees, his *shilwar* bulged out like knickerbockers. It made him look like a crazed yodeller in some Alpine farce.

We passed through a Nuristani graveyard. Carved wooden monuments marked the resting places of the dead – so different from the neglected graves of the Afghans and Pakistanis, who believe the souls of the departed are flown elsewhere – why commemorate what is nothing but a husk?

And now we began to find villages. But these were unlike villages I had ever seen. No one had ever reached them who had not first trekked on foot for weeks over the inhospitable mountains. Few of the inhabitants had ever left their neighbouring valleys. They were living a medieval life, untouched by the modern world, barely even aware of the ferocious war on their doorsteps that had already killed over a million of their countrymen.

Even mules and donkeys could only tackle the high passes in the summer months. Almost no one here had ever seen a motor vehicle; there were no roads within miles. Electricity and running water were nothing more than rumours.

The haunting tale of the Valley of Song seemed to come to life in this terrain, as valley after distant valley unfolded. The people who lived here could have only the sketchiest idea of what lay beyond the endless mountain range. I half expected to come across my own *doppelgänger*, or perhaps a facsimile of the Kentish village where I was brought up. Or maybe the constant walking, the lack of food and sleep were making me feverish.

The houses in this area were built of wood on two or three levels, like Swiss chalets. The animals lived below in hay-filled byres, while the family lived on the floor above. The roof was often used for storing grain.

People stared at our little band of men, although we were on foot and dressed in local clothes. Mostly they welcomed us, for we were a valuable source of news from the outside world. In return, they informed Zahir Shah, who was in terrible discomfort, that they were blessed with their own apothecary – a mere two hours' walk away. By now that seemed like no distance at all, so when Zahir Shah decided to pay the man a visit, I tagged along out of curiosity.

Sure enough, we found an immaculately presented little chemist's shop, run by a lad of about twenty. The medicines, it is true, were all out of date. Having been carried by donkey for weeks, then on the back of a man for another week or so over the mountains, they were also a bit the worse for wear. But to see them at all was a minor miracle.

The apothecary was called Hashem. He explained shyly that his father had trained as a pharmacist. As it is well known that such skills are hereditary, Hashem had been bequeathed his practice and title when he died.

Zahir Shah was in seventh heaven. He bought piles of antibiotic pills of many hues, and munched great fistfuls of them. 'This is very good medicine – it will cure all my pains,' he proclaimed.

Working on the premise that if one pill was a cure

then dozens were eternal life and prosperity, he also decided that he would have a penicillin injection. The hapless Hashem was forced to prepare a rusty needle – the only one he had – and an ampoule mixed with some dirty water from the stream. Zahir Shah disappeared into the next room to have an injection in his buttock. He emerged groaning enormously – the pain of the treatment had deepened his conviction that he was on the threshold of death.

Hashem was thrilled that we had paid him a visit. Now he was determined that we should all be guests at his home, no matter that there were a dozen of us. His wife would cook *pilau*. We happily agreed. But first we had to pay our respects to the village headman – the local Khan.

There was another two-hour walk; by now the sun was nearly touching the peaks of the great mountains that fringed this Shangri-La. When we arrived, the Khan was waiting for us. In keeping with his great status, he wore a splendid silk *chapan*, an embroidered robe. As I was by now heartily sick of Zahir Shah, I performed my usual trick of slipping off to the women's quarters, where the Khan soon joined me.

He introduced me to his two wives. One looked around sixty, but was probably only in her forties. Afghanistan has one of the lowest life-expectancy rates in the world – around forty-six years – and I was continually surprised to find that most people I met were a good twenty years younger than they looked.

The younger wife was in her early twenties. She already had three or four small children. The old wife watched wistfully as they played. 'This is Fatima,' said the Khan, pointing to his younger wife. 'She is very good – she breeds a lot.' He pointed to his poor older wife: 'Salma is not so good. She doesn't bear children any more.'

I felt indignant and angry on Salma's behalf. But Salma, listening to the conversation, smiled and nodded as though we were discussing the weather.

'Mind you,' said the Khan, 'she has borne me seven children already. So she, too, was good once.' This was all the commendation Salma received, but she seemed to draw comfort from it.

We trudged back to Hashem's house. As the mujahidin had, as usual, hopelessly miscalculated the time needed to do things, most of the journey was in darkness. We picked our way over flinty rocks on a dry riverbed, or along a tiny path etched into the side of the mountain. None of us had torches. The only light was from the intense green stars that hung like bunches of grapes, seemingly just an arm's length above us. Mountain stars: so close in the thin air that we seemed to be grazing the sky.

Hashem ushered us all into his guest room. After the hardships of the way, it seemed like the height of luxury. There were quilted *lihaf*, mattresses, laid on the floor around the room, and even embroidered cushions. There didn't seem to be any fleas at all. Tea was brought in bone china Gardiner teapots, manufactured in imperial Russia by an eccentric Englishman and much prized in Afghanistan.

Hashem asked me if I would come and see his wife

in the women's quarters. I was only too delighted, although the memory of the Khan's views on women was still making me simmer.

I followed him up the wooden steps and I think I might have gasped as I entered the room. I was standing in a painting by a Renaissance master. Everything needed for domestic comfort was there, but there was not a single object that could not have existed in the fourteenth century.

The walls were panelled with dark wood, and draped with curtains in rich colours. A shaft of golden light from the timber-framed windows illuminated a carved bowl and spoon standing on a wooden table. There were low chairs and an apparatus for spinning. Suspended from the ceiling, an ornately carved wooden cradle swung gently back and forth. The baby slept under embroidered coverlets, a flapped woollen cap upon its head. Outside, I glimpsed hens pecking on a wooden platform, a cooking fire and a clay oven. The whole effect was utterly charming. It roused in me an overwhelming sensation of *déjà vu*. This place seemed as familiar as a childhood memory. I felt as though I had come home.

In the midst of this empire sat Hashem's wife. She was very young, and extremely beautiful, with a heart-shaped face, deep grey eyes, rosy cheeks and a cream complexion. She was attractively plump in the muscular, mountain way. The only concession to twentieth-century life was in her hair. Kirby-grips had evidently just reached the valley, borne in the satchel of some itinerant tradesman. Karima wore dozens of them, carefully placed edge to edge, exactly as they are presented on cardboard in the package. She obviously viewed them as an adornment, to enhance her wavy hair and, on her, the effect was rather pleasant. However, they – and a determined glint in her mischievous eyes – hinted at a thwarted consumer.

It was clear that she was somewhat spoilt. Hashem visibly swelled with pride as he introduced me. 'My wife Karima is the daughter of a khan,' he said. 'Isn't she beautiful? I have married the most beautiful girl in the village.'

Three times in my life I have come across human beings with whom I felt an inexplicable affinity – a woman in an Egyptian village, a child in a Kurdish refugee camp and Karima. In every case, I have seen in their eyes an answering recognition, as though we have each realized, to our great surprise, that on some level we are connected. If my ancestors had taken a different path – if they had tamed their inner restlessness – I might have been Karima: mistress of this delightful room, the daughter of a khan, married to the local apothecary.

Karima was clearly as fascinated by me as I was by her. At first, she thought I was a boy, and made as if to veil herself, with a little murmur of surprise. Then I spoke, and she looked at me more closely. 'You're a woman,' she said. 'Why are you dressed like that?'

In her cultural framework, it must have been the equivalent of a man wearing stockings and suspenders or an old woman in fireman's gear, but she displayed neither censure nor mockery, merely an overwhelming curiosity about something so entirely out of the orbit of her daily life. Luckily, she spoke Persian, so we could communicate directly.

Carefully, I explained that I was in Afghanistan so that I could tell the world what was going on here. To do that, I had to travel with the mujahidin, and for that, these clothes were most appropriate.

'Do you not have trouble travelling alone as a woman with so many men?'

I told her that the mujahidin were engaged in *jihad*, a holy struggle. I could imagine no other group of soldiers where I could travel in such perfect safety.

She digested this for some time. Then she bade me tell her some of the things I had seen and learned during my journey. I told her how similar in many ways the people of Nuristan were to Westerners, while the majority of Afghans were quite different.

I wanted to know more about her life. But she was consumed with a wild curiosity, a hunger almost, to know about the world outside her valley, her village. What did women in the West wear? Did men and women talk together freely? Were there miraculous means of transportation that could move one about in the twinkling of an eye, through the air, even? How had I travelled to Pakistan? When would I return?

I answered her questions as best I could, realizing as I did so that, even where there is the will to understand, it is practically impossible to convey concepts outside somebody's cultural experience. For instance, as I told her about aeroplanes, I could see that her mind was on flying carpets and miraculous spells – the thought that such an object could be operated by mechanical means, like the water-mill in her village, was simply ludicrous.

'But how about the *jinn* of the upper air?' she asked. 'Surely this flying creature would need to obtain their co-operation – unless it was itself a *jinn*, and mightier than the rest.' About the existence of the *jinn*, there could, of course, be no debate.

We talked far into the night. Her husband listened at first, then slipped away to entertain the men in the visitors' room. In this fairytale valley, a remote and unique world was seen as standard – so the West became the fairytale.

Finally, she looked at me with a roguish expression and said: 'I shall dress as a man and travel with you back to Pakistan. I shall see all these wonders for myself.'

For a fraction of a second, I saw life through her eyes: the narrowness of existence in her valley, the exotic visitor from another world, more enticing by far, its mysteries beckoning, the way apparently clear. 'It's a long hard walk across the mountains,' I stalled.

'I'm stronger than you are. Look at my arm. I'm used to drawing water and milking goats.'

'Well, I really don't think that you'd like the modern world as much as you think.'

'I shall come with you anyway, and if I don't like the life there, I shall return.'

Again I was reminded of the story of the Valley of Song: just as the blacksmith was never able to return to the existence he had had before his discovery, neither would she. If she came with me, her experience would change her for ever, and bar her from this world.

That night as I drifted off to sleep under a soft eiderdown, I could hear Karima and Hashem whispering excitedly on their mattress at the other end of the room. They were obviously deeply in love: two souls perfectly matched, their bond sealed with a trust and mutual respect that is rare anywhere in the world. Their love somehow mitigated the Khan's casual selfishness and cruelty to his older wife. I remembered that Karima was a khan's daughter, realized it was probably the same one, and wondered whether she was ever afraid of ending up like her mother, once-loved but now neglected. I thought probably she was not.

I said a silent, fervent prayer that Karima would never follow her heart's desire and leave this mysterious valley, to follow a will-o'-the-wisp across the mountains. Poor Karima: years later, millions of your compatriots are still trapped in Pakistan. They all dream of their green valleys and clear waters, but they can never return.

The next day I said farewell to Karima and Hashem, and we left the Valley of Song. I often think of them, quietly living their lives in parallel to mine. And I think I know now what eluded me in the folk tale. For rather than sapping my will to live, their serene existence enriches mine. I sometimes wonder whether I could ever find my way across the implacable mountains again, and if I did, whether I would find them there – or whether the village and the valley would have melted away into the mist. If I did find them, I wouldn't let such a place slip so carelessly through my fingers again. I'd settle down myself and disappear for ever in the valley too remote to be touched by either time or war.

7. The Honour of a Man

The night is dark – but the apples have been counted.

Pushtu Proverb

My grandfather had only one vice. He was addicted to pulp novels about the American Wild West. His collection of yellowing paperbacks was full of titles like *Bones of the Buffalo* and *Shoot Out at Silver Mine*. I think he believed them to be literal accounts of historical events. They reminded him of the unruly Pushtun tribes, whom no man has truly succeeded in conquering.

In his own books, he described the proud men of the Afghan frontier in a style that owed as much to his treasured Wild West novels as to the *Arabian Nights Entertainments*. I lapped it up. This was a world where an imagined slight could spark a blood feud that lasted for generations. Where damsels were abducted – not always unwillingly – in the dead of night by their hot-blooded Afridi suitors. Where women took the precaution of wearing red trousers, lest they be shot by mistake during the frequent inter-tribal wars. Where men were apt to draw a hissing breath and curse: 'May you live to pay taxes.'

The Pushtuns, of course, abided by no man's law.

Yet they had their own unwritten code, *Pushtunwali* – and the penalty for transgression was worse than death: it meant dishonour. I was versed in the qualities and duties that *Pushtunwali* demands. Among other things, the law of hospitality means that, once you have eaten the salt of a Pushtun, you are entitled to protection and respect; *badal* requires blood in exchange for blood or insult; *mamus* imposes a duty to protect and respect women; and *ghayrat* establishes the right to defend one's property and honour by force if necessary.

My grandfather's reverence for the free-spirited lawlessness of the Pushtuns verged on the mystical. He tended to gloss over *Pushtunwali*'s outward face, dealing as it did with retribution for material loss, and the tedious duty of maintaining one's dignity in front of others. Instead he saw it as a metaphor for the refinement of which the human spirit is capable. In its insistence upon honour, generosity and nobility, he found a set of values capable of transforming the soul.

Until now my knowledge of Afghan frontier culture was entirely theoretical. Zahir Shah and his men were the first Pushtuns whom I had had an opportunity to observe at close quarters. We were marching again, and the way was hard. We were all exhausted, but there was still a long way to go.

Zahir Shah's bottom had been infected by the dirty needle. He had an abscess and could walk only with the utmost pain. I tried hard to feel sorry for him, but I was secretly amused by his self-inflicted plight. Now that antibiotics might be of some use to him, he had lost all faith in them. He used his large stock of coloured pills to pay for our lodging at *chai-khanas*, or to hand out as presents to children. Word travelled ahead of us, and soon, wherever we went, villagers rushed to meet us crying: '*Dawa*! *Dawa*! Medicine! Medicine!'

Back on the trail, we returned to our unrelieved diet of *yakhnee* and bread. I felt quite ill, and became hypersensitive. Zahir Shah's offers to help me over a tricky piece of terrain now seemed not just gratuitous but lewd. I snatched my hand back and could barely restrain myself from snarling at him.

In fact, after several weeks of marching, in constant tension, without privacy and with no control whatever over the pace at which we moved or our destination, I was approaching a state of mind known in Peshawar as 'Afghanistan burn-out'. One of the tell-tale signs of this is a conviction that you alone are completely rational, while the rest of the world is behaving in an inexplicable manner.

The march was taking much longer than I had thought. The mujahidin often got lost – it is a fallacy of the West that mountain-folk can navigate across such bleak terrain by some form of invisible radar. Worse, I strongly suspected Zahir Shah of making large detours, sometimes enduring days of deprivation, in the hope of wangling a comfortable stay and a good meal at a remote village.

I became disoriented and angry, without having any outlet or rational reason for my anger. I was now covered in flea bites. Every night I would feel dozens of little nibbles being taken out of my flesh. (When I eventually got home, I was horrified to see my emaciated, flea-scarred body; I counted more than three hundred bites before I gave up.)

One tea-house looked unusually comfortable. Then I noticed that the loose straw covering the floor seemed to writhe and crawl. It took all my self-discipline to walk in and sit down. There, I could see that it was just millions of crickets hopping about. Now, crickets are friendly little creatures, but that night my dreams were uneasy and I woke the whole room by shouting in my sleep – a sure sign that my thinking was disturbed. Zahir Shah leered at me, and offered to massage my feet. For some reason, I let him.

Another night I was woken by crying. It was the distressed howling of a child, but added to it was some other element I couldn't put my finger on. It sounded supernaturally anguished. I traced the source to little Gandom, the boy with cheeks like wheat. 'What's going on?' I asked, blearily.

'He was told off by the commander,' one of the men told me, avoiding my eyes. 'He is crying for shame.'

It struck me that I was now entirely at the mercy of Zahir Shah and his men. I could not so much as walk down the mountainside alone; an unarmed stranger stands a very poor chance of survival in Afghanistan. The adventure I had so blithely begun now held me in its thrall. As we trudged along, I took to mulling over every fragment of Pushtun lore I could dredge up from my childhood storehouse.

Now and then my father had injected a note of caution into my grandfather's steady diet of stories extolling the honour, bravery and fearlessness of the

Pushtuns. '*Zar, zan* and *zameen* – gold, women and land – are the three terrible failings of the Pushtuns. Watch out, Saira *jan*, they are dangerous people.' And again: 'Why do you think the Pushtuns make such a fuss about *Pushtunwali*? Not because they invariably adhere to it. It is there to remind them how they ought to be.'

The next day we arrived at the boundary of the area served by the mujahidin base to which we had, it transpired, been heading all the time. For Zahir Shah, this was civilization. For the first time we met other mujahidin. They were manning anti-aircraft guns in foxholes. It finally felt as though we might be in a war zone. There was, however, no sign of an offensive. Instead, I was invited to photograph a group of boys polishing their Kalashnikovs, while Zahir Shah lolled about and recounted tall tales of his heroism.

The main base was a mere two days' walk away. There, we were assured, was comfort and ease: the means to wash clothes, and good food. We set off along a dry riverbed. A look of indescribable cunning crossed Zahir Shah's craggy features. He fell into step with me. 'When we reach the base, you will be the guest of the mujahidin for at least a month.'

This was a new departure. Zahir Shah was evidently tired of walking. I realized, with a sickening plummet, that I was already behind schedule – I hadn't expected the trip to take more than a couple of weeks and we had already spent more than that going deeper and deeper into Afghanistan. By now my parents would have received the letter I'd sent them. With twenty-one-year-old drama, I had begun it with the words: 'By the time you read this, I shall be on the front line, inside Afghanistan . . .' Today the very thought of this cruelty makes me break out in a sweat of remorse – but at the time I was only just beginning to guess the effect it might have on my mother. Worse, my brother was due to visit Peshawar quite soon, and I'd promised in my letter to be back by the time he arrived. Now, that promise was all I had to cling to. 'Zahir Shah,' I said firmly, 'thank you for your hospitality. But, as you know, I have to be back in Peshawar by the end of this month.'

It was an absurdly Western way of looking at things. What was a day, a week, a month, a year here? The concept of time was ludicrous in this world, where we beat our feet against hard mountainsides, and where distance was measured in the amount of ground a donkey could cover in a day.

Zahir Shah gave a shout of laughter – but his eyes narrowed. 'What? You would walk all this way, then simply turn round and walk back again? Do you think I am a fool?'

'I know that you are a man of honour – and as such that you will honour your promise to take me back to Peshawar by the end of this month.'

We walked in silence for a while. Then he tried another tack. 'The mujahidin tell me that the snows have fallen early on the high passes. There have been six people killed in an avalanche. The mountains will not be traversable until next spring.'

This was a much more difficult assertion to counter. What if it were true, and the road was closed? I would have no other choice but to stay here until spring –

or whenever the mujahidin chose to take me back. I would not be able to get a message to my parents, who would suppose I was dead. I simply couldn't do that to my family.

I think I went a little mad. I invoked the obligation of hospitality and reminded him I was a guest of the mujahidin. Zahir Shah merely squinted: this had become a battle of wills.

I ranted and raved. Mujahidin hospitality was worth nothing. I had taken them for men who fulfilled their word. Had the people of his clan forgotten *Pushtunwali*, the ancient honour code adhered to by every freeborn man of the Hindu Kush?

Insulting the honour of a people as trigger-happy as the Pushtuns is a risky pursuit: in all my grandfather's tales of *Pushtunwali*, harming women was strictly forbidden but it seemed a huge leap of faith to stake my safety on the idealized myth that I had been spoon-fed as a child. However, I was out of control.

I tore off my money-belt, and flung the contents into the river. Five-hundred-rupee notes went bobbing everywhere. 'This is the *baksheesh* I intended for the brave mujahidin. Let the river drink it. It has more honour than they!'

When I was a child, Aunt Amina used to tell me of a princess, whose father was human and whose mother was a magical creature called a *peri*. When the princess grew up, her mother sent her back to the world of humans, where she belonged. But before they parted, the *peri* pulled out one of her tail feathers and told the girl that in dire emergency she should burn it. Under the right circumstances, this token would summon up the fearsome supernatural creature in person. My grandfather's tales of *Pushtunwali* were just such a token. They gave me the theory of Pushtun honour by which to conjure up its reality. I had spoken without thinking, and with no regard for the symbolism of my action, but Zahir Shah immediately surrendered. 'Even if we all perish in the attempt, I shall take you back across the high passes,' he roared. 'The honour of the mujahidin demands it.'

I found this sudden transformation disquieting. I had an uneasy feeling that I had unleashed forces I barely understood. My rage had boiled off as quickly as it had erupted. I now felt thoroughly ashamed. The mujahidin came cautiously to me, and handed back the wads of notes they had fished out of the river and dried off as best they could.

I wondered exactly what the outcome of this show of pique would be. I had an uneasy feeling that, although I might have achieved my immediate aim of returning to Peshawar, I had unleashed a train of circumstance I might live to regret.

We plodded on, and arrived at another base that night. Zahir Shah was now all sweetness and light. He lent me a clean *shilwar kamis*, and sent the mujahidin to wash mine.

I went off to a pool and managed to wash my hair in the icy water. In addition to the usual *yakhnee* and bread, this base had a tiny vegetable plot. I was beside myself with excitement. As guests, I knew we'd be served with whatever vegetable delicacy they were growing. Perhaps some baby carrots, a little spinach . . . anything but rancid sheep's fat.

But when the *yakhnee* came, it was only accompanied by a dish of large, white, knobbly roots. I bit into one. The flavour was unmistakable. For some reason known only to themselves, the mujahidin at this base had decided to devote their entire vegetable plot to growing radishes. They were so peppery and strong that I could only eat one before indigestion set in.

I retired to bed. Unlike the usual dormitory arrangement, the base had a series of cells. As guest of honour, I'd been given one that even had a couple of iron bed frames in it. I collapsed on to one, delighted to be in such comfort.

I don't know how much later I heard a gigantic thump and rattle. Zahir Shah had crept in and helped himself to the other bed.

'Get out!' I snarled, snapping awake. Zahir Shah crumpled a little, but flopped down sulkily.

'Do you know the meaning of the word *azzat*?' His voice came out of the darkness.

'Yes. Honour,' I said, wondering where this was leading.

'*Azzat* is the most important thing. The honour of a man. What people say about him. This business of the money, the *baksheesh* of the mujahidin thrown into the river. That will be spoken about – not outside, of course, but by our *qom*, our own people. It might be said that the mujahidin had not paid due attention to a guest – that is loss of *azzat*.'

I was now heartily ashamed. I told Zahir Shah that

he was an extremely honourable man, and that the temper of a weak woman might fray now and then in difficult circumstances.

Zahir Shah instantly pursued his advantage. 'Saira *jan*, why won't you let me come and lie down next to you?' he asked. That, coming on top of the lecture on honour, made me want to laugh. Then I heard the unmistakable click of a safety-catch being taken off and, with a sinking feeling, remembered the handgun he always wore in his waistband. In the silence that followed I thought over what I would do if he threatened me. I realized I wasn't frightened, I just felt stubborn.

'I have a gun, I could shoot you,' he said conversationally.

'Well, then, if your *azzat* allows you to shoot a woman, you'd better get on with it.'

There was a nasty moment or two in the darkness. Straining my ears, I heard the cartridge sliding out – was he reloading? He took a couple of paces towards me. I didn't think he'd dare to shoot, but I wasn't a hundred per cent sure. I thought of my grandfather, and hoped that his tales of Pushtun honour contained even a grain of truth.

Something thudded on to my mattress. It was the gun. 'You must shoot me dead,' said Zahir Shah, 'because in any case you will have been responsible for my death.'

With a sudden flash of intuition, I grasped that the sound I had heard was him emptying the magazine. This combination of drama with caution made it hard not to giggle. I put the gun firmly under my pillow. 'Good night.'

There was a sulky silence. 'If you're not going to shoot me, give me back my gun,' he pleaded finally.

'Promise on your honour as an Afghan, a commander and a Pushtun that you'll leave me alone, and I will.'

The next day we had, in an obscure way, come to some kind of understanding: we would be leaving for Peshawar without delay. Although I had trounced him in private, Zahir Shah's plan had worked. He had regained his status in the eyes of his men. All they knew was that I had remained alone with the commander for the entire night. I was obviously a Western prostitute, for all my fine talk. Zahir Shah strutted about in macho form – and I had gained some idea about the value of the *appearance* of honour.

'The mujahidin are strong and brave. For the sake of their guest, they will defy death by ice and falling snow,' thundered Zahir Shah. He struck a heroic pose, while his men looked on approvingly. Face had been saved. His reputation had been maintained.

When I saw the amount of snow in the high passes, I began to think that his talk was, perhaps, not mere polemic. In just a couple of weeks, the snowline had plunged down far below the trees, which meant that each mountain was twice as much trouble to climb. We slipped and slid on the ice. I tried to clutch the snow-laden branches to keep upright. I was beset by the thought that, if we were all killed in an avalanche, it would be my fault. Food was at an all-time low. Even the bread and sheep fat were hard to come by. We chewed pine resin to stave off the hunger pangs.

A few events leap out from what has become a blur of walking and sleeping, interspersed with pauses for flea bites and green tea.

Stumbling along the snow – nothing for miles but mountain peaks and gleaming whiteness. Then, in the opposite direction, a strange procession: around six men, carrying a bier, covered with blankets. The scene is like a medieval miniature. The silent intensity of the group stopped us in our tracks. We stood stock still as they approached – they took five or ten minutes to do so. There were none of the usual shouted greetings. Nobody said a word until we were face to face. What was happening? If this was an invalid, why were they taking him away from Pakistan, and medical help? If he was dead, why on earth risk this perilous journey?

The stone-eyed mourners told us, simply, that this was a man whom they had been carrying into Pakistan for medical attention. After a week of walking, and just across the border, he had died of his wounds. That made him a martyr, entitled to the greatest veneration. As his soul was now in the hands of Allah, they were on the long trek back to his home village with his earthly remains: one who had made the greatest sacrifice should not suffer the indignity of burial in a foreign land.

It was the first reminder in weeks for me that this was not a game. That there was a war being fought in these mountains, which meant more than the macho posing and boasting of the mujahidin. We stood and watched the procession out of sight. It seemed to represent the dignity of which the human soul is capable under the most unpromising circumstances.

It was also a grim reminder of the harshness of our situation. Here, still far from the border, a stomach wound was a death sentence. So was a medical emergency – appendicitis, say. And stepping on one of the uncounted landmines that littered the place could mean instant death.

We skirted round one village as dusk was falling. Normally it was just the kind of place Zahir Shah would have homed in on for food and shelter. I noticed a definite tension among the group. Two men went on ahead with Kalashnikovs at the ready. Two others guarded the rear. Zahir Shah and I remained in the middle.

'What's going on?' I asked.

'Blood feud,' said Zahir Shah shortly. 'The brother of this mujahid was killed, so he shot two men from the family of the murderer. Now they want to kill him. This village is not safe for our group.'

We had a long forced march in the darkness, picking our way blind along the steep mountain path. It seemed fitting in this mysterious world that, however hard I tried to lift an edge to peek into, there were still mysteries behind mysteries.

The lad who had killed the kinsmen of his brother's murderers was escorted along another path, further from the village. He had curly brown hair and soft, childish eyes. He was about seventeen.

When we were almost at the border, we passed a man herding goats, the first flocks we had seen for weeks. With my famished eyes, I no longer saw cute little animals but food. With sudden inspiration, I asked how much it would cost to buy one. The price was about forty pounds, a considerable sum in Afghanistan – and to me.

I bought it immediately. Instantly our group was on holiday. The mujahidin took turns to lead it along on a string. Its desperate bleating only added to our festive spirit. We smiled when we caught each other's eyes. Tonight we would have a feast.

With our guard down, we walked straight into the ambush.

By now the path had widened, as we crossed a valley. Mortar shells began to fall both in front and behind us, which I later came to learn is usually bad news: it means you are in the middle of the range.

My first feeling was a sort of indignation. I wanted to shout: 'I'm *nice*, you idiots, I'm a *nice* person – I've never harmed anyone. Why on earth do you want to waste good ammunition on me?' A few weeks ago I had been at university, going to student gigs and drinking cappuccino in the union café.

A shell crashed on to the road and topography rearranged itself in my mind. I flattened myself in a ditch I hadn't even noticed a moment before. The mortar crew had obviously got their range now because the shells were falling faster. As the adrenaline cleared my head, my brain speeded up. I had plenty of time to make decisions. I counted the shells under my breath. By the time I had heard eight or nine crashes, we had regrouped in the ditch and Zahir Shah at last had a chance to show us why he was commander.

'It's no use going back. They were watching us along the path, and waited for us to get too far into the middle of the kill zone. We'll have to go forward,' he said.

I understood the reasoning, but moving towards the fire still seemed an unnatural thing to do. Yet I felt a conviction that I would survive. There was a quite distinct moment of handing over responsibility. It was nothing to do with religion: it was more like reconciliation. Perhaps it is a survival mechanism. This level of alertness was exhilarating, like running on pure oxygen. I thought, This is how human beings are meant to be. So quick, and so sure.

At a signal from Zahir Shah we left the shelter of the ditch and pelted down the path. I ducked for cover more often than was necessary, but even in those few moments I was learning. My ear attuned itself to the cadences of the shells: that bang is loud, but you might as well keep on running. This whistle means a shell is passing close by – you had better take cover.

At one point, I heard a distinct whistle and, as there was no cover nearby, I flattened myself on the dust road. I actually saw a shell land. I can replay that moment quite precisely like a video in my mind's eye: it fell on the scrubby grass and flint on my right-hand side, bouncing as it hit the ground. Astoundingly, it didn't explode. This impressed me hugely: if it had gone off, I would have been killed. A few seconds later I passed a second shell that had failed to detonate.

Dimly I was aware of the panic-stricken goat bleating behind me. The Tunbridge Wells part of my mind thought: If we get out of this alive, I really ought to release that poor goat. Then, in a very few minutes, we had passed the point where a mortar's steep trajectory could hit us. The shelling died down as the unseen enemy realized that we were all past. We greeted each other like long-lost friends, amazed to discover that we had all escaped uninjured. As an ambush, it was negligible, using up plenty of shells to little purpose. I felt a guilty rush of satisfaction. At last I could say that I had seen something of the war.

The goat was frothing at the mouth and rolling its eyes. As the hungry part of me reasserted itself, I saw that I could never deprive the mujahidin of their first square meal in weeks, especially after they had risked life and limb to preserve it.

That night, we had a goat-feast. Making a great show of the duties of a host, Zahir Shah insisted I eat the first share of the brain. He pulled off a small piece for me with filthy fingers. It was delicious and very smooth. The commander gulped down the rest of it, in front of the famished eyes of his men.

The next morning we filled our pockets with cold meat. It felt wonderful to be walking along, alive, in the crisp late-autumn air, with pockets full of goat meat. We joked and slapped each other on the back, bonded at last. Zahir Shah, his tribulations and humiliations forgotten, was proud of the way he had led his group out of danger. He celebrated by assuming a triumphant pose on various boulders: his hand shading his face and his eyes gazing out over the mountain ranges. For once I was delighted to photograph him. It was the least I could do.

We got back uneventfully to the tribal areas, and the three days I had to spend there, experiencing Zahir Shah's hospitality before he would even think of sending me back to Peshawar, were difficult to be suitably polite through.

His wife, still scandalized by my male attire, which by now was very much the worse for wear, kindly gave me an Afghan woman's dress. As I finally put on my *burqa* to make the journey to Peshawar, Zahir Shah remarked: 'You are a very manly woman.' It was the highest accolade in his vocabulary.

When we arrived, we dropped in on the former Afghan army brigadier, now a mujahidin leader, who had arranged my trip. He was delighted to see me, and insisted we sit down on the spot to have *pilau*. As we were eating, my ashen-faced brother Tahir walked in. He had been trying frantically to discover my whereabouts for days. At about the same time that we were being shelled, he had stumbled across the brigadier. On making enquiries, the brigadier heard that we had been in an ambush. No details of casualties were available. He stalled my brother who, according to the rules of *Pushtunwali*, might well have been sent by my family to extract payment in blood for the abduction and loss of a sister.

When he heard that we were safe, the puckish brigadier told my brother that we had been in a skirmish and were probably dead. He then invited him to have *pilau* and talk it over. Tahir didn't recognize me at first: he was too busy trying not to look at the Afghan woman whom he was surprised to see had joined the men's meal. When I greeted him, an expression of huge relief passed over his face. 'Thank God,' he told me. 'Mum would have killed me if I'd had to tell her you were dead.'

I often think of that magical journey, and when I do, I always wonder what has become of the extraordinary women, like Karima, and Salma, the wife of the Khan, whom I met.

As for Zahir Shah, I never met him again but I did hear about him. Just over three years later, by a long chain of peculiar circumstance, I found myself working for a Swiss radio station in Berne, trying bemusedly to make sense of Swiss news. The duty editor handed me a wire: 'Didn't you say you know something about Afghanistan? Is this bloke important?'

It was only four lines long. It said that Zahir Shah had been shot dead in the tribal areas of Pakistan, in a killing with all the hallmarks of an assassination by a rival, radical Islamist, group of mujahidin. The only reason it could have made the wires was that some sub-editor must have confused his name with the former king of Afghanistan.

'No, he's not important. It's the wrong Zahir Shah,' I heard myself say, but my mind was elsewhere.

I thought of him posing on boulders, of getting us through the mortar fire, unloading his handgun before giving it to me, and rubbing lamb fat into his sleek black beard. I couldn't find it in my heart not to think kindly of him, or of his wife – who now does not need that pill to stop her having babies.

8. The Old Woman and the Hawk

A hawk belonging to a king flew away and landed at the
house of an old woman. She had never seen a hawk
before, and she decided to look after it. She trimmed the
hawk's curved beak into a straight line, cut off its crest and
clipped its claws. 'There,' she said, when she had finished.
'Now you look much more like a pigeon.'

Masnavi, Jalaluddin Rumi

When I returned from my journey with Zahir Shah, I
settled in Peshawar and set myself up as a freelance
journalist, stringing for several newspapers and magazines. It was the end of 1986, the chilliest depth of
President Reagan's Cold War. Pakistan was considered
to be a front-line state that needed shoring up now that
the Red Army had arrived on its doorstep. The military
dictatorship of General Zia ul-Haq received billions of
dollars of US military aid in return for playing host to
two and a half million Afghan refugees, and to the
squabbling factions of Afghan mujahidin.

The United States was so eager to see the conflict in
terms of Communism versus democracy that it didn't
notice its allies were fighting a different war. America
relied heavily on Pakistan's Inter-services Intelligence

to hand out its military aid to the mujahidin resistance. A shadowy group of Pakistani officers gave it to their own cronies. Thanks to the ISI, the US were nurturing a brand of extremist political Islam that, until now, had been almost unknown inside Afghanistan.

The lion's share of US military aid went to a Pushtun called Gulbuddin Hikmatyar, who had lived in exile in Pakistan for years. Gulbuddin had briefly been a Communist; then he had a road-to-Damascus conversion and became an Islamic radical. The two movements were paradoxically similar: both believed that only revolution could sweep away Afghanistan's outdated traditional society. Gulbuddin was driven by hatred – but not of Communism: he despised all infidels, including the ones who supported him. All this was well known to American diplomats, who would openly joke: 'Hell, the more a political faction loathes us, the more money we give them.'

I didn't need anyone to teach me how to see what I wanted to see. I didn't want this fractured, war-torn place: I wanted the lost homeland I had been told about.

It wasn't long before I found someone who personified my idealized Afghanistan. Professor Majrooh was an internationally acclaimed scholar. With his glowering beetle brows, he resembled a ferocious and sometimes grumpy falcon. But his sharp eyes had a twinkle in them, and they were kind.

He was a member of the educated élite who had now mostly used its influence to slip quietly abroad; his Kabul was a place of Italian restaurants, pleasure jaunts and cultural outings. He could have gone too, but rather than take up a lucrative teaching post at some American university, he remained in Peshawar, in a poky office with the one gnome-faced servant who had fled with him from Kabul.

I would drop by his office, ostensibly to listen to his views about the conflict, but I wasn't really there for journalism. I wanted a mentor, and perhaps another storyteller father figure to replace the one I had left in England.

Majrooh was one of the few people who complained that US dollars were fostering Islamic radicalism. 'This fundamentalism is foreign to Afghanistan. It is not Islam,' he would say.

I nodded adoringly, but I wasn't really listening. I had taken to stalking the professor. He alone seemed to have the key to the Afghanistan of my beloved myth. Majrooh was immensely patient with a naïve and pestering twenty-one-year-old. Often he would wink and tell me: 'Come back after four o'clock.' At that time, armed with a bottle of whisky, he became expansive. For a while, his dingy office would fade away, and I became his attentive university student. I never knew whether I would get a political analysis or an exuberant treatise on the classical Persian philosopher-poets. His eloquence soared on the wings of the enigmatic Hafiz, the lyrical Khayyám, and the awe-inspiring Rumi. Whatever the subject of his thesis, it would somehow come flying back to our present situation.

'. . . The poet Hafiz could not set pen to paper unless he had had a glass of wine. Yet the spiritual power of his poetry still astonishes people today. We have our own tradition of Islam in Afghanistan. It looks to the internal, the absolute, rather than the externals: what clothes you wear, what rituals you perform. What does any of that matter compared to the real state of the individual?'

At that time Peshawar had a dangerous edge, a Wild-West-meets-Casablanca feel, as if it was teetering on the brink of a nameless chaos that might engulf it at any moment. To drink alcohol in one of the town's few bars you had to swear in triplicate that you were both an infidel and a habitual alcoholic. This lent an illicit air to the whole undertaking.

Among my drinking companions were propagandists, spies, drug-dealers, gun-runners, do-gooders, hacks, drifters and the seriously deranged. I rubbed shoulders with the kind of people you never meet in Tunbridge Wells. There was a Pole who just wanted to have a crack at the Russians. There was a New York narcotics cop, who was doing something secretive involving heroin. There were lots of former public-school boys, keen to make a quick trip into Afghanistan with the 'muj', and to pick up a few shell casings as trophies for their Fulham flats. There was a floating population of grizzled American war reporters, who had done 'Nam and 'Bode and who thought they might as well do Af before they retired.

And then there was Hank. He could often be seen propping up the bar of the American Club. He was a stringer for a US television channel, but he liked to hint that this was just a cover for his work as a CIA operative. He went to great lengths to further this image, maintaining a villa beyond his income, over which towered an enormous satellite dish. Strategically placed on his dining-table stood a picture of Hank greeting a puzzled-looking President Reagan.

I have often wondered what pleasure life can hold for Hank now that the Soviet Union has collapsed. Who else can he possibly have found to hate with such vehemence? Hank feared political pollution as the devout fret about spiritual defilement. He went to great lengths to avoid those whom he suspected were not 'on our side'. When I first arrived in Peshawar, he would hiss in my ear: 'Do you know so-and-so? He's a Communist! Do you know such-and-such? KGB! Do you know him? He's KHAD, Afghan secret service!' I believed it all, until a new acquaintance opened a conversation with me by saying: 'So, I hear from Hank that you're a spy . . .' I doubted that even the CIA would have employed Hank.

A short man, with bulbous eyes and tombstone teeth, Hank saw himself as a romantic Lawrence of Arabia figure. He took to wearing Afghan clothes, to growing a beard, and to telling other reporters what they should and should not write. Later, he kept birds of prey and could often be seen, a leashed falcon perched nobly upon his wrist, striding in lonely splendour around the grounds of his vast, empty villa.

Just as he needed the Soviets to be evil, Hank required the mujahidin to be noble. They had to be good and, what was more, they had to be good in a way he could understand. He had no patience with an increasingly factionalized conflict in a country with a delicate religious and ethnic balance. He wanted to believe that the mujahidin were fighting because they detested Communism, just like him. Hank wanted a myth – and he wanted it so badly that he intended everyone else should be made to believe it too.

As for me, no one challenged my description of myself as a reporter, although when I started I was so broke that if I didn't sell a story I sometimes went into Afghanistan just to eat at the mujahidin's expense.

Everyone in Peshawar lived in a strange, parallel world to the war in Afghanistan; shadow puppets of the real actors across the border. We all kept a wary eye on the road that led to the border. We all dreamed that one day, when the war was over, we would drive down it. And we all feared secretly that war, plague and pestilence might one day come swirling up it instead.

For now, the road was blocked. At the city limits, a Pakistani checkpoint turned back foreigners. The Afghan refugees didn't need a checkpoint to tell them they were stuck there, in this dustbowl. There was a suffocating feel to Peshawar, as if every breath might make your chest constrict and your lungs collapse. Or perhaps that was just me: hyperventilating and drunken at this wild new world into which I had cast myself.

By day, my hangout was Lala's Grill, the restaurant of a seedy hotel called Green's. Newspapers rustled as you went in. They belonged to the legions of spies from Pakistan's many intelligence services who kept an eye on foreigners. You soon got to know the Pakistani spooks: they were the ones wearing regulation thick-soled *chappals* – sandals – and sunglasses. The idea that I was important enough to be watched by the secret services merely added to the palpitating excitement of the place. I loved walking into Lala's Grill.

Hermetically sealed in its fishbowl interior, I would gaze through tinted glass at the glorious roaring madness of the world outside. There was usually some kind of demonstration going on: 'taking out a procession', as it was called, was the accepted pressure valve for Peshawar's unbearable and contradictory tensions. Sometimes opium producers marched past, demanding the legal right to grow poppies. At other times students from the university called to be allowed to cheat in exams. Every now and then Islamic radicals – their hearts expanded by Friday prayers at the mosque just up the road – cheered for Allah and fired Kalashnikovs into the air. Once, a happy and excited crowd stormed past on its way to burn down the offices of the local newspaper, the *Frontier Post*, which had heretically published nude portraits of those venerated Islamic figures Adam and Eve.

Hour upon hour, I sat in my safe bubble, like a spectator at the dawn of creation, and I watched this exhilarating, mystifying new landscape unfold. Even from inside my fishbowl I guessed that, when it came to making sense of this place, I was up against far more subtle barriers than dirty window glass. Just ordering a drink at Lala's Grill was a daily ordeal.

'A *lassi*, please, with salt,' I would say.

'OK, madam. So, is that saltish or sweetish?'

'Er, saltish.'

The waiter would write triumphantly in his pad: 'Sweet . . . ish.'

It seemed, always, terribly important to get my message through; at least here – at least in my bubble. So, for a while, we'd be locked in a Punch and Judy parody of attempts at cross-cultural understanding.

'Sweetish?'

'Saltish!'

'Sweet-TISH!'

'SALTISH.'

When my *lassi* arrived it was, of course, always sweet. In Peshawar the worlds of East and West would frequently collide, but they never managed to communicate.

At around that time, my nineteen-year-old sister Safia came to work for an aid agency and, for a while, we shared a shabby room in the Peshawar Club – the only place, aside from his own villa, where Uncle Mirza could tolerate the thought of his nieces living.

The club – a petrified remnant of the British Raj – was the hangout of retired colonels, and immensely respectable. Ancient uniformed waiters teetered from clubhouse to bungalow with silver trays held aloft. The menu consisted of 'short lunch', which was chicken and chips, and 'long lunch', which was the same, with the addition of green jelly. A substance called yellow cake was served for tea.

However, with delightful Oriental irony, behind its sober façade the club was a den of vice. Many of the colonels had taken rooms there to gamble, drink whisky and entertain prostitutes. This outwardly decent, inwardly decadent domain was the perfect setting for our paradoxical suspension between East and West.

In my persona as a dutiful Muslim niece, Uncle Mirza introduced me to middle-class unmarried girls of my own age. My mixed background played in my favour – *outré* enough for rebellious teenagers yet perfectly respectable from their families' point of view. I was plunged into the shadowy world of young women who were exerting their utmost ingenuity in making themselves unmarriageable. Akila wore only men's clothes and cut her hair short like a boy's. Nargiss had gone to the other extreme: she wore bright red lipstick and high heels to horrify the mothers of potential suitors. My favourite was Samira, who knew that her family would die rather than arrange a marriage for her with a man of inferior education. She was currently studying for another degree.

When young men dropped in on Safia and me, their visits were given extra piquancy by the possibility that our Peshawari relatives might arrive unannounced at any time. An American called Jim Lindelof often used to come round with illicit beer. Jim was a big, sun-bleached, good-natured guy who was waiting in Peshawar to make a trip into Afghanistan. In a place where everyone spent their time hatching plots, suspecting the worst of each other and maintaining a paranoid secrecy, he had an endearing and particularly American quality of being totally trusting. It was lovely to hang out with somebody so laid-back. Safia, Jim and I would sip our beer, have light, easy conversations, and bask in the little part of California he brought into our lives.

It was inevitable that one day our irreconcilable worlds would collide. We were sitting drinking beer with Jim when there was a furious honking outside. I looked out of our window and saw Uncle Mirza's car drawing up, laden with relatives. In the passenger seat, telling her prayer beads, was Auntie Soraya. There was no time to explain to Jim. Without consultation or speech, Safia and I acted as one: I opened the wardrobe door and she thrust Jim inside, complete with his six-pack of beer. Seconds later, relatives rushed in like the tide. For an hour the room became an outpost of our extended family. My auntie sent for yellow cake, babies were suckled, ablutions and prayers performed. Every now and again, Auntie Soraya glanced around suspiciously, as though prompted by an inner intuition that something was amiss. But however closely she peered she saw nothing except two demure Muslim girls.

The moment our relatives left, Safia and I sprang to the wardrobe to release Jim. He emerged with barely a sun-kissed hair out of place and only mildly puzzled at our strange way of treating visitors. His own tolerant nature had protected him from the distressing scene that must have unfolded had he opened the wardrobe door. When he finally ambled off to Afghanistan, I hoped the same naïve all-American goodness would envelop him in its protective haze.

Gradually, too, my rebellious Muslim teenagers drifted out of my life. One by one they had succumbed to the determination of their families to arrange a match. Akila, the tomboy, was cudgelled into marrying a pimply youth who could not expect a beauty. Nargiss, the vamp, was despatched to marry a polo player in Lahore where morals were loose. And poor little Samira fared worst of all: her family dredged up a decrepit old professor from Peshawar University, who was delighted to have such an academic young bride.

Deep in my mind, a little voice warned me that my own impunity could not go on for ever. As my balancing act between East and West became more and more intricate, the likelihood grew that I would end up flat on my face.

By 1987 there were explosions in Peshawar almost every night and quite often during the day, but we didn't take them seriously. At the dinner parties I attended, we played a game. When the inevitable detonation came, somebody would guess: 'About half a kilo of plastic explosives, two klicks away.'

The next person said: 'No – a kilogram at three kilometres.'

Then we'd all pile drunkenly into some aid worker's Land Cruiser to find out who was right. We would come across a crater, perhaps a baffled Pakistani cop or two, and every now and then a bit of shredded flesh. After a while, we got bored with it. The explosions carried on, but we had ceased to register them. They were part of the background soundtrack to our existence in Peshawar, as ubiquitous and unobtrusive as Muzak.

We tut-tutted when dead bodies with lacerated throats came floating up the canal, but I don't remember writing a single story about this unexplained slaughter. Nobody thought it was important. We were thinking in terms of a superpower conflict, so we never put together the pieces. As in Rumi's fable of the elephant in the dark, we called its trunk a hosepipe and its ear a fan, but we missed the elephant itself.

The tussles in Peshawar were, as ever, merely a pale reflection of the growing rivalries inside Afghanistan. There, a battle was going on for the heart and soul of the resistance, which had nothing to do with the current war against the Soviet Union. Gulbuddin's Hizb Islami party was locked in competition with another faction of mujahidin called Jamiat Islami, whose most famous commander was Ahmad Shah Massoud. Many Westerners used to visit him, and that year Gulbuddin's mujahidin began to kidnap foreign aid workers and journalists.

Months after he disappeared into Afghanistan, we heard terrible news about Jim Lindelof – sweet-natured Jim, who had brought us beer and hidden in our wardrobe. He had been killed, along with his colleague Lee Shapiro. They were travelling with Gulbuddin Hikmatyar's men but – somewhat to the surprise of many people in Peshawar – their deaths had nothing to do with mujahidin rivalry. Soviet helicopter gunships had ambushed them; Jim was cut in half by a rocket. Lee did not die instantly – a witness reported that a Soviet officer delivered the *coup de grâce* with a pistol. There was, after all, a superpower conflict going on.

The US, of course, thought that compared to the battle between Communism and the free world, petty rivalries among the mujahidin were irrelevant. It wasn't as though their ideologically or ethnically based squabbles would ever matter. Although America packed Peshawar with expensive CIA spies, although it talked up the heroism of the resistance, and although it handed them some five billion dollars in military aid, fundamentally it believed in the myth of the invincible Red Army. Unlike their Afghan allies, the Americans never imagined that the mujahidin were going to win.

The Reagan administration was represented in Peshawar by the US High Commission. You could tell whether you were in or out of favour by whether you were invited to their cocktail parties.

I had never been to a cocktail party before I went to Pakistan, so I didn't grasp just how eccentric the ones at the US High Commission were. There were never, strictly speaking, any cocktails: America's allies, the Islamic radicals, would not tolerate them. It was left to the discretion of the High Commission's ancient Pakistani retainer whether or not one found vodka in one's orange juice or gin in one's lemonade.

Professor Majrooh was smart enough to get himself invited to every expatriate party in town. I think he went to relieve the tedium of his exile from Kabul's cosmopolitan society, as well as to replenish his supplies of whisky. But I always got the impression that he looked on the mujahidin's superpower patrons with an independent eye.

'There are too many fundamentalists about,' he grumbled at one event. 'The Coca-Cola in my whisky is giving me a stomach ache.'

To cheer him up, I pointed to a collection of fine Mughal miniatures on the wall. 'Aren't they beautiful?' I said.

It was the wrong remark. The professor was furious. 'You haven't really looked! Examine them more closely!'

The pictures showed scenes from a more light-hearted Islamic age: huntsmen pursuing wild boar, black-eyed *houris* frolicking under canopies. Every detail was there, although you needed a magnifying glass to see it. In one picture, a sultan sat upon an elephant. When I looked more closely, I saw the beast was a collage of thousands of other animals. They were crammed so tightly that some were biting each other's tails. But they were more than just a tiger, a fish, a fox, a boar, a dog and so on. Together, they were also the elephant. There was writing on the outside of the print. I tried to make it out. 'Oh,' I said. 'It's been torn from a book.'

Professor Majrooh's beetle brows lowered. 'Exactly my point. To frame this single print, a book has been destroyed. In pulling out an individual picture, these vandals have desecrated the whole. This picture is merely one in a series of prints and words that together tell a story, contain wisdom. In the name of Art, its original function has been lost.'

'That's a shame,' I said inadequately. It did not pacify the professor.

'Back home in Kabul I had a magnificent collection of such books, full of miniatures far more valuable than these you see on the walls. I had to leave them behind.

Murderers and thieves though the Soviets are, I have no doubt that they will preserve those books. The Soviets at least know the value of knowledge.'

During this period, Peshawar played host to a stream of highly paid American dignitaries. They were generally treated to a game of *buzkashi*, the violent Afghan national sport, which is itself a parody of warfare, and perhaps the only game in the world more dangerous to watch than it is to play. For the visitors it provided a neat metaphor for all that was noble in the Afghan love of battle, without the inconvenience of its messiness and death.

Buzkashi, which literally means 'goat-pulling', has been called 'rugby on horseback' but is actually a wild precursor to polo. In place of a ball, the players scrum over the carcass of a calf. At that time Hank was gleefully spreading rumours that inside Afghanistan they now preferred to play *buzkashi* with the heads of captured Russians. The thought must have driven a Kiplingesque fear into the hearts of the Soviet conscripts huddling in their bases.

Just as I am persuaded that *pilau* is the food of the gods, I passionately believe *buzkashi* to be the most exciting team-sport devised by man. Any number of players can play, on any size of ground. To win, a team must pick up the carcass, ride with it round each end of the pitch, and drop it back in the middle. There are few rules: the opposing team members may do just about anything to impede their rivals' progress and seize the carcass. The brave little horses, the direct descendants of the Mongols' mounts, are trained to perform all sorts of manoeuvres and even to bite the horses of the opposing side.

A particularly important official was due in town, and for weeks Hank had threatened anyone who would listen with instant deportation if they dared to print a negative story about his visit. When the great day arrived, the inevitable *buzkashi* match was laid on. The foreign guests were seated under a canopy at what was deemed a safe distance from the mêleé.

I could not bring myself to join the Westerners under their canopy. Instead, I drifted down to the edge of the makeshift pitch to watch the game warm up. Even this was exhilarating; the horses feinted and swerved, and scuffles broke out between players. The air was full of shouts, whistles and the thudding of horses' hoofs. I felt exposed, in danger of being trampled, but it was a heady danger: the price for a close-up view of the writhing bodies of horses and men.

A friendly *buzkashi* player offered me his horse and, as I joyfully climbed on to the back of the little grey mare, my world was transformed. I was now on the same level as the riders. I had become part of the game, rather than a mere observer.

My horse responded to a complicated range of hand and foot movements and shouts. A light tug on the reins sent it moving in a straight line. A mere touch would turn it right or left. A shout and it ran full pelt. A certain type of kick and it would stop dead on the spot. There was not the slightest delay. I worked out the commands by trial and error as we progressed. It was exhilarating, a primeval force pulling me back towards my ancestry.

When I was a child my father told me – on no authority whatsoever save the poetical – that the dark patches on my insteps are hereditary stirrup sores. Our ancestors galloped over deserts, mountains and plains for thousands of miles, arriving in Afghanistan in the eighth century with the Arab invaders. *Buzkashi*, it seemed to me, was an encapsulated memory, just like my hereditary stirrup sores, just like my family's saga. On the back of my horse, I was part of something larger, not just in space but also in time.

The horses ebbed and flowed, split and merged. I tried to stay out of the fray, but my mare moved to their tide, a satellite in thrall to the greater mass. The horses' movements were too rapid to detect individual wills. We became one will, one body and one move-ment. I thought: This is what battle must have been like – no room for fear, just a swooping, heady rush.

I could feel these riders joining with others, the first *buzkashi* riders of all: the terrifying, inexorable Mongol hordes, sweeping over the steppes from the north like locusts, destruction pulsing in their veins. 'The greatest joy,' said Genghis Khan, 'is to conquer one's enemies, to pursue them, to seize their property, to see their families in tears, to ride their horses and to possess their daughters and wives.' At that moment, thundering across the field, I understood him.

Afghan culture is as steeped in its Mongol heritage as its earth is steeped in all the blood they spilled. The great Afghan poet Jalaluddin Rumi was born as the forces of Genghis Khan were gathering to consume Central Asia. The barbarians swore to exterminate all who did not belong to their race, and they nearly succeeded. They killed thirty million people – in battle, in civilian massacres, and by the famine and disease they deliberately unleashed. It was the worst man-made catastrophe the world had ever seen.

Rumi's father and his young son fled their home-town of Balkh in northern Afghanistan and joined the tide of starving civilian refugees being pushed before the invaders. They took refuge first in Nishapur, in present-day Iran. But the Mongols were hot on their heels. Behind them the entire population of the Afghan city of Herat was massacred. The Mongols hunted down and killed any survivors and then – to make sure that those they missed would die slowly of famine in the bitter winter – they burned the grain in the gran-aries. When this carnage was over, just forty people gathered in Herat's great mosque. They were all that remained of one and a half million inhabitants. Six months earlier, people had joked that you could not stretch out your leg in Herat without kicking a poet or a philosopher.

Rumi's father and his young son hurried on to Bagh-dad, where they heard that their hometown had been destroyed and its inhabitants massacred. Not long after-wards, Nishapur, where they had first sought refuge, fell to the barbarians. All living things, including dogs and cats, were slaughtered, the city was razed and its site sown with barley.

Eight centuries later, Central Asia still bears the scars

of that holocaust. Barley still grows on the site of Nishapur's ruins. Afghanistan's population has never recovered. The Mongols' systematic destruction of the delicate system of irrigation channels has left barren vast tracts of once-fertile farmland. To those who lived through those terrible days, it must have seemed as though the lights of civilization were going out.

But Rumi, who had lost his family, his home, his country, his future – and all hope of peace or stability during his lifetime – refused to be limited by the parameters of his collapsing world. 'From the point of view of a man,' he says in his *Discourses*, 'a thing may appear to be good or evil. But from the point of view of God, everything is good. Show me the good wherein no evil is contained, or the evil in which there is no good. Good and evil are indivisible. Good cannot exist without evil.'

The world of the West was telling me there was a battle going on between good and evil. The Soviet bloc saw things the same way – it just reversed who was good and who was evil. But here, on the back of a *buzkashi* horse, was a view gleaned from the sowing and reaping of countless invasions: there are no absolutes in our fragmentary world; the divisions we create and believe in are artificial. Time itself is no straight line of ordered progress, but an endlessly repeating cycle – throughout our lives and throughout history – from which we are at liberty to learn if we wish. The rest is a swirling mass, a primal force, a dustcloud of thundering feet and shouting voices, the thrill of the chase, the cutting down and the building up.

The plants that the Mongols had pruned so harshly grew back. The memory of their ravages has become part of Afghanistan and we are stronger for it, as all our gore-drenched history has made us stronger. Even our beloved national dish, *pilau*, is said to have originated on those wild rampages, when the troops of Genghis Khan laid out their round shields to catch the dripping from the carcasses they had pillaged, and threw in a little rice – a grain they had never seen until they came to Afghanistan – to mop it up.

I gazed at the Westerners under their safe canopy and I thought: However much they love us or hate us, and however much they want to believe the myths they have invented about us, they will never clip our beak and our crest and our cruel, cruel talons and turn this hawk into a pigeon.

A rider plunged into the ocean of hoofs like a pearl diver, disappearing except for one foot still in a stirrup. When he emerged, he had the carcass under his arm. He rode like the wind with the horde at his heels. The crowd of foreign dignitaries oohed and aahed from beneath their canopy.

The front rider wheeled to throw the horde off his back. The mass turned too, throwing up dust like a mobile whirlwind. They were flung off-balance, de-stabilized by their own force. The game shifted far from the edge of the designated pitch, and came thundering straight towards the canopy: the very canopy under which sheltered the great and the good of Europe and America. Just before it tumbled down – scattering the political élite of two continents before a mass of thundering, charging hoofs – I saw a freeze-frame of shocked American faces.

They had thought that in this sport, in this country and in this war there was such a thing as a safe distance. They had trusted in their canopy. They were unable to believe that it had not protected them from the fierce and noble, proud and warlike Afghan people, who were leading their battle against the Communists. That the force they had unleashed had seethed and risen to engulf their tenting and their banners, their gilded chairs and the trappings of their civilization, and had sent them all tumbling into the mud.

9. A Shooting War

If you cannot stand a sting, do not put your finger into a
scorpion's nest.

Sheikh Sa'adi of Shiraz

By the beginning of 1987, the US was at last starting
to deliver sophisticated weapons to the mujahidin. In
particular, hand-held anti-aircraft missiles, called Stingers, were altering the balance of the war. They were
capable of knocking a Soviet jet out of the sky.

Hank believed that reporting the effectiveness of
controversial new weaponry was just doing the Com-
mies' work for them. He threatened to use his intelligence contacts to cancel the visa of any foreign reporter
who covered the Stingers' deployment. So, of course,
I decided that for my next trip to Afghanistan I would
try to do just that.

But, first, I had an urgent errand. When I had got
back from Kunar, I'd entrusted my precious black-and-
white films to one of Peshawar's makeshift photographic labs. Days later the prints simply faded away.
The lab had used outdated East European chemicals. If
I was going to get pictures of a Stinger in action, I
needed to find somewhere I could process my own

films. A Swiss journalist, Beat Kraettli, was rumoured to have a darkroom, so I set off to find him. Down a winding, sewage-filled alley, I came across a sign that announced in large, but slightly irregular letters, 'Swiss Information Office'.

Almost before I could knock, the door burst open with terrible force. A small man in a felt hat stormed out like a gale. Then I found myself propelled into a tiny office littered with papers that looked as though they had been blown about by the furious activities of my host. A resigned-looking Afghan sat in a corner, making newspaper cuttings with an oversized pair of scissors. Without bothering to ascertain whether I spoke German, Beat began reading to me the article in a Swiss magazine that had precipitated his rage. While he did so, he impatiently rifled through shoals of papers on his desk, as though even in the act of reading he couldn't bear to be still.

When, eventually, I managed to splutter out my request, he exclaimed: '*Tscha*! You mean you actually know how to process film? Teach me at once!'

I was amazed that he had gone to the trouble of setting up a darkroom without knowing how to use it. His laboratory had been fitted out with Swiss attention to detail. Bottles of developer and fixer stood un-touched on shelves. There were trays for paper prints, tongs, clips, and an impressive modern enlarger. The walls were lined with ranks of drawers. Nothing was missing. I collected together everything I would need. It was good to measure out the chemicals, to smell again the familiar odours of developer, stop bath and fixer.

Beat watched all these preparations enraptured. They seemed to have taken away his compulsion to speak, or even to rush about. When I was ready, I switched off the light.

'I'm unloading the film from the canister,' I told him, aware that I was supposed to be instructing him. 'Now I'll wind it round the spiral.' This was usually a tricky operation. For those few moments, the film would be exposed to the light outside; the least chink would destroy it. I got the film on to the spiral, but when I felt on the bench for the developing box to put it in, I realized I'd forgotten to locate the lid. Now I couldn't turn on the light to find it.

I opened drawers and poked around inside. They were full of strange objects, none of which felt like photographic equipment. There was a small, plastic, double-bladed thing, which was full of liquid when I shook it. There was an odd wooden box, about six inches long, and a variety of spherical metal objects that were quite heavy. 'Beat,' I said, 'what on earth have you got in these drawers?'

I could hear him shuffling guiltily in the darkness. 'Oh, that – that is only my unexploded bomb collection.'

I flung open the darkroom door, and fled into the garden. Behind me, Beat lamented the fate of his film. When I'd recovered, Beat showed me his collection. The bladed thing was a butterfly mine – the liquid I'd heard was explosive. Beat had been given it by a mujahid and he admitted he wasn't sure why it had not detonated on impact – he thought it must be faulty. The box was an old wooden booby trap. Its package of solid explosive was old and unstable, but Beat could not bear to throw it away. I was clearly dealing with a madman. There and then, I decided Beat was all right. I didn't know it at the time but I was beginning a major chapter of my life.

Beat and I decided to share stories. For our first joint project, we organized a trip into Afghanistan to try to document the Stinger missiles in action. A commander from Jaji, close to the Pakistani border, agreed to let us see his newest weaponry. A mujahid called Engineer Jan was to be our guide. For an Afghan Engineer Jan was something of an eccentric. In a country where the average lad picks up his AK-47 automatic rifle at puberty, he refused to carry a weapon. A slight man, with flame-red hair and an attractive, buck-toothed smile, he was rumoured to have attended the first year of a course at Kabul University. War had interrupted his studies and turned him into a foot soldier for the resistance. He never complained about his shattered dreams, but every now and then a misty look would come into his eyes, as if he was dwelling for an instant upon a higher plane. In token of his status as an intellectual he wore sky blue *shilwar kamis*, and he was unfailingly referred to as 'Engineer'. Although he had lost everything he held dear, it was impossible to imagine Engineer Jan succumbing to hatred or fanaticism. I liked him from the moment I met him.

On the day of our departure for what was then probably the hottest front line in the war, Engineer Jan arrived to collect us wearing his blue suit. In preparation for a fray in which both sides were deploying state-of-the-art weaponry, he had armed himself – with an air rifle. It seemed suicidal, absurd. When I broached the subject, he merely smiled, and that misty look came into his eyes. 'Whatever Allah wills,' he said, as he shouldered his toy weapon. 'Afghans are not afraid of death.'

I hid beneath a *burqa* to slip past the Pakistani guards on the edge of town. Inside my tent, I was woozy from lack of air. As we reached the border, there was the unmistakable roar of a shell. Our bus was drawing fire. From the men, I could hear the sounds of chaos, panic and shouting; I could not see their faces. There was another shell, then another: muffled inside the *burqa*, I could feel their reverberation. My one thought was: If we have to run for it, I'll never make it without my boots! I was nearly trampled by the others scrambling out as I fumbled in my bag for them. The laces were knotted, and I was forced to jump out still wearing fluorescent pink plastic shoes. In my panic I couldn't remove my veil. Through its grille, I made out the rest of our group disappearing up the hillside out of range of the guns.

Outside, shells were landing in clumps: the signature of a multiple rocket launcher, heavier than the mortar fire I had experienced in Kunar. I was imprisoned in a world of criss-cross shadows and stifled sounds: a bad dream under the blankets. For an instant I stood stock still in the kill zone, faltering, clinging to the *burqa*'s illusory protection, as if this flimsy piece of fabric could stop shrapnel. Then I ran for my life.

I heard gasping, and realized it was my own breath. Trying to run in a *burqa* – even when it is pushed back off one's face – is rather like running a marathon wearing a human-sized tea-cosy, complete with fancy embroidery. Worse, the *burqa* was orange, my trousers were red, and I thought I must be terribly conspicuous. The others became tiny points in the distance, as I wrestled with the *burqa*. I managed to untangle it and for a while its voluminous silk streamed out behind me like a landing parachute.

The plastic shoes were more of a problem – I could hardly keep them on. But the ground was stony and possibly mined. Would it be wise to go barefoot?

Several more shells landed close by. I wondered whether the unseen enemy was even now taking aim at my red trousers. The thought made up my mind about the plastic shoes. I flopped out of them, and sprinted across the stones to where the others had now passed the firing zone. They were sheltering safely out of range on a large boulder.

I reached the others. Beat's look suggested that my tardiness was exactly what he expected from a girl. I blurted: 'I think they were aiming at my trousers.'

'What complete nonsense. They were going for the bus.'

Shaking with delayed shock, I changed into my Afghan men's clothes. Beat and I were both panting: winded by our brush with death. Engineer Jan seemed unruffled.

We started to climb. We had entered the desolate landscape one sees sometimes in dreams. This had once been a living forest. Now it was a shattered plain, dotted with blackened tree stumps. Eerily, a couple were still burning, crackling in the still air. There was no birdsong, no sound of life at all. Now that the shelling had stopped, an oppressive silence settled over us, broken every so often by a sharp crack and a feather of smoke from a butterfly mine. The area was sown with them.

We picked our way round bomb craters. It seemed the most abandoned and sinister place on earth. None of us knew it then, but we had wandered on to the battlefield for the spirit of Islam itself.

Although the world tends to view divisions within Islam in terms of schools and creeds, I believe there is a much more fundamental conflict. It is between those who cling to the literal letter of the Islamic law, and those who stress its inner values. At one end of the spectrum are the fanatics, the religious zealots; at the other, the Islamic mystics, who have historically been enormously popular in Afghanistan.

As a child, I was told that no true believer should ever claim to be a Muslim. The word means 'one who is resigned to the will of God' – and who can live up to that? This sort of approach, refusing to allow someone to hide behind a religious label, is typical of Afghanistan's Sufi heritage.

Before he set out on his pilgrimage to Mecca, the saint Bayazid met a man who was dying of hunger. 'Let me be your pilgrimage,' begged the poor man. Bayazid handed over the money he had saved for his journey, circled around the beggar seven times, and considered that in spirit he had fulfilled the obligations of pilgrimage.

In the nineteenth century, the austere Wahhabi movement arose in Saudi Arabia to cleanse Islam of this sort of contamination. Now Wahhabi volunteers were flooding into Afghanistan to fight the infidel – and clear up the lax religious practices of the Afghans themselves.

After a couple of hours, we passed a gigantic military installation carved into the sheer rock, which rose like a wall in front of us. Daubed on its flat surface, a patch of graffiti said, in English, 'Down with Israel.' I laughed aloud. What had Israel to do with this conflict?

We were witnessing the birthplace of a worldwide Islamic movement. We had just passed one of the military installations sponsored by the CIA, funded by Saudi Arabia and engineered by an idealistic young Islamist firebrand. His name was Osama bin Laden.

The volunteers were known to the Afghans as Arabs, although they were actually Islamic radicals from all over the Muslim world. The bulk of them joined the extremist mujahidin factions belonging to Gulbuddin Hikmatyar and a Wahhabi Islamic scholar called Abdul Rasul Sayyaf. Once in Afghanistan, they began to formulate a new hybrid political Islamic doctrine.

The foreigners were not generally considered to be good fighters. 'They don't mind strapping explosives to themselves to become martyrs, but they are afraid of a bit of shelling,' one disgusted commander told me.

However, they came with fringe benefits. There was a famous – and certainly apocryphal – tale of how emissaries from Saudi intelligence had turned up with suitcases of money, looking for suitable mujahidin factions to support. One after another, the resistance leaders welcomed their Arab guests, throwing parties for them, forcing them to eat vast mounds of *pilau*, showering them with gifts, firing guns into the air and generally behaving in an uncouth Afghan manner. Sayyaf's group was small and militarily insignificant, but he understood the mentality of the sober men of the desert. When the Arabs sought him out, the grey-bearded scholar was sitting alone under a tree, apparently in deep contemplation. Far from welcoming his guests, he did not even look up. A disciple explained that his master could not be roused until the hour of prayer. When that time came, Sayyaf invited his guests to join his lengthy devotions. Only then did they all share the handful of dates that made up the sage's meagre fare. As they headed home, tired but elated, the Arab emissaries' suitcases were empty but their hearts were full. Beyond a doubt they had selected the worthiest recipient for the lucre they had accumulated by selling the black blood of the desert to the dissolute West.

It was a good story, and it might have been inspired by a tale of Nasruddin, the Afghan folkloric figure of a village *mullah*, with which I grew up. Sitting outside his humble shack, with a fishing net wrapped round his shoulders, Nasruddin put on a similar show to attract the largesse of a sultan. The *mullah* was duly rewarded, but his benefactor returned unexpectedly, to find the supposed ascetic eating sugarplums, cavorting with young maidens and generally living a life of unbridled luxury.

'Mullah,' he exclaimed, 'whatever happened to your fishing net?'

'Ah,' replied the mullah, 'what need is there of the net now that the fish has been caught?'

We passed a checkpoint manned by unfriendly mujahidin. Instead of the usual warm greetings, there were hostile questions. There was something else different about them, but for a while I couldn't put my finger on it. Then I got it: there was no laughter, and none of the disrespectful banter that usually accompanies any group of Afghans. These cold-eyed men didn't relax until they had watched us leave.

It struck me that a sense of humour may be the opposite of fanaticism, or at least its antidote. It is difficult to dream of martyrdom if you can see the funny side of life. Of course, the great Afghan poet Jalaluddin Rumi got there centuries before me, and said it better: 'If you have no sense of humour, then you have an incompleteness in your soul.'

Most ordinary Afghans feared and mistrusted the radicals. Although much too kind to criticize his fellow human being directly, Engineer Jan muttered something about their lack of humour. Then he told an Afghan joke: 'Every Afghan fighter wants to be a *ghazi*, a hero, but the Arab wants to be a *shahid*, a martyr. That's why we try to help them along by putting them on the front line!' He giggled, in the curiously girlish Afghan fashion.

We laughed too. It was a good summing-up of two very different approaches to the war, religion, everything.

The mujahidin base we had come to visit was right on the border: we could see the electric lights of Pakistan glimmering far below.

On the other side of us artillery fire was targeting an Arab post across the valley. We had a good view of white smoke glinting in the morning sunlight. As we watched, the direction of fire changed and, inch by inch, it worked its way round the mountain. They were using a grid, methodically covering the ground. Every couple of hours, it was our turn. For ten minutes or so, all hell broke loose. Shells whined through the air and crash-landed around us as we cowered in our inadequate foxholes. Then the roulette wheel would turn again, and for the next hour or two the shelling would shift to another part of the mountainside. Each time it came back to us, it seemed statistically more likely that sooner or later they would hit the jackpot and blow us all to smithereens.

At one particularly loud bang I dived into a nearby foxhole. Lying in the narrow trench, it gradually dawned on me that I was alone. I crawled out, to roars of delighted laughter from the mujahidin. The noise that had so terrified me was their own BM-12 multiple rocket launcher. My embarrassment at least taught me the basic skill of distinguishing between incoming and outgoing fire.

After a while, shelling in the distance no longer made me jump. I barely registered it, until it got to a level where some invisible sentry in my mind would suddenly warn me that it was time to be afraid. My hosts would amuse themselves by whistling at exactly the right pitch just behind my ear, in the hope of tricking me into another embarrassing leap into a foxhole.

The Stinger was an odd object, square and boxy. It

looked as if it had been fashioned by a BBC props department out of spray-painted cardboard. One young man had been on a special CIA course to learn how to use it, but the expensively trained operative had been relegated to making the tea while his superiors took turns with the new toy. In the early days, the mujahidin had been delighted at how easy it was to pull Soviet jets down from the sky. Of late, however, the aircraft had taken to flying high and dropping flares to confuse the Stinger's sophisticated heat-seeking device. The mujahidin were usually enticed into loosing off a few precious missiles at them anyway, whooping and laughing as they did so.

The CIA and Pakistani intelligence gave most of the Stingers to the extremist factions of mujahidin. Perhaps the dour-faced fanatics were easier to deal with – they might have had a tedious obsession with martyrdom but at least, in their own way, they treated death with the level of seriousness it deserved.

The routine of the base became my world. During the day, I watched plumes of Soviet artillery smoke rising in the distance, and the mujahidin shooting futilely at planes. In the evenings, we gathered round the stove, away from the cold night air, and played cards; Beat always won. Safely under cover of darkness, the jets came back for a couple of low-altitude bombing runs every night. The roar of their engines and the crashing of ordnance reverberated through the mountains like a summer storm.

One night, I heard an extraordinary popping sound, like thousands upon thousands of firecrackers. After the usual thunder of bombs, the racket seemed almost frivolous. We rushed outside, and I saw the most astonishing sight: the mountains were alive with tiny flashes of light. Even when the jets roared off in a shower of flares of their own, the lights and noises did not subside.

The planes had been dropping butterfly mines, like the one in Beat's darkroom collection. Now I learned more about their uses at first hand. Their 'wings', plastic flanges, allowed them to spiral softly to earth like sycamore seeds. A gentle landing was important, because each mine contained a quantity of liquid explosive and a detonator. It would blow up if anyone trod on it.

The mines were used to soften up and demoralize an enemy: pinioning him in one place while he was pounded with artillery fire. As well as contact detonators, they also had timers, clearing themselves in forty-eight hours so that eventually ground troops could move in for the kill.

After he had explained all this to me, Beat said carefully: 'That's what it looks like they're trying to do here. Soften up the base for a ground offensive.'

When the others had gone in, I sat outside on a rock overlooking the valley. I had seen enough wounds caused by butterfly mines to know how dangerous they were. But I hadn't expected them to be so beautiful, like millions of fiery living creatures, or the haunting flickers of lost stars. Their unreliable illumination lit up the craggy mountain peaks behind them. As, for a fraction of a second, each one brought forth its frantic blossom of light and sound, the mountains, too, seemed to be watching. They had an eternity to do so, I thought. They would be here long after all our lights had died away.

We had our story, one of the first accounts of Stingers in action. The only problem was that we were trapped on the base. New butterfly mines were sown every night. The route down to the road leading to Pakistan had become a minefield, and the road itself was under constant shellfire. The mujahidin's supply lines to Pakistan were cut off.

After a few days I was numb. Looking back, I wonder why I wasn't overtly terrified. Perhaps it was my inexperience: in this new world, I was just a toddler, capable of wandering off a cliff without realizing the danger. Or perhaps I had failed to recognize the insidious effects of traumatic stress. When the shelling got close, some primitive mechanism would click into place, and for a while I was utterly absorbed in the task of survival. But for the remainder of the time, my brain shut down into a resting mode of anaesthetized boredom. It was as though my thinking, my emotions, and anything else I did not urgently need, had been packed away in cotton wool.

I passed the time recording the sound of explosions for a story I hoped to sell to a radio station, and squabbling with Beat. 'Do you have to photograph *every* bloody shell? Your shutter clicks every time one lands. It's spoiling my tape.'

'*Tscha* – you are spoiling my picture.'

'You've taken a million already. What's the point? One plume of smoke looks exactly like another.' I pointed at one next to our forward gun position, and we both stared at it. It looked different from anything we'd seen before: dense and greasy, cumulose, almost solid. Possibly to relieve the tedium, we speculated that it might be a cloud of some kind of chemical gas.

'I shall go to have a look,' announced Beat.

'I'll come too,' I said.

We told ourselves that we would easily be able to spot the butterfly mines on the stony path. Engineer Jan volunteered to be our guide. He was tired of the other men laughing at his blue suit.

We didn't speak. We were all too busy scouring the ground for butterfly mines. By the time we reached the mujahidin's BM-12 multiple rocket launcher, the gas cloud had mercifully disappeared. A head, clad in a brightly coloured turban, poked out of a cave. This apparition addressed us in the poetical Persian of the north: 'Become entombed!'

It took me a moment to realize that he was telling us to take cover. He had just fired off a salvo from the BM-12 and was expecting the return fire at any minute. As we made our introductions, crouching together in the narrow granite cave, explosions buffeted outside.

There were two mujahidin operating the gun, both Afghan Turkomans. Yes, they were very far from home here among the Pushtuns but, in *jihad*, all men are brothers. They had done a stint up in the Panjshir valley with the legendary Ahmad Shah Massoud, then with Ismail Khan in Herat. After that they had meandered slowly down south, availing themselves of the village *hujras*, the free guestrooms that each community maintains for visitors. If it had not been for *jihad*, they said, they would never have seen so much of the world.

When the shelling quietened, we emerged cautiously from the cave. Our new friends cast a supercilious eye over Engineer Jan's air rifle. One may have sniggered behind the fold of his turban. Engineer Jan took the insult quietly. 'See that stone?' he asked, pointing to the tiniest of pebbles, some distance away. They nodded their huge, beturbaned heads. Before they had finished nodding, the pebble whizzed up into the air. Engineer Jan was a crack shot.

Their radio crackled and a loud conversation followed. I gathered its drift: the enemy had nearly succeeded in plotting their co-ordinates. They should not reveal their position by firing the BM-12 and, as soon as it was safe to do so, they should withdraw. But the northerners were not prepared to neglect the duties of hospitality.

'Travellers are the guests of God!' shouted the one with the biggest turban, and the maddest gleam in his black eyes. 'You have come all this way to visit us. We shall not fail you. We shall disobey orders and demonstrate our rocket to you.'

When we tried to dissuade them, they told us, with a hint of menace: 'We have a saying in Afghanistan. The guest chooses when to arrive, and the host chooses when he shall leave.'

We retreated about thirty yards as they prepared their BM-12 for firing. The contraption, which resembles a kind of elongated egg-box with numerous barrels, had to be front-loaded, then fired by pulling a piece of string. The Turkomans performed a Keystone Cops routine, forgetting to run clear and diving away at the last moment. Under the circumstances, it was not as amusing as it might have been. Finally, there was a deafening bang and the BM-12 ejected its missiles with a force that sent the launcher skidding backwards.

'Now we have performed the duty of hospitality incumbent upon all Muslims,' shouted our hosts. 'If we are killed in the counter-attack, we will get our reward directly from Allah, in Paradise. You may go now. May you live for a thousand years.'

'May you live for ever,' we replied grimly, and left at a run.

While we put as much distance as we could between the gun position and ourselves, the mountainside reverberated to the most forceful attack yet. When we reached the mountaintop, we found a solitary tree that had not yet been burned. We sheltered under it, while we paused to catch our breath, as one would from a storm. A figure on a horse came galloping up. It was a man, with his right hand under his *shilwar kamis*. A butterfly bomb had blown off half of it and he was hurrying to Pakistan, quite matter-of-factly, to look for treatment. A saying of the Prophet flashed into my mind: 'Treat this world as I do, like a wayfarer; like a horseman who stops in the shade of a tree for a time, and then moves on.'

It was a moment of unexpected tranquillity. I felt a flood of affinity with the understated Islamic values of my childhood – now almost forgotten in the changing world of Islam. As I'd grown older, and discovered how liberal my upbringing had been, I'd even wondered whether I was entitled to call myself a Muslim at all.

Once my grandfather met a Unitarian minister, and was fascinated to learn that here was a Christian who did not believe in the divinity of Jesus. He asked: 'Do you agree with the statement "There is no God but God and Muhammad is the Messenger of God"? The minister said he did. 'My dear sir,' said the Sirdar, 'in that case, I should like to inform you that you have in fact been a Muslim all along.'

Now, as the horseman and we sheltered together in companionable silence – fellow travellers waiting for a lull in the shelling before we went our separate ways – I felt at peace with my own faith, however the outside world might label it. Perhaps, I thought, I too had been a Muslim all along.

Back at the main base, the latest shelling had disturbed even the card games. As we arrived, a shell landed near the Stinger position. Shrapnel hit the cook, who had been having a go with the new US weaponry. As we tried to help him, another shell almost grazed us, coming down about twenty feet away. Luckily the side of the mountain was so steep that it landed far below the base. The boys with the grid reference seemed to have got their act together on our co-ordinates.

There was even more demoralizing news: now that we were considered to have been 'softened up', a substantial Soviet land convoy was making slow but steady progress towards us. The word was that any day now they would mount the ground offensive they hoped would result in the fall of Jaji. If they succeeded, it would wipe out resistance in this key area altogether. We were running out of heavy ammunition, out-flanked and outnumbered.

And we were still trapped. A fresh drop of butterfly mines had seen to that. They severely restricted movement on or off the base. Far below us, we could see the road we had arrived along. The downhill return journey would not take long, but between the road and us lay a stretch of ground peppered with butterfly mines. Part of this was a grassy bank, upon which they would be impossible to spot.

'We can call the bus by radio,' said Engineer Jan, 'but reaching it might be a problem.'

'Not a very good plan to be on the wrong side of a battle,' I said.

'Especially when we've already got our story,' Beat agreed.

I looked at him. 'You'd lose a foot, perhaps, if you were unlucky.'

Beat nodded. 'Half a foot probably.'

Engineer Jan was disappointed that we weren't staying for the ground offensive and probable rout of the forces of Islam, but he agreed to radio for the bus.

The next morning, we assembled with our ruck-sacks. We could see the bus waiting for us, a tiny speck down below. From somewhere in the mountains, an unseen mujahid took a pot shot at it – that Afghan sense of humour again. But his bullet bore a serious message: we should get going.

The mujahidin said goodbye, then quickly melted

away. It was clear that the commander wasn't prepared to risk putting a fighter out of action to conduct a couple of crazy journalists off a base before the real fighting had even started. We bade an emotional farewell to Engineer Jan. 'Are you sure you won't come with us?'

He looked – wistfully, I thought – at the bus, then shouldered his air rifle. 'No. I'll stay for the offensive. After all, I am a mujahid.'

The bus seemed a long way away. A wisp of smoke from a mine whose timing device had just expired shot up out of the bank, as if to remind us of its presence. I wondered if I'd have the nerve to do it. A whole lifetime without a leg, never to be whole again – not to mention the immediate pain and the chorus of 'I told you so' from my family.

Beat caught my hesitation. 'All right, then,' he said briskly. 'I'll go first – you tread in my footsteps.'

He shouldered his rucksack and set off down the hill. When we reached the grass bank, I unashamedly stepped in his tracks. That part of the journey seemed to go on for hours, but probably lasted no more than five minutes. I kept my eyes glued to the long grass. A couple of times, little whooshes of explosions and the telltale wisp of smoke a few feet away made me jump. But we reached the bus in safety.

Beat's action was the most understated act of bravery I had ever seen. After that, although I was often reminded that he was excitable and frequently reckless, I never forgot that he was also full of generosity and courage.

10. The Man who Trusted in God

Go higher – behold the human spirit.

Jalaluddin Rumi

The time had finally come when I could no longer juggle my contradictory worlds of East and West. I had to choose between them. After we got back from Jaji, in summer 1987, I moved out of the Peshawar Club, and Beat and I set up house together. I knew that, by living with a man to whom I was neither married nor related, I had brought disgrace upon my family.

Uncle Mirza visited my new home only once. I was used to his flamboyant arrivals at the wheel of his Toyota packed with relatives: master of his domain, his horn tooting gaily, his English hat perched jauntily on his head. This time it was different. He came alone and on foot. As I watched him make the long trek up my driveway, he seemed diminished and diffident, an old man lost in a foreign land.

He came as far as my veranda. He preferred not to come in, he said; he just wanted to tell me something. I braced myself for the storm: how disgraceful I was and how, if I persisted in living this independent life, I would be banished from the protection of my kin.

But he hadn't come for that at all. He just wanted to tell me about Jamil Haidar; the man on the white horse who had epitomized for me all that was noble about the mujahidin; Jamil Haidar, who had sat smelling Bukhara roses in the garden, whose wife we had saved and whom my uncle had been supporting for years with instalments from his savings. This year, those savings had run dry. In their fury, Jamil Haidar and his band of mujahidin had torn down my uncle's home.

Uncle Mirza refused my offer of tea. After he had delivered this bombshell, he put his English hat defeatedly back on his head, walked down my driveway and out of my life. We never had the dramatic falling-out I had dreaded – but as I watched his beloved figure disappear into the distance, I knew that we were on two different planets, whose orbits were drawing us further and further apart.

Beat's and my new home was beside the canal that divided the city of Peshawar from the sprawling Nasir-bagh refugee camp. One day, when I was walking in Nasirbagh, a refugee accosted me. He said simply: 'Madam, I need a position so that I can feed my wife and small children. Kindly furnish me with one.' He might have been asking a department-store attendant for some trivial item, or seeking directions from a well-disposed stranger. To refuse him would have been churlish.

His name was Rahim, and although I had made a private pledge never to have household staff, something in his black eyes seemed to pierce me, and before I knew what I had done, I had engaged him on the spot.

I told myself it would be good for my Persian to

listen to his poetical utterances. Rahim spoke the dialect called Dari, which means 'of the court'. It is the language of the historical kings of Persia and of the thirteenth-century literary classics. Nowadays it is considered unbearably rustic in Iran, but it survives in the mountains of Afghanistan. It was rather like taking on a manservant who persisted in speaking Shakespearian English.

Rahim did not walk, he 'beat the feet'. He did not talk, he 'hit words'. He did not grow old, his 'years were eaten'. He was constantly afflicted with adventures, things that 'passed upon the head'. Even something as prosaic as an orange took on new meaning to my ears when Rahim spoke: *narang* – probably the origin of the English word – literally means 'no sorrow'. Persian proverbs and flowery quotations tripped off his tongue – usually to trounce me in our frequent arguments.

I soon discovered that Rahim was in uncontestable control of our lives. As he took his first pay cheque, he sternly reminded me: 'My wages really come from Allah, even though He may direct them through your agency. If it is His will, Allah will provide. Either through you, or through someone else.'

Rahim reminded me irresistibly of a commanding figure in my family's mythological corpus: my grandfather's faithful Pushtun retainer, Ahmad Shah. It was he who had stolen the maharaja's grandmother from her fishpool in the palace all those years ago. My father remembered him as being over six foot tall, with the straw-coloured skin and the grey-green eyes of the true frontiersman. He was never separated from his Lee

Enfield rifle or from his long Afghan knife, and his favourite means of relaxation was to polish them both until they shone.

Bobo wrote about him in her memoirs, too: 'He would work well and faithfully for three months or so. Then he would say he must go. He never asked whether he might go. The word was must. If you asked him why he used so strong a phrase, he would place his hand over his heart, and throw a far-flung glance southwards, the direction of his homeland.'

I can picture my gentle Scottish grandmother, who had exiled herself for ever from her blood family, looking wistfully through her window at Kabul's spectacular mountain range, as she continued: 'If you belong to the Highlands yourself, you will understand what he meant. You would appreciate that inward loyalty to your own hills, although you might be surrounded by other, higher ones elsewhere. You would know that, assuredly, there comes a time when the heart remembers, regret asserts itself, and back you must go.'

One morning, I discovered that a new group of refugees had taken up residence on the bank of the canal beside my home. It was not a good spot. The canal was fetid with the excreta that poured into it from hundreds of shanty-huts, latrines and restaurants. Like the rotting tentacle of a vile sea-beast, it lay suppurating in the sun. Until now, no refugee had been desperate enough to settle next to its sluggish waters, but that morning a little group of four or five families had already pitched a ragged camp next to it, in a bowl of choking white dust that reflected the sun without mercy.

When I went down to visit them, a flurry of women's hands tugged at me like ferns and burrs, pulling the hem of my dress, stroking my face. They were not begging; at least not for money. They were soliciting something more fundamental: my time, my attention, my sympathy.

Their leader impressed me. He was a frail, white-bearded old man, who looked like a schoolbook illustration of a biblical prophet. He sat still, and with perfect dignity, his hand upon his wooden staff, his hooded eyes gazing back in the direction of the mountains they had left. You could not see the mountains from this dustbowl. But the old man had something of the seer about him. I was sure he could picture them quite clearly.

'Where are you from, Father?' I asked him.

'By God's grace, we are from Kunar province.'

As I had been to Kunar – with Zahir Shah on my first trip to Afghanistan – we talked about the various villages I had visited along the river Pech. The old man's eyes lit up when I spoke of his hills and streams, of the houses clutching the sides of the mountains, the flocks of sheep and the shepherd children dashing up and down the slopes.

'What brings you so far from your homeland?' I asked, as soon as it was polite to do so.

'God is generous. There was an offensive somewhere on the other side of our mountain. Our village was bombed the next day, although we have never had anything to do with the fighting forces. We began to walk to Pakistan. On the way it was Allah's will to take

180

from me my little grandson, the blessing of my old age.'

We both fell silent. Eventually he continued: 'If a tree could move on foot or feather it would not suffer the agony of the saw or the wounds of the blade. Allah has brought us here and, as we can walk no further, this is where we shall stay. We shall await whatever He has in store for us.'

'Father, you cannot stay here. You must be registered as refugees, then you will be assigned to a proper camp and you will be given food and shelter.'

'Whatever Allah wills.'

I told him how to begin the process of registration: first they must get identification from one of the mujahidin political parties, linked with the various armed factions. They could use this to get a ration card from the United Nations High Commission for Refugees.

The old man looked bewildered. 'But we have never been involved with politics or armed factions before,' he said, 'and I have never asked for help.'

'Don't worry, you are in Pakistan now,' I told him.

He smiled, in a manner I could not get out of my mind. 'We are, and we always have been, in the hands of Allah.'

The old man didn't know it, but just metres from his squalid camp lay the nerve centre of the world's largest refugee aid effort, dedicated to helping people like him. Nestling in the plush suburb of University Town were the headquarters of more than fifty inter-national agencies serving some two and a half million dispossessed Afghans. Few of the recipients of their charity ever penetrated this oasis of tree-lined avenues, luxury villas, off-the-record briefings, satellite dishes, irrigated gardens and air-conditioned Pajeros.

Foreign-aid money was sloshing into Peshawar: around eighty million dollars a year to the UNHCR alone. But as the myths the West wished to maintain diverged more and more from Afghanistan's reality, political strings tied the aid effort in knots. The myth said that every able-bodied Afghan was involved in the armed struggle, so to get a ration card refugees had to become affiliated to an armed faction. The myth said that the refugees would soon be going home, so camps remained transitory and bereft of hope.

The next day, as I returned from the bazaar, I saw that the new refugees were still in the dip beside the canal. I went to ask the old man why they had not yet been moved to a better camp.

'My daughter, we went to the mujahidin political party most active in our area. There, we waited all day for registration. The official demanded a huge bribe, so we gave him the jewellery my wife received on her wedding day. He has told us to return to his office tomorrow.'

'What will you do?' I asked him.

'The Prophet, peace be upon him, adjured us to trust in God. We shall go tomorrow to wait at the party office for our identification. Then, if God wills, we may receive some rations.'

The old man insisted on carrying my shopping-bags back home for me. He was frail, and he staggered, straight-backed, under their weight. By now, I was desperate to help him, so I tried to press money into his hand. He looked at me with the closest to anger I had seen in his eyes. 'Are you not ashamed to offer payment for what was done for God?'

For the local economy, refugees were big business. Peshawar was booming. If you were a local entrepreneur, a war profiteer or a Westerner, it was difficult not to prosper. Even I did. The international press had a voracious appetite for news about the war, and Beat and I had also picked up several lucrative contracts for aid-agency publications. We opened a joint journalists' office in our villa, which Beat grandly christened the International Information Office.

Within an hour, a lonely figure made the trek up the drive. He was wearing a billowing brown *shilwar kamis*, and his hair was neatly brilliantined back. He carried a satchel.

'Is this the International Information Office?' he asked.

'Yes.'

'In that case,' he said, 'give me some international information.'

We thought this interview was amusing, but it had a profound effect upon Rahim. A few hours later, I found him striding sorrowfully up and down the road outside the gate.

'Madam,' he said, 'my heart has become narrow.'

I waited for this to be explained. Rahim let his remark sink in for just long enough, then announced: 'The vegetable seller informs me that our neighbour on the left has been robbed by *badmarshis*, bandits. This house is unguarded. All manner of people are permitted to walk up to the door without even being kept waiting. It gives a low impression of the status of the owners.'

Sensing my impatience, Rahim cut to the point: 'Madam, in short, we need a *chowki dar*, a man with a gun to watch the door. I would do it myself, but I have other duties. However, I shall arrange a good man. To ensure he is reliable, and as brave as a lion, I shall give you my own brother.'

The next day, Rahim's brother, Shafi, arrived. Contrary to expectation, he did not have a gun. He didn't seem all that bright either. His eyes didn't focus in one place, although his fixed smile of ineffable sweetness made up for it.

'Rahim!' I said sternly. 'Where is the gun?'

At that moment, there was a hesitant crunch of gravel from the driveway. An ancient man was hobbling towards us. He was so emaciated that I feared he might collapse under the weight of the seventy-year-old Lee Enfield rifle he was carrying on his back.

Rahim drew himself up to his full height. His chest swelled with pride. 'This good grandfather fought the *feranghee*, the British foreigners, when he was just a boy. He earned the title *ghazi*, hero, before he was ten. Now Shafi is his pupil. He is learning the secrets of battle from this great warrior. Both pupil and master will come and guard your house. Rahim has arranged it.'

'But, Rahim, he is very old,' I said.

'And Shafi is very young,' said Rahim smoothly. 'Now you have the benefits of both: the strength of youth and the wisdom of age combined.'

It was an unanswerable argument. I agreed to take them both on a month's probation. As I went back into the house, the old man stuffed a rag into the barrel of his rifle, stretched out on a *charpoy* and fell asleep.

Rahim began to consolidate a minor empire. With such a large household to care for, he now needed a woman to wash everyone's clothes. He procured from somewhere a toothless old hag who took up residence in a corner of the kitchen. He also acquired a stunted personal assistant whom he never permitted to stand in my presence. This servant of a servant crawled from room to room sweeping up with a single twig. It left Rahim free to do the jobs he excelled at: supervising, handling the money and running his own ingenious and lucrative recycling business.

All our rubbish was carefully sifted, sorted by type, and passed on to his confederate, the vegetable seller, to be sold in the bazaar. One day I found that the public letter-writer had a note from my mother pinned on to the wall beside his stall. His disciples were sitting in a semi-circle around it, earnestly trying to copy her negligent scrawl. Their own notepads were made from bundles of my draft articles. Rahim had sold the blank space on the back.

Bits of tin foil and elastic bands were lovingly collated and sold on, while objects of which Rahim disapproved (foreign canned goods, audio cassettes and, for some reason, paper-clips) would slip mysteriously into the bin and be wafted away for ever to the bazaar. Items that he felt should never be thrown away (used cotton-wool balls, the disposable containers for my contact-lens solution and any form of medicine, however out-of-date) would be lovingly retrieved and presented at inconvenient moments – between the second and third courses of a dinner party was considered a particularly auspicious time. It was an end to privacy of any kind.

As neither of the *chowki dars* was up to the job of protecting us, Beat decided to get geese to guard the office. One day he returned excitedly from the market with a couple of vicious-looking specimens. Rahim pored over them. His face had become the colour of a prune: I realized that goose-buying was definitely in the category of chores that were his exclusive domain.

'Rahim! Get the *chowki dars* to dig a pond!' cried Beat, oblivious to the tremendous hurt that Rahim was suffering. Wordlessly, and with great dignity, Rahim picked up the geese. He carried them down the drive and vanished into the seething bazaar that started just beyond the front gate.

Three hours later, he returned. In his arms were not two but four geese of gigantic size. They completely eclipsed the pair that Beat had been rash enough to buy.

Rahim's face shone with joy. In the manner of one telling an *Arabian Nights* fairy tale, he declaimed: 'Sir, you are a foreigner. Therefore it was not your fault that you were swindled in the bazaar. However, the villain from whom you bought those geese of inferior aspect did not know that he would have to answer to Rahim. I have myself been to the market and, after many incidents falling upon my head, I discovered the thief in question. I beat him until he agreed to take back the birds. With the money he gave me in compensation for trying to cheat a foreigner, I have purchased four geese worthy of your standing. They are the bravest and fiercest geese in the Hindu Kush and until this moment they were in my own backyard, since it was I who brought them from my home in Jalalabad. Note: they are not Pakistani geese, but Afghan geese. They will cackle like an army when intruders approach and, if it is Allah's will, thine enemies will be put to flight. That is all.'

He set about building them a special pond with his own hands. Thanks to his own swift action, the water of his face had narrowly escaped being spilled.

Over the next weeks, I kept a close eye on the Afghan refugees beside the canal. For shelter, they knotted a couple of rags over some sticks, and from somewhere they procured a blackened iron kettle. Otherwise, the spot they had chosen remained as inadvisable as ever. I sent Rahim down with food for them. One day, he returned in fury. 'Before the antidote arrives from Iraq, the snake-bitten one will be dead,' he fumed. 'Those unfortunate people say that they attended the offices of the UNHCR. They were told that the Peshawar region is full up with refugees. If they wish to receive aid, they must be transported hundreds of miles away to the plains of Sindh. Now these people are waiting for others from their village to join them. They agreed that the first to arrive would wait in Peshawar for the rest. And, besides, they do not wish to move to the blazing plains.'

I was aghast. 'But what are they going to do?'

'Madam, they will wait where they are. They say they will rely upon God to protect them.'

The next time I went to visit the old man and his family beside the canal, he said: 'It is not seemly that you leave without taking a little *nush-i-jan*, life-giving sustenance.' Accepting so much as a cup of tea made with the canal's slimy water was deeply inadvisable, but to refuse refreshment would be an insult. There was no way out.

Tea and bread appeared from nowhere. A rag was spread, and we sat upon it as delicately as if it were a silken cushion. Now that he had the dignity of a guest, the old man became confident and expansive, even slightly sanctimonious. I glimpsed the person he must have been before his life was turned upside down: a grand old sheikh full of elegant courtesies, wise saws and moral discourse. Now that he had lost everything else, I hung upon his every word.

We talked of the times in which we were living, through what Afghans were already calling the *musibat*, the calamity. He reminded me of other calamities the people of Afghanistan had faced: the coming of Alexander the Great, the century of war when the Arabs invaded, the horrific onslaughts by the barbarians from the north. So much fighting, misery and death, all for what the invaders merely imagined would quench their thirst for riches.

Once, he said, a poor man approached the great Afghan king Mahmud of Ghazna and asked him to fill his begging bowl. But the king's money disappeared, as if the bowl had no bottom. The haughty monarch called for more gold to be brought. When half of the treasure of his kingdom had vanished, Mahmud admitted defeat. 'This bowl represents the desires of man,' said the beggar-sage. 'There is no limit to man's capacity to devour.'

One day, I found a brightly painted bus standing in the dip where the refugees were camped. Clustered round it, with their meagre belongings strewn about them, were the women and children I had come to know. There was an excited hubbub about the place; it was clear that something was going on.

When I hurried down to the dip, they greeted me cheerfully. Only the old man, their leader, remained sitting impassively on a stone, surveying the scene. 'May you never be tired, Father,' I said. 'I am glad to see that the bus has finally come to take you to Sindh.'

'May you be well, my daughter. This is not the bus from the refugee authorities. Nor is it taking us to Sindh.'

'What is going on, then?' I was startled into asking a more direct question than is polite by the strict rules of Afghan etiquette.

'The Prophet, peace be upon him, said, "Trust in God, but tie your camel." We trust in Allah, but what we can do for ourselves, we must. The people from our village have not arrived; perhaps they have met with misfortune on the way. Here, in Pakistan, our children are becoming ill. Every day we have to sell a few more of our belongings to buy food to keep alive. Our hearts ache for our own hillsides and orchards. I have therefore resolved to return. My eldest daughter, who is a widow, has consented to sell her gold earrings, and we have hired this bus. It will take us to the border, and from there we will walk until we reach our village. Be it however destroyed, it is better to die there than to be buried alive in this dusty grave. Every breath we draw here is a slow death. In our own village we may starve without owing anything to anyone. Here we starve, as objects of charity, in thrall to people who tell us how and where we should live.'

I watched as the last of the women and children bustled aboard the bus. When he was satisfied that everyone was seated, the old man himself, with stately dignity, rose unaided from his stone. He walked slowly to the bus, saluted me, and climbed on board.

I waved goodbye and stood there, reflecting, long after its horn had blared, and its garish fat belly had disappeared from view.

11. Lost in the Desert of Death

I fear you will never reach Mecca,
O traveller,
For you are on the road to Turkestan.

Gulistan, Sheikh Sa'adi of Shiraz

In 1988, Beat decided it would be interesting to visit the region around Kandahar, Afghanistan's second city. I was more cautious. Few journalists had visited the area since an American, Charles Thornton, had been killed in a Soviet ambush two years before. In the south, everything was different. The terrain around Kandahar was flat, offering the mujahidin none of the natural protection of the mountains. To top it all, even among a people as bloodthirsty as the Afghans, the Kandaharis have a certain reputation for ruthlessness. As a child, I was told how to spot a Kandahari: he will cut your throat with a rusty knife because it hurts more.

We had no inkling of it then, but six years later, the religious student movement, the Taliban, would emerge from this region, combining the unpredictability of the local tribesmen with the zealotry of purist Islam.

We paid a visit to our old friend, Hamid Karzai, who came from Kandahar. He was as urbane as they came.

In Peshawar, a town in which to leave the house was to be instantly drenched in sweat and covered in grime, he wore a pristine white silk *shilwar kamis*. Almost alone among adult males who wished to command respect among the guerrilla fighters, he shaved not only his beard but his head. He had intelligent, slightly protruding eyes and a fine mind. He also had a fondness for what he liked to call the Big Picture.

'I'm so glad you came . . . I was working on a little paper – one of the more importunate French institutes has been pestering me to do it – about the Common Man in Afghanistan. I would be so interested to hear your views.'

Karzai loved talking about the Common Man. In times of peace, he might have been a leading academic or a social reformer. Here, in exile, he was a spokesman for a small, moderate opposition political party. After half an hour or so, he asked: 'Now, how may I be of service to you?'

'We'd like to go to Kandahar.'

Hamid did a visible double-take. 'Both of you?'

'Yes,' we said firmly.

'It's very dangerous.'

The way he said it, I knew we were going to go.

A few days later a wiry, unhappy-looking man, with a thin face and darting eyes, somehow got past all our defences. We found him perched on a wicker chair on the veranda. He wore an outsized black silk turban in the Kandahari manner, and he was shouting: 'I Ghaffar Khan – you come now Quetta. We go Kandahar. Bang! Bang! Ha! Ha!'

Ghaffar Khan had come to take us to the headquarters of a mujahidin commander in Arghandab, close to the city of Kandahar. The rest of our travelling companions seemed to bear out my childhood warnings about the madness of the southerners. Their eyes, glittering and wild, were thickly ringed with kohl. They laughed at nothing in particular. Their beards were long, black, and woolly to an extraordinary degree. Their huge silk turbans had dangling ends, which they liked childishly to suck. They seemed quite untrammelled by any form of human convention. Along with the usual ammunition belts and AK-47s, they toyed with roses in a manner that suggested they might decide to shoot you, then smell their roses afterwards.

We visited their armoury – a series of caves packed with Kalashnikovs, heavy machine-guns and rocket-propelled grenades. Stimulated by the sight of so much weaponry, the men loosed off random bursts of machine-gun fire. Eventually, they began to load supplies into the pickup truck. They seemed to be enjoying themselves – they formed a human chain and threw RPGs from man to man. The last person in the chain sent each one flying with a satisfying crash into the metal back of the truck. The RPGs were stored without detonators, but it seemed reckless all the same. Next they hauled a gigantic open drum into the back of the truck, filled it to the brim with fuel and left it without a lid. Beat and I found ourselves sitting on top of several layers of RPGs, while an open barrel of diesel splattered us every time we hit a boulder.

The sun raged down on us, and copious fumes rose

from our diesel can. The sands of a vast, flat desert stretched out in all directions, offering no cover. A couple of times, we heard the dull buzz of planes. Fortunately, they were not jets but light reconnaissance aircraft, presumably armed with cameras and sophisticated heat-imaging equipment. The amount of money, men and hi-tech matériel at the Red Army's disposal was an interesting topic for reflection as we jolted along in our soft-shelled truck with a group of what I could only describe as enthusiastic amateurs. We were sitting ducks.

The men seemed unconcerned. They left such details in the hands of Allah, along with most of the responsibility for organizing our route. As we rumbled on, possibly in circles, Beat and I watched our supply of mineral water disappear. Nobody else had thought to bring anything to drink.

In the time of Alexander the Great, this arid desert was a place of gardens and flowers. Pomegranates grew, and figs, and there were many splendid towns. Then a great devil of a beast appeared and laid it all to waste. Alexander consulted his ministers, but nobody knew what to do. Finally, the philosopher Aristotle made a gigantic mirror, and mounted it upon a carriage, which he drove towards the monster. As soon as it glimpsed its own reflection, it gave a terrible howl and died.

Aristotle explained that the people of the area were wicked and unclean. The monster had been created out of their evil thoughts and actions. When it saw itself in the mirror, it was killed by its own evil eye.

After he had finished telling me this story, our driver gave me a wink. A dashing figure who wore a lime green turban and plentiful black kohl, he was taking no chances with the evil eye. Half of his rear-view mirror was obscured by a verse from the Qur'an. The other half was covered by a fluorescent sticker of a large blue eye, a potent device against the harmful effects of the envy that either his splendid truck, or his handsome person, might excite. The wing mirrors and the base of the truck were tied with ribbons and jangling chains. They were anti-*jinn* devices, for it is well known that *jinn* detest fluttering and jangling things.

With such precautions in place, the driver felt no particular responsibility for our safety. He often neglected to put either of his hands on the steering-wheel. Nor did he bother to look at the road, preferring to entertain us with amusing stories, at which he would throw back his head and laugh lustily. At other times, he swivelled round in his seat to give me long, soulful looks.

I was becoming more and more certain that he was flirting with me. This was puzzling because, as an extra safety precaution, I was pretending to be a boy. Ghaffar Khan had shown me how to tie my black silk turban, and I wore it partly covering my face. I had shadowed my upper lip and tightly bound my breasts, which were in any case disguised by my loose waistcoat. Whatever I looked like, it wasn't a woman.

At sundown, we stopped at an oasis, where a muddy pool of water provided some greenery. The men went to great pains to cover the truck with branches, apparently unaware that it would still be visible to heat-imaging equipment. Only Ghaffar Khan's eyes had been opened to the risks we were running: during the whole day's drive, he had sat in the truck, hunched with fear. 'I am an educated man,' he said. 'I have attended mullah school and done Red Cross first-aid course.' He demonstrated his first-aid skills by poking at a comrade's septic leg wound with a pair of blunt, unsterilized scissors.

After prayers, the mujahidin taught me how to play a game called Stone the Mullah. You set up a row of five or six stones, with one in front. The first is the mullah, the rest are his congregation. As in a game of marbles, you have to use another stone to try to knock them down. There are extra points if you hit the mullah.

Everyone in Afghan knows a joke or two about the mullahs, Islam's unofficial clergy – and the men who would one day lead the Taliban movement. No village is complete without one. He might be an erudite religious scholar or, more often, an illiterate local bigot. I grew up with stories about the Afghan folkloric figure called Mullah Nasruddin.

Nasruddin decided to unseat the mullah of his village. He challenged him to an open competition, to test who was the more knowledgeable. Nasruddin asked the first question: 'What is the meaning of the Arabic word *marafsh*?'

'I do not know,' said the mullah, translating.

At that, the villagers rose up and threw him out, welcoming Nasruddin as their new spiritual guide. As he was leaving, the disgraced mullah said to Nasruddin: 'You have tricked me.'

'How many years have you been mullah in this village?' asked Nasruddin.

'Thirty-five,' said the old man.

'And in thirty-five years,' said Nasruddin, 'the only wisdom you have taught these people is how to be tricked?'

That evening, we arrived at a village as the local mullah was saying his prayers. Rather than greeting his guests, he prolonged his devotions to underline his piety. To emphasize further his spiritual rank he wore an enormous turban, but his eyes were greedy and shrewd.

The mujahidin were worried about introducing Western journalists to this venerable bigot. Before I could stop them, they were pretending that Beat and I were young Arabs, here to fight for Islam. A rustle of excitement rippled through the villagers. They told us their mullah was fluent in Arabic. He often complained that none of them could converse with him in the language of the Holy Qur'an, which was, after all, so peculiarly fitted to discussing the burning issues of Islamic jurisprudence.

I could just about hold up my end of a conversation in Arabic, but not enough to fool an Islamic scholar. When he had finished his devotions, the mullah and I sat in the centre of an expectant circle of villagers.

'*As-salaam aleikum,*' he intoned. 'Peace be upon you.'

'*Wa aleikum as-salaam.* Upon you be peace.'

An uncomfortable pause followed. I decided to allow the mullah to make the opening remarks. He darted a quick look round the faces of his flock. Then he began to speak.

For a few moments, I stared at him in amazement. I thought he had gone mad. This was not Arabic, or any other language of this world: it was complete gibberish, with the occasional pious Arabic phrase thrown in. Then I understood: the poor mullah spoke not a single word of the holy language of Islam. In a last desperate stand, he had resorted to this stratagem.

After about five minutes, he stopped and inclined his head to me. I took a deep breath. 'Esteemed, sir,' I began in Persian, 'when I hear my language spoken so well, I know I am in the presence of a true Muslim. But I am trying to learn Persian. Will you forgive me if we speak in that language?'

The mullah beamed. His face was saved. Now he could appear generous in front of the whole village by forgoing a discourse in Arabic for the sake of a guest.

The mullah's knowledge of Islamic law was as shaky as his Arabic. When the villagers waded into a nearby stream to perform *wudu*, the ritual wash before prayer, I noticed that rather than take off their shoes — as is done from Albania to Indonesia — they splashed water on to their boots.

'In Islam,' said the mullah loftily, 'you may keep your shoes on to do *wudu* as long as they don't come above your ankle.'

'But many of the men are wearing boots that do cover their ankles,' I pointed out.

'They,' said the mullah, 'are *not* good Muslims.'

I often thought of that mullah as the Taliban rose to prominence. His attitudes explained a great deal about the Pushtun cultural values underpinning their Islamic theories. After prayers, he lectured us about the evils of the West: 'Do you know that in America women are even permitted to marry dogs?'

'I take refuge in Allah! How appalling! Are you quite sure?'

'Perfectly sure. They take the dog to their church and the priest will marry them. The next day, perhaps they wish to divorce the dog, and the priest will allow that too.'

In 1928 King Amanullah Khan took on the power of the mullahs. He was a forward-looking king, who dreamed of establishing a haven of European culture in the Hindu Kush. His court was modelled upon the salons of Paris, he rattled along the highways of Afghanistan in a dusty Rolls-Royce and, on the outskirts of Kabul, he built his great monument to progress, a splendid aerodrome.

Amanullah decreed that everybody in the cities should wear Western dress. His wife, Queen Soraya, publicly uncovered her face, while his soldiers ripped the veils off women in the street. Outside Kabul and Kandahar, vast flea-markets grew up, hiring out Western clothes by the hour. It was a humiliating farce. Peasant men trudged to market in tattered ballgowns, and women tried to cover their shame with crumpled bowler hats.

But the mullahs fought back. They circulated pictures of Queen Soraya, wearing a shoulderless gown, and dancing with a man to whom she was not related. They roared from the pulpits that if the king could not even control his own wife how could he hope to rule a man's country like Afghanistan?

Amanullah did not survive this public disgrace. The backward traditions he had tried to sweep away rose up to engulf him. In the streets, people made great bonfires of European clothes. The king was forced to flee in his Rolls-Royce.

Just as the Taliban appeared in the anarchy following the Soviet withdrawal, the chaos that followed Amanullah's retreat allowed a brigand to take power. Bacha Saqao – the son of a water-carrier – turned Amanullah's beautiful aerodrome into a torture chamber. The splendid European palace was occupied by ruffians, who slept upon the billiard tables and held cock-fights in the gilded Louis XIV audience chamber.

It is as if there is an invisible corrective to the West in Afghanistan, a force of nature, dragging it back to its roots.

The next day we saw two more reconnaissance planes overhead. They were still circling but the loops were much tighter. They seemed to have more idea where to look. Perhaps the villagers of last night had ensured their own safety by tipping them off.

Worryingly, we found ourselves driving along proper earth roads, which could be easily ambushed. Ghaffar Khan, with a certain feral cunning, had decided that the safest place to sit was in the back of our truck, with his legs dangling over the tailgate. He reasoned that a front wheel was the most likely to hit a mine. In this position he might be thrown clear. Hunched in his thin black turban and ragged black *shilwar kamis*, he looked like a crow.

'Please, what is "puck you"?' he asked.

'What?'

'Puck you, puck you, I always want to know what is "puck you".' For a moment I was genuinely confused, then Ghaffar Khan said: 'Meester Charles, he always used to say: "Puck you, Ghaffar Khan. Puck you, you no good bastard." So what is "puck you"?'

'Who is Meester Charles?' I asked warily.

Ghaffar Khan shook his greasy head, and clicked his tongue in a gesture intended to denote sorrow, but which only revealed rows of rotting teeth.

'Meester Charles Pornton. He say: "You pucker, you gonna geddus keeled."'

'You mean to say you've travelled with Charles Thornton?'

'Yes, poor Meester Charles, I take him to Kandahar.'

It was worrying enough that Charles Thornton had been killed two years previously in the same area. Now, I realized, we were with the same guide. When we eventually got back to Peshawar, I found a picture of Ghaffar Khan with Charles Thornton in a copy of the Communist magazine *Kabul Today*. It had been developed from an unexposed roll of film found at the site of the ambush.

Ghaffar Khan admitted to having been with Charles Thornton when he was killed, but when I asked for more details, he just hunched further over the tailgate. I could get no more out of him than: 'Poor Meester Charles.'

We passed a group of mujahidin, who told us to be careful of ambush on this road because the resistance in this area had become very weak. 'The United States has stopped delivering Stinger missiles to this part of the country,' they said. This was an extraordinary piece of information, and we asked why the CIA should withhold these weapons from such a key area.

The mujahidin's casual reply amazed me. They said two commanders from an extremist Islamic faction had sold their Stingers to Iran. The men had made it look as though Iranian troops had captured their arms convoy, but the word around here was that the weapons had been sold, all right.

Beat and I both knew at once that, if true, this was a major story. In the wrong hands, a Stinger missile could easily bring a passenger plane plummeting out of the sky. At the time, Iran was the USA's most ferocious enemy. For all their flaws, I still didn't want to believe that the mujahidin were capable of such treachery. We decided to treat this rumour with extreme caution.

That evening, we stopped at a village. It seemed prosperous – there were melons and grapes growing and animals foraged about the mud houses – but the villagers gave us a frosty welcome. The headman told us without apology that their land had been ruined because of the war, they could only spare us a few grapes; then we would have to go. Our band of men made a point of stopping to pray in the village square, their Kalashnikovs within easy reach. A gaggle of villagers watched us sourly until we left.

We slept in the back of the truck, on top of the knobbly RPGs. The desert air was very cold and, although we were easy targets for an ambush, no one wanted to stay up to keep guard. Despite my worries,

I was so bone-tired I fell asleep almost immediately. Three or four hours later I woke in pitch blackness, illuminated only by the fat desert stars, to find someone groping me. I gave the offending hand a furious slap, and fell back to sleep.

The next morning, the driver had obviously realized that I was a woman. Far from leering, he could now barely bring himself to look at me. It was obvious that he was suffering from severe loss of face. Instead of turning round to regale us all with stories and jokes, and to bestow upon me flashes of his gleaming white teeth, he kept his hands firmly on the steering-wheel and his eyes on the road. From now on, he pointedly directed his attentions to the youngest lad in our band instead.

Things were starting to go seriously wrong for us. We had not eaten properly for two days, and we were utterly lost. But as night fell the hamlet we arrived at was more hostile than ever. As if to make it clear that we were not welcome, the villagers put us in a decrepit shack with an unexploded shell peering in through one of its mud walls.

We waited for some kind of refreshment. It never came, not even a glass of water. I watched Ghaffar Khan grow pale. Under *Pushtunwali*, you may not kill a man if he has eaten your bread and salt. Conversely, until you have been offered food or drink, you cannot count yourself among friends.

The village elders began to arrive. I could tell by the tenor of the Pushtu conversation that things were not going well. The kindest Pushtu greeting sounds like a fight, but this was a real argument. I had never seen a situation like this; only force of numbers, it seemed, was keeping us safe.

'What are they saying, Ghaffar Khan?'

Ghaffar Khan seemed to be moaning in fear. Finally I got from him: 'These very bad people, no respect mujahidin.'

The villagers had banded together to form a militia of their own. They had made a deal with the Soviet-backed army under which they were left alone provided they gave no shelter to the mujahidin. Now, they informed us, the news had spread that there were foreign journalists with our party. That was a great propaganda prize, and there was a big operation in place aimed at catching us.

The villagers wanted us to leave right away. Resting for the night was out of the question. More troops would be airdropped into the area tonight. The rumours flew that they included the dreaded Spetsnaz, highly trained Soviet commandos. The road we had intended to travel along was ambushed. We would have to take a back way and hope that it had not been blocked as well.

Blearily, we got to our feet. We were being hunted. Artillery fire had never driven fear into my heart like this. There was something comfortably random about shelling. I could calculate how many billions of cubic metres of empty space there were and how tiny a target I was in comparison. But this was different. There were pilots up in those jets, looking out for us specifically, and dozens, perhaps hundreds, of soldiers spending the night on those cold plains with no other objective but to catch us. If the villagers were to be believed, they included top commandos from the mighty army of a superpower. How could we, a bunch of incompetents, outwit them? The thought clawed at my heart and I was truly afraid.

I couldn't blame the villagers for throwing us out. They had had enough of the war, they wanted a quiet life. What was it to them who held sway in Kabul or even in Kandahar? Central government wouldn't touch their village life, but war could.

12. Increasing Your Necessity

Since new capacities come about through necessity
Therefore, O man, increase your necessity.

Masnavi, Jalaluddin Rumi

We took the back roads, skirting warily past ruined villages and giving inhabited ones a wide berth. Then, just before dawn, we heard the sound of jets.

We held a *jirga*, a war council. In this area the flat plain mercifully gave way to gentle hills, which offered a bit of cover. However, the truck was still too conspicuous. We decided to split up: we would cut across the hills on foot, and the driver would make his way alone to a prearranged rendezvous, posing as an innocent traveller.

We set off up the hillside, through pre-dawn blackness so deep that we couldn't see our own feet on the stones. When we were nearly at the top, we heard a helicopter hovering on the other side. We ducked back down the side of the hill while one man from our group went to have a look. He came back to report that troops were being dropped in the valley below.

The net was closing around us. All that night, and the day that followed, we skirted round a series of sandy plateaux and hills. This whole area seemed to be unpopulated. We had been forced to make a wide detour and, as usual, the mujahidin were lost – they kept stopping to argue among themselves about the route. By the evening, we were exhausted and very hungry. I didn't think that I could spend another night walking, but I worried that, if we stopped, we would freeze when it grew dark.

Then, on the flat top of a ridge, we saw grazing sheep. The little girl tending them had dark skin and fine bones, and her colourful costume was all in rags. She was a Kochi, one of the nomadic Afghans who resemble the Romany gypsies. We eyed each other cautiously as we passed; the Kochis keep themselves to themselves.

We came to their encampment, a tattered collection of black tents. In my despairing state, it seemed like a miracle. We sat and waited, while two of our men went to ask for food and shelter for the night. They returned ten minutes later, to say that the Kochis couldn't risk helping us. We would have to continue on our way.

The rebuff was like a physical blow. The Kochis are the outcasts of Afghan society. Now even these pariahs were shunning us. In other parts of the country the mujahidin were a popular movement, which could count on the support of civilians. If the local people were frightened of the resistance, what was the point of them existing at all?

The mujahidin fingered their Kalashnikovs, and for a moment I thought there would be a fight. Then they simply got up, collected their weapons and walked away. We moved about six hundred metres from the

Kochi encampment and sat down again. We were all too tired to walk another step.

This was a camp of the worst kind. No fire, no water for tea or to perform *wudu*. No shelter from the wind. We watched the sun set in chilly silence. There was no question of food. The desert night was freezing. We had hit rock bottom.

Somewhere in my brain, a slow wind rose and mounted to a hurricane. Here in Kandahar, the myth of the noble mujahidin was finally blowing apart. Snowflake fragments whirled in my brain: all the things that I had ignored because they didn't fit in with what I wanted to see. The bodies with their lacerated throats, sailing down the canal in Peshawar, and the bombs exploding there night after night. Jamil Haidar destroying my uncle's house. Above all, the possibility that the mujahidin had sold Stingers to Iran.

I had been ready to blame everyone – the West, the Arabs, the Islamic extremists – but I could not let go of my noble mujahidin. Because they belonged to my myth and, in a sense, they were a part of me.

I fiddled with my hair and discovered that a strand of it had turned white. It seemed like an omen.

We marched on at dawn and, within five or six kilometres, found a small stream where we could get water. We had simply been too demoralized to make camp in a more sensible place. The men got a fire going and we boiled a little water for the last of our tea. I went through my rucksack and discovered a stock cube hidden in a sock. This was treasure. I slipped some into the tea that Beat and I were drinking, pretending it was medicine. 'That is a very delicious-smelling medicine,' grumbled Ghaffar Khan.

The morning air was cool and sunny and an absurdly cheerful post-dawn glow lit up the hard white rocks. The fear of the chase didn't leave my mind, but it seemed somehow postponed at such a magical moment.

For another day we wandered, apparently aimlessly. Towards late afternoon we at last neared the village where we were supposed to meet our truck. We approached it cautiously, skirting fields of tall maize so that we would not be seen.

There were small ears of unripe corn on the plants and, suddenly, I couldn't restrain myself. If I stole one, who would see? I quickly snapped one off and munched it as I went. It was gone in just a moment; I would take just one more to put in my pocket. As I reached out, Ghaffar Khan spotted me.

He was about to give me a reproving look, when I saw, visibly crossing his face, a terrible temptation. Instead of chiding me, he deliberately reached out and took a couple of ears for himself. We were accomplices. But then, of course, the other men saw what was going on. They had barely glanced at the corn, but now they too began plucking the green ears. Within seconds, they had made a little fire out of corn-husks, and jiggled the corn on it. It smelt delicious. As if to excuse their felony, they mimed that they intended to give me the first piece. For the first time in days, there was cheerful joking and laughter.

Just as the corn was ready, an old woman came hobbling through the field. She saw the men, and gave them a terrible tongue-lashing. Sheepishly, they put out the fire and handed over the stolen ears. We hurried on again in silence, terribly ashamed.

As I walked I thought of a tale of the great hero of the Pushtuns, the legendary warrior king Mahmud of Ghazna. Once, becoming separated from his hunting party, he wandered around lost in the forest for hours. When he was tired and famished, he smelt delicious cooking and discovered an old woman in a clearing, stirring a pot of beans over a fire. When the king asked humbly for a few beans, she refused, saying: 'Your kingdom is not worth what these beans are worth. Look at all the enemies who threaten it. I am free and I have my own beans.' And the mighty Mahmud thought of his disputed kingdom, and wept.

Miraculously, the truck was at its rendezvous. It was wonderful to see our driver, and even to be reunited with the terrible vehicle, the barrel of diesel and the knobbly RPGs. Possibly to encourage us to leave, the villagers gave us some bread. It was made out of maize and very coarse, with a faint taste of nuts. Because it had no gluten, it crumbled to the touch.

Back in the truck, I was so ill with motion sickness that I took an anti-allergy pill, hoping it would help. It wasn't a good place to discover that I react severely to some forms of antihistamine. It sent me into a deep stupor.

Dimly, I heard Ghaffar Khan shouting: 'Keep at back of truck! Many mines!' Then I crashed down into the RPGs and passed out. Ghaffar Khan made intermittent attempts to wake me up, telling me it wasn't safe to sleep, we were in a very dangerous area; there were mines and the villagers were hostile. I knew I should keep awake, in case we had to jump and run for it. But it was too late, I had already taken the pill. It was the best sleep I had had in days.

I was woken by the unmistakable rattle of Kalashnikov fire: set on automatic and sounding panicky. None of us seemed to have been hit. A warning, then. There was angry shouting from the darkness, and answering shouts from our men.

Almost as punctuation, a hot-headed mujahid fired off a single shot, which prompted another burst. A bullet ricocheted off the side of the truck, narrowly missing the diesel barrel. Ghaffar Khan, always the panicker, shouted: 'Jump!'

I realized that this was probably exactly the kind of scenario that Charles Thornton had faced. The whole scene had a dreamlike quality. Still doped from the tablets, I jumped off the side of the truck and my legs packed up. I staggered to the side of the road and took cover. Then, I think, I lost consciousness again.

It was villagers, angry that we were passing through their land. They told us that the road ahead was mined. After some discussion, it transpired that they had mined it themselves. They didn't want the mujahidin to pass that way. It would only bring trouble to the village.

We knew that if we went back the way we had come, we would fall right into the arms of our pursuers. Our choices had been cut off one by one and now, like rats in a maze, we had to go on.

We stayed for a long while, pleading with the villagers to tell us the positions of the mines. They were stubborn.

No one had travelled down that road for three years and it had kept the village in peace. They didn't want anyone going down it now. We must turn back.

There was a slim chance that they were bluffing. In any case, it seemed certain that the mines would be anti-personnel ones. The Kandahari mujahidin hatched a plan.

Our driver proved himself a hero. He would drive the unloaded truck ahead of us. We would all follow on foot, in the tracks of our vehicle, hoping that our weight was too light to detonate the mines if the truck had not done so already. He leaped into the driver's seat, as unconcerned as if he was going on a little pleasure jaunt. As he did so, the nerve of one of the villagers broke, and he jumped into the cab as well. We had a local guide, but would he be of any use? I knew that mines could shift their positions in the earth.

I heard the driver whistling as he vanished, inch by inch, into the gloom.

Nobody needed to say it, but the mujahidin's thought was: This too, like all things, is in the hands of Allah. Now it was our turn. I followed in the newly furrowed track of the truck. We had no torches, and the driver drove without headlights, so I had only starlight by which to see my feet. As my eyes got used to the darkness, I found it was more than enough. My senses were heightened to an extraordinary degree, and I thought that we must live most of our lives using just a fraction of our potential. But it is there, waiting, for when we need it.

We plodded on: thirty-odd people, somehow

linked, as though we were one organism. I didn't feel afraid and I didn't pray, as such, but I felt a closeness: to my group, and to what I can only describe as existence. A certainty that life or death were not problems that need concern me. That this certainty would keep me safe, beyond life, beyond death. They say there are no atheists at sea. Perhaps the psychological phenomenon of faith is catching, and I had caught the faith of those around me.

We carried on at this snail's pace for a couple of hours, until we were well past the furthest boundaries of the village. There had been no mishap, either to us or to the truck. Had all this talk of mines been a bluff? In this psychological war of attrition, I couldn't be sure, but the road hadn't been used before by local mujahidin, and it usually takes more than a bluff to keep away a bunch of crazed Afghans. Had we been lucky? Possibly. Were we under the protection of One greater than ourselves? The mujahidin assumed we were, in the same way one assumes the sun will rise in the morning.

When we were sure the villagers were far behind us, we all piled back into the truck. The driver was as cheerful and loquacious as ever. I eyed his anti-*jinn* talismans and Qur'anic verses with new respect. They obviously worked for him.

The walk had got rid of the last traces of the allergy tablets, and Beat, Ghaffar Khan and I all sat in the back, watching out and ready to jump. It was now that very dark time before dawn. The moon was gone and the stars were vanishing one by one. The truck drove without headlights. The darkness edged past us, and we rushed into ever-deepening darkness ahead.

I felt the jolting and juddering of the truck smooth out, like the change in a horse's rhythm from trotting to cantering. It seemed an unnatural sensation. At first I couldn't work out what was happening. Then it struck me – we were on a Tarmac road. As my body almost wept with gratitude, my head told me how dangerous this was.

There are very few metalled roads in Afghanistan. We must have been on a major highway, one of the main arteries linking key towns. These roads were closely guarded military sites, used for troop convoys. Mujahidin might sneak up to them for hit-and-run raids or ambushes. Trundling down one apparently aimlessly was bad news.

'Do you hear that?' asked Beat.

'What?'

'A slight whining . . . very faint.'

We strained our ears in the cold air. Above the wind I thought I heard it too, a familiar, high-pitched drone. 'Tank?' Now I was afraid again.

Beat nodded. 'Look,' he said. Round the bend, far away, was a light.

Our driver saw it too. Without slowing down, he made an abrupt detour down a dirt track. Behind us, the whine got louder, then faded away.

With its headlights off, the truck coasted back on to the metalled road. We were still trapped on the Kabul–Kandahar highway. As Beat said: 'At least this way we know where we're going.'

'Yes,' I tried to joke. 'Either Kandahar or Kabul, right?'

After the past few days' jolting, it felt as though we were flying. The mujahidin took turns to stand ready with an RPG launcher in case of ambush. We watched the craggy black hillsides slip past, looking for the flash that would signal an attack had begun. Our ears strained for the whoosh of a rocket. By the time we either heard or saw a weapon, our fates would have been decided. If we saw the flash, the shot would have already missed us, and we would have time to try to jump clear before the inevitable second try.

The monotony of this concentration was mesmerizing, and somehow peaceful. The old man whose turn it was on the RPG launcher was singing to keep himself awake. We seemed to be gliding along on the blackest velvet, the mountains behind; darkness upon darkness. We passed the burned-out shells of tanks. As dawn broke, the ridges got darker and craggier, and the old warrior with the launcher was silhouetted against the lightening sky. A few plump dawn stars appeared and the wavering voice wound on and on: an endless, wordless song. It might have been the same Pushtu war song his ancestors had sung as they waited to ambush the British invaders in the nineteenth century, or the Mongols of Genghis Khan in the thirteenth century, or the Arabs in the seventh century, or the Central Asian hordes in the fifth century, or even the Greeks of Alexander the Great, four centuries before Christ.

All at once I knew that there was no end to this song, or this road, or these mountains, or this war; either now, or ever. Nations and political systems, issues and ideals were secondary and irrelevant. This was eternal, and we were just visitors, passing through.

13. The Rumour Officer

O Heart! until in the prison of deception,
You can see the difference between this and that.
For an instant detach from this well of tyranny.
Step outside.

Jalaluddin Rumi

Everywhere we went in Kandahar, the story was the same: Stingers had fallen into the hands of Iran. Some people said that they had been ambushed, others that they had been sold, but everyone agreed that the CIA had secretly suspended supplies of the weapons to this area. Two commanders, both of whom had links to Iran, were involved. Sixteen missiles had disappeared.

When we made it back to Pakistan, we found sources to corroborate the story. For me, this was far more than just a journalistic scoop – it was the smoking gun that finally convinced me the myth of the noble mujahidin was a lie. And, if that one wasn't true, how could I believe any of my other myths about Afghanistan?

When it came to writing about the sale or capture of the Stingers for a British newspaper, I stuck strictly to facts. I tried to build a picture that was balanced and fair. 'In most areas the mujahidin are a popular movement . . .' I hedged. 'The overwhelming majority of commanders are honest . . .'

I was hopelessly naïve. A sub-editor on the paper removed all of the context I had so carefully included. The result was a sensationalist piece that I barely recognized. But there was nothing I could do: the facts were correct.

For a while, I thought I had got away with it. The mujahidin were briefly embarrassed; the Westerners in Peshawar, backed by US officials, assumed the allegations could not be true. Then, three weeks later, Stinger parts were found on an Iranian frigate in the Gulf, and the glue that held my world together began to come unstuck.

One of the men I had accused of selling Stingers wanted to see me. Abdul Haq, a mujahidin commander for whom I had a great deal of respect, arranged a meeting. Haq was a close ally of the United States; a sober, decent man, who refused to shell Kabul from his military base in Sarobi because he didn't want to cause civilian casualties. At that time, he was in Peshawar recovering from an injury by a butterfly mine, which had blown off half of his foot. He greeted me amicably, but he took care to leave the room before my adversary arrived.

I was left alone with a man who looked like the village mullah I had met on the way to Kandahar, at once angry and avaricious, with the dirty grey turban and wispy beard of a religious bigot. I could easily picture him selling Stingers to Iran – and quite possibly believing that in America women are permitted to marry dogs. He was shaking with rage, and perhaps also with humiliation at having been insulted by a mere woman. When I asked him if the allegations against him were true, he seemed genuinely puzzled. 'But that isn't the point,' he said.

In his terms, of course, he was right. His personal honour had its own existence, quite separate from the facts. Regardless of whether or not he had sold his Stingers, I had made him lose face. His political party had stopped his weapons. In order to regain his dignity, he needed to take revenge.

Abdul Haq, the peacemaker, had been at work behind the scenes. The commander was prepared to compromise. 'Tell me the name of the person who told you that story about me.'

'Why do you want to know it?'

'So that I can kill him.'

Through the haze of my Western indignation, the choice was easy. Perhaps I was even relieved to find a question of ethics so black and white, after thrashing around for so long in a forest of grey.

'I can't possibly tell you.'

'If you don't tell me his name,' said the commander, 'then I will send people to kill you instead.'

Later, when the commander had left, I asked Abdul Haq if he would protect me. He shrugged sadly; there was nothing he could do. 'It is between you and him,' he said. 'I am only an intermediary.'

Many of the mainly right-wing Western expatriates in Peshawar would have forgiven me for publishing lies, but I had done something much worse: I had exposed *their* truth. Hank, the pretend CIA man, led the onslaught. I had impugned the mujahidin's honour, and the quicker the mujahidin killed me, the better. In the American Club bar, there were murmurs of agreement.

At the time the town's handful of educated Afghans was being systematically wiped out. We all believed that a key ally of the West, the extremist mujahidin leader Gulbuddin Hikmatyar, was to blame. His victims – writers, doctors, journalists and lawyers – were moderates; exactly the people the country would need one day to rebuild its war-ravaged society. Although they were fêted in Europe and America, nothing could be done to save them. They lived in a shadowy world-between-worlds, sheltered by neither the Afghan nor the Western tribe. They were the unprotected, and everyone knew it. It had never occurred to me that I might become one of them.

Now the Westerners, too, wanted me dead. It's hard to explain how that feels. When I went to the American Club, conversation stopped. It was suggested that I was not a proper foreigner and there were moves to expel me. Hank spread his old stories about Beat and me being KGB agents, and this time people believed him. Someone photocopied my article, underlined my by-line, and helpfully sent it to the offices of Gulbuddin Hikmatyar. Half a dozen dogs were found hanged in a disused lot in University Town, close to our home. A gloating rumour swept round – it was a warning that Beat and I would soon follow their example.

In Corsica, until quite recently, groups of villagers claimed to share the same recurring dream. In their sleep, they were a pack, hunting together. They rushed through the darkness until their quarry became apparent. Sometimes it was a fox, sometimes a hare, but always at a certain point they perceived that the animal embodied the soul of a member of their own community. At the dream's invariable conclusion, the pack caught and tore to shreds its prey. Everyone in the village knew that that person was doomed – in real life – to die.

Their victim never lasted more than a few weeks. It would have taken superhuman strength to survive the guilty glances, the pointed questions, the hastily silenced gossip. That's the best way I can describe how it feels to defy the desires and expectations of the community in which you live. Something inside you tries to crumple up and die.

When I looked out of the window of Lala's Grill, I no longer saw delightful madness, but lurking threat. In the public morgue, an assistant pulled open a drawer, and there was the body of a girl like me – the last young woman who had broken the rules.

The line between life and death is fragile; I have seen corpses, newly dead, which look as though they are asleep. But after three days in the patchy refrigeration of Peshawar's morgue, she was swollen to twice her size, mottled with purple welts. The curve of her mouth and nose were shocking; the eye recoiled to discover a person inside this thing.

She had been found with the back of her head caved in, eyes protruding. Bruises ran down her arms, her upper thighs and her stomach, thickening and merging in the area around a tuft of ginger pubic hair. There was matter under her fingernails that might have been skin. An autopsy cut – roughly sewn up – ran from her navel to the top of her chest. Her head had been sliced open in the same way. Clubbed to death then carved up afterwards in autopsy like a piece of meat, she had been doubly abused. Her body lay in its fly-infested pool of blackening blood like a physical warning.

Until I looked into her life, I had not understood how easily you could get yourself killed in Peshawar. She was a Swiss anthropologist, fearless, outspoken. She was studying Afghan sexuality. She believed that Afghan women were oppressed by an out-of-date, macho culture. She wore revealing clothes defiantly. She was rumoured to be promiscuous. Sometimes she collared strange men in the bazaar and quizzed them about their sex lives. She was left-wing. She had researched the drugs trade. She had befriended, then fallen out with, a Maoist group. The difficulty was deciding which of the many people she had antagonized might be to blame.

Now a representative of the macho culture she despised was in charge of her case. Captain Gul Aga showed me the police photographs of her body as it was found, naked from the waist down. A makeshift noose had been fastened round her neck and loosely connected to the ceiling fan. There were signs of a struggle. I suggested that she might have been raped, but Captain Gul Aga pooh-poohed that idea. He had his own theory. 'You must understand her psychology,' he sneered. 'This is a woman of werry low moral. Werry low moral indeed. There is a knock at her door. She goes to answer it naked . . .' He paused to relish

222

this lascivious image. 'It is a man, so of course she invites him into her room to have sexual intercourse. They indulge in violent procreation, during which he kills her, then puts the noose round her neck in an effort to convince us – the Pakistani police – that she has tried to hang herself.'

He was triumphant at this piece of deduction. 'Really, it is the fault of Western girls. I am a married man. I have four wives. When I go home at night, I enjoy one of my wives. That is how it is arranged in Islam. A husband shall enjoy his wife. But a single girl, to travel alone, to behave the way she did, it inflames men's desires. That is why Allah cannot allow such things.' He fingered a damp pair of knickers lovingly. 'These were found next to her on the bed.'

I felt an urge to scoop up whatever I could of her, to protect her from his coarse hands. Her cheap hotel room was strewn with her intimate possessions. My eye fell on her notebooks lying on the table. They were written in German and, hesitantly, I offered to translate them. Captain Gul Aga, still engrossed in the knickers and in his own lewd thoughts, waved a hand carelessly at me. 'Take them, take them.'

When I got home, I realized that they were her diaries, handwritten, in soft-backed exercise books. I felt guilty for prying, but I was consumed with curi-osity, a thirst to know everything about her. She didn't bother to write about what she did, instead she recorded her thoughts, impressions and emotions. Reading them was like looking into her mind. Like me, she was obsessed with a quest to discover, to learn. But we were

223

so different: she was free, and angry, and she wanted to fight.

As I sat there, deciphering her handwriting, a change came over me. My familiar Peshawar ebbed away and I was living in a different version of the same city – a place of narrow alleys, overflowing sewerage and tantalizing doorways. I knew this town, and yet I didn't. Everything I saw was filtered through her eyes. We strode through the streets, sure and invincible. She was outspoken, she wanted to solve problems, she wanted to put all the injustices here to rights.

I was still in a reverie, when the Rumour Officer arrived. His position at the US High Commission was never precisely defined – I called him the Rumour Officer because he had a habit of spreading stories, usually by appearing to deny them. I was very surprised to see him; all the time that Hank had been subjecting Beat and me to his vilification, US officialdom had pointedly ignored us.

Just now he seemed particularly tense, although he was always nervous. He had a painful trick of blinking before he spoke, and his skin was so thin you could see the watery blood throbbing beneath it. 'Did you hear about the offensive at Nangrahar?' he asked, by way of small-talk.

'What about it?'

The eyelids fluttered like trapped moths. 'Let's just say,' he said, in his slow way, 'that it didn't happen. There was no offensive, and particularly no chemical-weapon attack by the Soviets. In particular, it is untrue that a group of seventeen Afghan pre-school children, their faces melted like mozzarella, were buried at sundown in a deep pit just across the border.'

There must have been something of the dead girl hovering around me, because I said rudely: 'You can hardly have come here to tell me about something that didn't happen. What is it you want?'

He looked panicked. 'Er . . . I hear you have a kinda inside track on the investigation of the murdered Swiss woman. Those her diaries there? Anything interesting in them?'

'Nothing to interest you, no facts.'

'Stream-of-conscious stuff, I guess? Rather like mine.'

I looked at him dubiously. There was an embarrassing pause, and then he said: 'You see, the thing is, we've heard that she had some links that could make her very interesting. Very interesting. We think she may not have been all she seemed. Some friends of mine were wondering if you'd come across a kind of ruler in her possession. It's about so long,' he indicated a length of about ten centimetres, 'for codes.'

I am diplomatic by nature, but I felt a far more confrontational personality welling up inside me. My violence, as I sent him packing, startled me. It was as though her passionate views couldn't just disperse but needed somewhere to lodge for a while. I doubted I would have liked her if we had met, but that seemed as irrelevant now as whether I liked myself. For a while, bubbling inside me, I could feel her arrogant, ignorant, heroic conviction that she could make a difference. In my place, she would never have given in.

I stopped going to the American Club. I slept with a gun under my pillow. I left the veranda light switched on. I began to believe that everyone hated me. I remembered how kindly old Professor Majrooh had brandished his walking stick at the mention of a journalist who had criticized the mujahidin, and how he had shouted: 'I will hit him with my stick!' Now I became convinced he must think the same of me. I could face the threats of the Islamic extremists and the contempt of the Westerners, but I couldn't bear to see disappointment in the professor's eyes. So, I did the cowardly thing. I stopped visiting him.

One afternoon, not long afterwards, when Majrooh's little servant had gone out to buy food and the professor was alone, there was a ring on his doorbell. Majrooh opened the door to a gunman, who riddled him with Kalashnikov bullets. That month, a colour photograph of his blood-soaked body, contorted and desecrated by death, appeared on the first page of the information bulletin he edited.

Notables from most of the mujahidin political parties attended his funeral, but none of Gulbuddin's men. It was generally supposed that Gulbuddin had had him killed. But, of course, this was Peshawar. Nobody ever bothered to find out for sure.

For weeks after Professor Majrooh's death, I was consumed with grief. I had lost much more than a friend, a mentor, a father figure: for me, the professor was the human being I had picked to personify the fairytale Afghanistan in which I had so desperately wanted to believe. His murder was the final blow that marked the death of my own personal myth. I spent hours staring at the picture of his corpse. For the first time since my world had begun to disintegrate, I wept. I suppose I was crying for a lot of things: for him, for the lost Afghanistan he represented, for my helplessness – and for fear of what would become of me. It seemed that the lights in my life were going out, one by one.

14. End Games

'O foreigner, do not attack – attacking is our job!'

Proverb

I didn't leave Peshawar right away. I thought that that would have seemed like an admission that I was frightened, that my enemies had won. But when, in 1988, the Soviets suddenly announced that they were withdrawing, I seized the opportunity to plan my return to Europe at the beginning of 1989. I told myself that I would do better pursuing my journalist career in the mainstream; that this story was nearly over. Abdul Haq appeared on US television, saying that the mujahidin were massing for a final onslaught on the capital. Most people believed him. America – all of us – wanted it to be true.

The Soviets retreated first from Afghanistan's extremities and, as they left, surging masses of revellers flooded in, like blood returning to a cramped limb. For ten years, they had lived amputated lives and now, with dizzying speed, the border was open, the artery was flowing. I joined a tide of people moving towards a newly abandoned base at Ali Khel, close to the Pakistani border. The retreating Afghan Communist forces were still shelling it now and then, but the crowds didn't care. They had come to celebrate, to sightsee and to indulge in an ancient Afghan tradition – *ghanimat*, looting.

Down from the mountains came woolly, wild-eyed, wide-eyed men. Some had been in the hills for years. Most of all I remember their amazement: eyes stretched open, as if they couldn't cram in enough looking. Ali Khel was one of the first abandoned bases, and they drank in the sights with sheer, childlike joy. For nearly ten years, since some of them were twelve or thirteen, these men had lived in the mountains launching raid after raid upon this base. They had sacrificed education, clothing, jobs, home, marriage and family to capture it. This was their first glimpse inside.

In their haste to quit, the Communist forces had left behind a mountain of equipment. The mujahidin turned it into an impromptu funfair. They took turns riding on the abandoned tanks. They fired the heavy artillery as though they were at a coconut shy. They gorged themselves on canned rations.

Bushy-bearded Pushtuns strode around in Soviet gas masks. A select few – mostly elders – swaggered about with officers' canes. I walked past a boy guarding hundreds of tins of processed peas. A toothless mujahid tried on a trademark Russian army striped undershirt over his *shilwar kamis*. In the spirit of the day, I looted a gas mask.

The men raised great cries of '*Allah Takbir! Allahu Akbar!*' 'Glorify God! God is Great!' They had won. The miracle had happened: Afghanistan was finally free.

The mujahidin made great effigies of Soviet officers,

paraded them about cheering and – almost as an after-thought – burned them. I remembered Uncle Mirza saying all those years ago: 'When we saw the British scared, we realized that they weren't invincible after all. It was then we knew that we would beat them – eventually.' On the faces of the mujahidin was the same wonder. The myth of the unconquerable Red Army had evaporated – just as that of the invincible British had before the eyes of their grandfathers. The children's children of these men would learn that here, on this bright wondrous day, on this windswept hillside, one of the great empires of our age collapsed. It had taken madmen to puncture the monster with eyes of fire, and their prize was to discover that it was full of nothing but air.

The Afghans had left the accommodation of the Soviet military advisers superstitiously untouched. They didn't need to see the human face of their enemy – but I did. You could still feel them here, cowering in this half-underground warren of mud walls and empty ammunition cases, sandbagged for protection against artillery attacks. So this was how they had lived – cooped behind a mined perimeter fence in a mystical, mountainous country where the population was blood-thirsty and wild. Vodka bottles were strewn every-where. There must have been moments of utter despair, and months of tedium. One man had built a gym from pieces of scrap metal, another had constructed a sauna out of ammunition boxes. This prison was their refuge: from the strangeness of the mountains, the cold, the enemy lurking to cut their throats. I never imagined, as we skirted fearfully around this base, how deeply they must have feared back.

From a pile of abandoned ID cards, the bogeyman stared at me. The faces were pensive, sad, homesick, frightened, cocksure. Above all, they were absurdly young. I picked up a photograph of a straw-haired, fresh-faced boy. Was he dead, or was his mother even now welcoming him home? Did he still look innocent, or had Afghanistan changed him for ever – the way it had changed me?

War had changed Afghanistan. A million and a half people – nearly eight per cent of the population – had been killed. Four million more were banished to squalid refugee camps. A generation of children had been left uneducated, their future as good as destroyed. Agriculture was bombed to shreds, the terraced mountain fields – hand-built over generations – were shattered, and the eroding earth sown with untraceable mines, as the Romans sowed salt. Victory had not come cheaply. My feet threw up dust from the eroded soil. This land had not been dug for years. Now even the habit of digging had been lost. The shaggy men romping like children in the sunshine had become accustomed to the rush of battle, the thrill of martyrdom. What did they know of sowing or of harvest, of painstakingly repairing what war had torn down? I had thought that this was an ending; it was only a beginning.

As around me the mujahidin whooped and cheered and looted, I picked up my stolen gas mask, and walked towards the border.

BOOK THREE

The Day it Rained Fire

From each heart is a window to other hearts,
They are not separated like two bodies,
Just as, even though two lamps are not joined,
Their light is united in a single ray.

Masnavi, Jalaluddin Rumi

15

11 September 2001

Smoke is blossoming from the World Trade Center. It is beautiful in the morning sunlight. The sound is turned down.

I am in a newsroom in London, which is slowing to a stop all around me. Nobody here quite believes what is happening. On television we are used to things that are not real. We feel awe and, yes, excitement. The world has been turned upside-down. It is a film, momentous and grand. History in the making.

I hear my journalist's voice, professionally cynical, saying: 'This is an extraordinary news day.'

At that moment, a plane flies into the second tower. Behind me somebody gasps: 'But it was such a beautiful building.'

Then, from the window of the tower, we see hands waving. One woman has left a message on her husband's answerphone. They play it on the news. She says, agonizingly: 'We've been told to go back into the building.' Her voice is shaky with tears.

And suddenly this isn't film, or history, or grandeur, or beauty. And we are weeping – because finally, finally we have understood that there are people down there, and that we cannot help them.

But I am not weeping entirely for the people waving

from the window of the World Trade Center, because none of us suffers in a vacuum; because experience comes in cycles. Then images rush into my mind, of things I have spent years trying to forget.

Smell: cordite and blood. Sound: a rushing noise – maybe blood in my ears – maybe the swooping of shells. Feet running? It is hard not to project, the mind tries to fill in the gaps. Sight: a shell plunges nose down, embeds itself in the road, quivers there like a dart. Tarmac melts, enfolds it like an envelope. Sparks fly out of its nose, a daytime firework. I stand and watch it, numb. Surely it is fizzing, but on my tape it is mute. A woman runs by, and her mouth is moving. She is shouting, but I can't hear her.

When I see, there is silence; when I smell, I am deaf; when I hear, I am blind. In my memory, the evidence of my senses is stored on different tapes. They contradict each other – random, out-of-sync scenes from a movie. Nothing is connected.

Point-of-view shot, looking up. The air is full of spears. Their tips glisten like raindrops. They fall in an arc, towards me, graceful.

The overpowering smell of blood.

It is noisy: firecracker noisy. Somebody, in the darkness, is screaming.

I am standing on a road in the Pakistani capital, Islamabad. On the kerb beside me squats an old woman. Shells rain softly down around her.

A *charpoy* under a tree, a man asleep. Or is he dead? A shell crashes in slow motion through the branches and spears him through the groin. He looks absurd: an ill-proportioned African fertility god.

I don't know what happens before or after any of these incidents. The tape of my mind has come unwound. I'm left with vignettes, mute and repeating. A video on a loop, spooling, spooling.

A wave of people is silently running. They have fused into a single entity, an ocean of people, moving as one. Even their expressions are uniform – everyone is wrapped up inside a personal world of fear. There is none of the usual human interaction; no one speaks or catches anyone's eye. A woman stumbles, and no one stops to help her.

Beat and I are in a jeep, struggling against this vast, slow-moving tide. I am trying to find out what is going on, but I can't get anyone's attention. I have rolled down the jeep's window and I am shouting at people, trying to catch their eyes, but no one will stop to answer my questions. I grab a man's arm, and he looks as though he has been rudely awakened. 'Israel is attacking!' he gasps, and breaks free to run on. But when I stop others, they say: 'The Soviets are coming to get us!' or 'India has invaded!'

Really, they don't know why they are running. They are fleeing from their own fear.

Beat and I were sitting with the Communist Afghan press attaché in Islamabad on the day, in 1988, when the explosion happened. Many of Peshawar's press corps disapproved of having any contact with the

Soviet-sponsored government, but being an outcast makes you free. We had decided to apply for official visas to Kabul.

'War? In Afghanistan?' the attaché was saying, with an oily smile. 'The bandits have been subdued and the entire country is at peace.'

As if in retort, there were two deafening blasts, a fraction of a second apart. The press attaché dived under the sofa with practised speed; he was also the first to regain his composure. 'You see?' he said triumphantly. 'Islamabad is far more dangerous than Kabul.'

The initial blasts were followed by a constant, subdued pounding. We made hurried excuses, and left him to drive towards the sound.

We are heading towards the airport. On the horizon is a column of smoke. It is like nothing I have ever seen before: thick, grey, almost three-dimensional, stretching up vertically into the sky. From closer up, we can see minor explosions, white flashes in the sky, fragments of light dislodging from the central column. A weak roman candle. It sounds like there is an artillery battle going on. It gets louder and then, as we approach, subsides a little. We pass a man running, blindly, his hands over his face. He is covered with blood. Now there are signs of damage: houses with collapsed roofs; an unexploded shell in the road, and then another. It looks like there has been an artillery attack here just seconds ago, and in the streets bodies lie, sliced in bits. The noise from the smoke column is getting louder again – we are still roaring directly towards it.

I say to Beat: 'Do you think it is a good idea to keep on driving towards the explosions?'

The ammunition dump at Ojri military camp was a storage depot for many of the weapons that the USA had given Pakistan to distribute to the Afghan mujahidin.

It never became clear if what had happened there was an accident or sabotage. When it blew up, a US audit was due, and there were rumours that some of the weapons had gone missing. The country's civilian Prime Minister ordered an investigation into possible foul play by Pakistan's Inter-services Intelligence. But the country's military ruler, General Zia ul Haq, sacked the Prime Minister, and the report has never been released.

The official death toll was a hundred. Thousands more were injured. The shells were stored without detonators, so few exploded when they landed. Instead they fell like heavy brass raindrops, and skewered people.

Beat wheels the jeep round and we flee back, driving fast, zigzagging. It is like trying to outrun a tornado: as the funnel of smoke behind us gets higher, the trajectory of the shells it is throwing out is getting wider. Can you make it through a hailstorm without being touched by a single shard of ice?

Then, through the smoke come ghosts. All the streets are full of children. They are very young – some as little as four or five. Too young, many of them, to be afraid. They are dazed. One little boy is crying, the rest just look confused. They are wandering – aimlessly wandering – through the smoke and confusion. Later, I discover that their teachers have panicked and sent them home from school. But just now I can't understand where they all come from. I feel quite clear-headed but I, too, must be in a state of confusion, because I think that perhaps it has been raining children. They are like beings from another planet. It never occurs to me to help them.

A white television van drives up to the hospital. The crew slides open the door, and as they get out they are already filming. They have brought their own material – an injured woman. Galvanized by the presence of the camera, medical staff rush to load her on to a stretcher. The producer gropes beneath his seat, takes out her severed legs, and places them on top of her. Then, camera still rolling, the crew follows her into the hospital.

The power has been cut, the hospital is in darkness – the light of the television camera is our guide. Everyone piles into the operating theatre, but this is too much for me. I turn and flee blindly down another corridor, feel my way through a door, and grope my way to sit down on a bed. In the darkness, I sense that I am in a room with many people. I can smell blood.

Then the dazzling light of the television crew comes on – and reveals that I am sitting in a charnel house. There is gore everywhere – on the floor, on the beds, on the walls. From every bed a face – numb and catatonic with shock – is staring. Some have been

240

bandaged, most have not. I cannot speak or move. I stare at this freak-show of the maimed and bleeding, and their unseeing eyes stare back. The television crew moves from bed to bed, filming.

Outside, a man has been brought to the hospital. Four men are carrying him, each holding an arm or leg. Protruding straight through his stomach is a metre-long shell, about ten centimetres in diameter. It has made a surprisingly clean wound, punching neatly through him like a gigantic drawing-pin.

At the door of the hospital, a white-coated doctor bars the way. This man isn't just a patient, he is wrapped round an unexploded shell. The hospital and its grounds are packed with people, the doctor cannot take the risk of admitting a human bomb.

The bearers argue. They are tired, but they can't find a way to put the man down. Half of the shell is sticking out of his back, the other half out of his front. Everyone is becoming bad-tempered and – now that the possibility of the shell exploding has been raised – a little nervous. It is an impasse.

It is then that I realize the patient is still conscious. He is paralysed, but I can see he is listening to the discussion. His wild black eyes fix themselves upon me. There is no way I can describe the power of another human being concentrating all his force upon you in utter desperation. It feels as though I am looking into my own tormented soul.

My eyes veer away. Behind him is a grass bank. It is full of people, sitting, lying, writhing. Everyone has lost a limb, or is clamping a hand over a bleeding wound. The further I raise my eyes, the further I can see – they stretch beyond the boundaries of this garden, this city, this country, this age. In that instant I understand that normally our senses are scattered, divided. At rare moments we catch a glimpse of what is real; we are the same, we are all connected.

In front of me is a man who is obviously an Afghan mujahid. Blood is streaming down his face from a head wound, but he is sitting upright. Still shaking with the momentousness of my discovery, and the terrible duty it imposes, I lurch up to him, and say in Persian: 'Brother, how are you? Can I help you? What is your name?'

His face contorts with anger. 'You do not know my name – but I know yours. You are Saira Shah, you have written lies about my commander, and if I have an opportunity, I will kill you.'

His wound is pouring blood, he is dazed, he is nearly dead; but his hatred is still alive. The shock of it hits me like a physical blow, and I reel backwards into the masses of the injured and dying.

16

For years after the ammunition dump explosion at Ojri, I would wake up at night, drenched in sweat, shaking from a recurring nightmare: the endless, bloodied people stretching before me in an infinite sea of need, and the clenched, venomous hatred of the single man I had tried to help.

I told myself there was nothing I could do for them. By then I thought I had escaped: I was safely back in Europe. As the West breathed a sigh of relief and decided it could forget about Afghanistan, I married Beat, and went to start a new life in Switzerland. I had found a new identity to hide behind. As a Swiss, I could be neutral. Like the rest of the world, I watched from the sidelines as Afghanistan disintegrated.

Contrary to Western expectations, the Afghan Communist government continued to fight on after the Red Army withdrew. By that time, a whole generation of Afghans had grown up under Soviet occupation – they had had vastly different experiences from the refugees and mujahidin I had encountered. It took years of military and diplomatic offensives to dislodge the Communists.

It wasn't until 1992 that I visited the capital of my father's country for the first time. The television channel I worked for sent me there just after the mujahidin entered Kabul. As I drove into the city, I couldn't help shouting, 'Look! A street sign! A traffic island! And there's even a telegraph pole!' My colleagues must have thought I was insane. In all my years of trekking across mountains and creeping round the outskirts of Afghan towns, I had never seen telegraph poles or traffic islands; I had never properly understood that the mujahidin's Afghanistan was just a fragment of the whole.

All my patriotic sense of Afghan-ness came flooding back. I was soaring – far above the left-over bomb craters our vehicle kept getting stuck in, above retribution and suffering – as far as my imagination could carry me. I would give up my job and come back to my homeland. I would help to rebuild it. We'd have those villas and flowers again that my grandmother Bobo knew. We'd export apricots and *karakul* lambskin instead of war.

After thirteen years of Communist domination, the staff of Kabul's Intercontinental Hotel had evolved into shrivelled, Eastern-bloc Westerners, with dyed moustaches and servile, bell-hop uniforms. Around these vanquished creatures surged people who might have been from another planet. The victorious mujahidin army – bearded, ragged men who smelt of goat – whooped through the corridors, joy-riding up and down in the elevators and forcing the hotel restaurant to give them free *pilau*.

Every gun in the city was firing for joy. The spent bullets tumbled down and bounced off the pavements with little pinging noises. At night, great arcs of red tracer bullets flew above our heads like welding sparks.

If I'd been looking more carefully, I might have seen the friction of worlds colliding. But I thought they were just sparks of happiness, pulsing into the sky.

Almost as soon as the mujahidin took over, the rivalries between the leaders of various factions exploded into civil war. In particular, Gulbuddin Hikmayar and his old enemy Ahmad Shah Massoud began to fight for power. Technically, the two men belonged to the same government: Gulbuddin Hikmatyar was prime minister, and Ahmad Shah Massoud was defence minister. But that didn't stop them.

Gulbuddin Hikmatyar installed himself in the suburbs of Kabul, and tried to take power by shelling the city centre with heavy artillery, tank cannon, mortars and RPGs. In return, defence-ministry planes, trying to dislodge him, blanket-bombed the city's residential suburbs. Neither side made any attempt to avoid hitting civilians. Twenty-five thousand people were killed.

In 1994 Gulbuddin imposed a blockade on Kabul. For eleven months no food or relief goods could get in. People were starving. One woman crept out in a lull in the fighting to scavenge for food. She was caught by a gang of former mujahidin and raped by twenty-two men for three days. Finally she staggered home to discover that her children had died of hypothermia. Her story was featured in an Amnesty International report – but nobody took a blind bit of notice.

It began to matter what ethnic group you were from. Gulbuddin was Pushtun and Massoud was Tajik. So Gulbuddin's men burned down the homes of Tajik civilians; Massoud's allies raped Pushtun women. No one's hands were clean: other ethnic groups, such as Uzbeks, joined in.

Gulbuddin's men arrested two women and showed them a number of containers. The men opened one. Stuck all the way around the insides were gouged-out eyes. The women couldn't tell how many, maybe fifty or sixty. This, said the soldiers, was what happened to those who opposed them.

Bodies and body parts turned up everywhere in Kabul – stuffed down wells, in brick kilns, in abandoned buildings, even in the basement of the Faculty of Medicine, where around twenty corpses were found stacked neatly on the laboratory shelves. At the Institute for Social Sciences, a group of armed men raped and killed sixty women. Nobody ever worked out which militia they were from.

I read about all of this in Amnesty International reports, and on news wires. Even though I covered a great deal of international news, I didn't visit Kabul once during this period. The television programme I worked on was serious and liberal. We prided ourselves on looking at things from every angle. At one of our morning editorial meetings, there was a debate about whether we ought to report the Rwandan genocide. A senior journalist argued that there were few British interests in the country, the killing had nothing to do with our lives, and it was unfair to upset viewers with the sight of suffering that they couldn't do anything to help.

When I proposed that we should cover the civil war in Afghanistan, the honest, good eyes of one of my editors said silently what he put into words a few seconds later: 'Is any of this our fault? Can you convince me that we should care?'

In 1994 an obscure Muslim cleric called Mullah Omar began his political career by saving the lives of two young girls. One of the former mujahidin commanders had kidnapped them, shaved their heads, and taken them to his military base near Kandahar to rape them. While everyone else stood by, too frightened to intervene, the mullah and a group of his religious students stormed the base. They freed the girls, strung the commander from a tank gun, seized his weapons – and the Taliban were born.

Unlike the marauding mujahidin, Mullah Omar and his Islamic army weren't interested in money, property or sex: they wanted to stop the war and set up a just Islamic system. They soon came to the notice of Pakistani intelligence. Pakistan had long wished to install a Pushtun government in Afghanistan and until now it had been supporting Gulbuddin Hikmatyar. But it was finding the war on its doorstep increasingly destabilizing and, in the autumn of 1994, it quietly switched sides and helped the Taliban to take Kandahar.

Before the world had woken up to what was happening, mujahidin commanders in the south were defecting to the Taliban. Eventually even Gulbuddin Hikmatyar's Pushtun forces deserted him, and he was forced into exile. In province after province, the Taliban didn't need to fight the wild Pushtun commanders, they simply absorbed them. Pakistani and Saudi money bought them off.

Warlords from other ethnic groups – like the Tajik

Ahmad Shah Massoud, and the Uzbek General Abdur-rashid Dostum – retreated north. The country was split along ethnic lines, with the Taliban controlling the Pushtun south, and the Northern Alliance, a loose coalition of different ethnic groups, opposing them in the north and parts of the centre.

In 1996, Afghanistan was once more in the news. I returned to cover the Taliban takeover of the capital. This time, Kabul was eerily quiet: I found a moonscape of broken stones, bricks and twisted girders. Once I saw a woman who had survived an acid attack. In profile she was still beautiful, but the flesh on one side of her face had melted, exposing sinews and a ghastly structural mess of tooth and bone. That was what Kabul looked like after four years of rocketing.

There were people in the West who pointed out that while the Taliban had imposed the world's most draconian restrictions on women, while they publicly executed those who transgressed their laws, and privately persecuted religious and ethnic minorities, they had at least succeeded where everybody else had failed. They had stopped the shelling.

Western aid agencies were having to choose whether to withdraw, or to work within the limits imposed by the new regime. I visited an aid worker who had decided to stay. He ran a centre that gave food and a few lessons to Kabul's street children. The civil war had created huge numbers of orphans, who tried to keep alive by begging. But in Kabul hardly anyone had enough to eat, so it was easy for a beggar to starve.

The aid worker told me that the Taliban had given

permission for him to carry on feeding the boys, but they refused point-blank to let him feed the girls. He agonized about his presence in Kabul: up to a third of the city survived on food handouts and there was no doubt that foreign aid was helping to keep the Taliban in power. But if it was withdrawn, people would starve.

When I arrived, the boys were sitting in a circle receiving their meal. The little girls, who used to be fed there too, stood peering through the locked gates and watched them while they ate.

In the evenings, the foreigners gathered in the UN club bar. No one there stayed sober for long. The first to arrive was always a French photographer, rake thin, with the hollow cheeks of a war junkie. He knocked back whisky until curfew. I only heard him speak once.

Two aid workers had begun the perennial argument about whether it was morally right to pull out or necessary to stay. The French photographer lifted his eyes from his glass and said, 'In Sarajevo, I struck up an acquaintance with a sniper. One day he agreed to let me photograph him at work. As we were sitting together on top of a roof, two women passed in the street below. Suddenly he asked, "Which one shall I blow away?" I told him I couldn't do that – I couldn't choose. But he just laughed. "Well, if you don't choose one, I'll shoot both. You can save one. It's up to you."'

The photographer looked around the room with empty eyes; he had stood by and watched so many terrible things that there was nothing left inside him at all.

He shrugged. 'What could I do? There was nothing I could do.'

17

The stands of Kabul's stadium are crammed full, and there are moans of excitement coming from them. This is not the sound of a crowd watching a football match. It is the noise – at once eager and fearful – that a mob makes when it is about to see a person killed.

Even though the video is snowy with repeated copying, it is easy to make out the Datsun pickup doing a triumphant tour around the pitch. Hunched on its open back are figures shrouded in pale blue *burqas*. One of the women is taken down and led across the pitch. A soft gasp, almost a sigh, runs through the crowd.

Encased in her *burqa*, she must be disoriented, unable to see, yet dimly aware that many eyes are watching her. She must be able to hear the crowd, to feel their pulsing excitement, as she is steered on to the penalty line and made to kneel down.

A man walks up to her, casually aiming his Kalashnikov. Perhaps she senses him behind her. She turns, peering through the *burqa*'s grille to catch a glimpse of him. Her posture is one of religious supplication: kneeling, arms outstretched as if in prayer. Then he pulls the trigger and, as the crowd gives a last orgasmic moan, her brains fly splattering on to the pitch.

★

Years ago, the day before I left for Peshawar on my very first trip to Afghanistan, my father summoned me to his study. I felt guilty of betrayal: I was travelling to a forbidden realm, checking up on his dreams. I was secretly terrified, but I was not going to be thwarted – not even by the dreamer himself.

I told him grandly that I was going to find out the truth about Afghanistan. He didn't try to oppose me. Fear was not something one spoke of in my family. He did not admit his, or I mine. He just looked tired and – oddly, for so forceful a personality – resigned. There was something else in his eyes, which I could not decode. Did he know all along that by chasing the dreams, I would banish them? That truth isn't something you can grasp in your fingers, and the closer you get to a myth, the further it retreats?

He waited patiently until I had finished speaking. 'You need to learn how to compromise,' he said. 'Otherwise you'll get yourself killed.'

Since then I had often thought of this interview, but it was too late now to heed his advice. Some experiences change you for ever; some journeys, once started, cannot be stopped.

A sharp-eyed producer at Channel 4 Television in London spotted on the Internet the video of a woman accused of murder being executed in Kabul's football stadium. The channel decided the time was ripe to take a closer look at the Taliban's atrocities.

In February 2001, producer/director Cassian Harrison, cameraman James Miller and I arrived in Nawabad in northern Afghanistan. It was one of the last pockets of the country held by the opposition Northern Alliance. We were filming a documentary for Channel Four called *Beneath the Veil*, and we had come to investigate rumours that the Taliban in this area had massacred people from different ethnic groups.

I was determined that this time I would remain detached, a scrupulous observer. I would conduct my investigation in the Western manner; through a logical examination of the facts. But even as I stepped off the plane I must have known that, however hard I have tried to abandon it, Afghanistan has always found a way of dragging me back.

Thirty thousand people were crammed into this corner of north-eastern Afghanistan, pushed right up against the border with Tajikistan. In aid-workers' jargon, they were Internally Displaced People. In practice, they were people who were unfortunate enough not to be Pushtuns like the Taliban, who were gradually taking over the country. When the religions army encountered other ethnic groups, it burned their homes, killed their menfolk and seized their lands. A massacre here and there – and whole communities fled north. Now this retreating tide of the dispossessed had been pushed right up to Afghanistan's northern border. They were trapped: there was nowhere left to go. This enclave might fall any day; it was only a matter of time. When it did, there would be carnage but the world seemed struck blind and dumb.

This was a holiday, the feast marking the end of Ramadan. Ten families had each cooked a dish. Their elders, grave-faced at the importance of the occasion, left their own celebrations to eat with us. The grass was dotted with tiny flowers. We sat in the graveyard because the refugees could not agree on who would have the honour of receiving us in their tent. Now the elders fretted that we might feel slighted at having been asked to sit outside. 'Isn't this view beautiful?' they said.

White flags marked the graves of those killed in the war. Most of the graves had one. As a reminder that the fighting was getting closer, in the soft grass next to our picnic site there were twenty new mounds of earth: victims of a Taliban shell that had landed in the field behind us just the other day.

The refugees brought a goat for the sacrifice. Its face was washed, its eyes were lined with kohl and salt was placed in its mouth. Prayers were chanted as the elder raised his knife. The blade bit through the hair, deep into the flesh. Rich red blood gushed out, but the old man's aim had faltered. The goat drew long heaving breaths through the spluttering wound. Nobody spoke: we all watched the hole in its neck open and close in a ghastly parody of a red–lipped mouth, gasping for air.

Just before I had come out here, I had watched a video of a woman lifting a knife, and sawing through the throat of a man accused of raping her. The man's blood pumped on to the earth. He had made the same noise: an agonized, bubbling wheezing. Despite their hatred of television, the Taliban allowed his execution to be filmed to show that they would not tolerate crimes against women, that they stood for Islamic justice, and that they were determined to clear up the corruption, the breakdown of law and order, the orgy of abductions, rapes and killings that the mujahidin – those pawns of the West – had unleashed.

'Welcome to Afghanistan,' said our hosts. 'Are you Chinese?'

'Ha ha – the killers wrote their names on the wall . . .' Our interlocutor was a Western aid worker. He had evidence of a massacre in Yaqolang, in central Afghanistan, carried out by the Taliban upon members of the Shi'ite minority. He had been out here too long, seen too much. His brain could no longer process the evidence of his senses. He had come here to do good, but what he had seen had pushed him to the brink. He was trying hard to go native, but he had not yet managed to reach the oblivion of total resignation: he still cared. He laughed a little bit loud and a little bit long at inappropriate points.

'Ha ha – Taliban graffiti. Their own names, geddit? Pretty stupid. War-crimes tribunals and all that . . . Ha ha.'

Both of us knew that there would never be a war-crimes tribunal to bring the killers to justice. The killers knew it too. That was why they had written their names.

Perhaps he was traumatized. Perhaps he had seen things that facts cannot explain. Perhaps he was just tired of trying to understand why. As we spoke, the world was in a flap because the Taliban had decided to blow up Afghanistan's ancient Buddhist statues. He had spent two years failing to get the international community interested in a famine that had cost thousands of Afghan lives. This man, who hated the Taliban to the point of psychosis, found himself asking along with them why the West cared more about statues than about human life. We had reached the point where logic fails.

'Ha ha – the Taliban: tough on statues, tough on the cause of statues. I've got a good one. Why don't we package the dust from the Buddhas, sell it to the Japanese and buy food aid?

'Ha ha. They tied my assistant to my office chair, shot him in the kidney and left him to die! Ha ha! They skinned a boy alive. They used bayonets.'

His smile no longer denoted amusement, cynicism or humour. It was a rictus. It was the way he coped. Of course I knew this. I knew his jokes were not tasteless: they helped him to keep paddling desperately in a whirlpool that threatened to suck him under. But I could not laugh along. My horror showed. He stopped laughing and, for a moment, I saw panic in his face. 'Ha ha,' he said. 'Ha ha.'

Like him, I was at a loss to understand. My knowledge of Afghanistan was too fragmentary. I should have listened harder when my father buried snippets of information and Persian vocabulary in his tales. 'Once upon a time,' he would say, 'when flies flew backwards, and the sun was cool, there was a land called Hich-hich, which means "nothing at all".

'The Queen of this country wanted to have a little boy. So Arif, the wise man, gave her a magical apple, called *seb*. But because the Queen was absentminded, she dropped it half-eaten.

'Nine months later,' said my father, 'she gave birth to a boy. He had only one eye, one ear, one arm and one leg, and he hopped wherever he went. So they called him Nim, which in Persian means half.

'When he grew up, Nim longed for just one thing: to be whole. Arif, the wise man, said that he must go and find Tanin, the terrible dragon. If he drank the *dawa*, the special medicine, in the back of its cave, he would grow another arm, another leg, another ear and another eye. And from that day on, he would be *kull*, which means whole . . .'

As a child, I had always assumed that, like Nim, one day I would set off on a journey of my own. When I reached the real Afghanistan, fact and myth would slide together like a jigsaw, my two warring selves would make peace – and I, too, would become whole.

From the Northern Alliance post at Ai Khanom, close to the Tajik border, you could look down past a wide, lazy river into a valley where, six weeks ago, it was rumoured, a massacre had taken place.

The river was called the Koksha. Down on its banks was a cluster of four villages, caught between the Taliban and Northern Alliance lines. The valley was bursting with almond blossoms, and with blossoms of artillery smoke, too. From this distance, you could not tell them apart. In January, the Taliban had pushed forward briefly and had taken the villages. As they withdrew – almost as an afterthought, the locals claimed – they had shot a dozen or so civilians in each.

A young Northern Alliance fighter called Usman

agreed to take us down to one of the four villages, a place called Mawmaii. He was young, good-looking and – as far as was humanly possibly for an opposition soldier trapped on the front line – he was cooler than cool. When we met him, he was trying to shoot down Taliban jets with a Russian sniper rifle. This seemed physically impossible, but it looked good and he knew it.

He begged us for Madonna tapes and bottles of whisky. In another universe, he would have been a spoilt rich kid – mobile phone, fast car, lots of girls. He seemed to realize, through some holistic intuition, that he had been robbed.

The closest he had ever come to the debauchery he craved was at medical school in the Tajik capital, Dushanbe, a haven of Western sophistication. 'There were girls in my class,' he said. 'I used to talk to them.' Once, he even went to a disco. He had to drop out after just one year: he was needed at the front.

One evening, Usman posed strategically on top of a tank, and sang a soulful, catchy song about the bitterness of war. The setting sun highlighted his chiselled Uzbek cheekbones and his dark, almond eyes. When I complimented his voice and his leading-man good looks, he said: 'Yes. If it was not for the war, I would have been a great star.'

The road to Mawmaii lay across an implausibly green plain, ringed with white-wisped mountains and dotted with sheep. I stood in the open back of the truck and inhaled its loveliness.

There was a swooping, singing beauty about this

place. The light had a marvellous golden translucency I have only ever come across in Afghanistan. Shepherd girls waved from the side of the road. Their dresses were emerald, ruby, turquoise, amethyst – living, sparkling jewels. Every tree was bursting with blossom. A grey-bearded mullah with a white turban trotted past us on his donkey; his disciple walked respectfully behind.

How can I explain the beauty of this place? It was beautiful, like a song that makes you want to weep. There was magic in the fields and the mountains and the people and the trees.

Once, when we were flying over Córdoba, a Spanish friend of mine said: 'Welcome to my beautiful country.' I felt a pang of anguish, because I had no country to be proud of. Now I felt a surge of joy. I hugged myself and whispered: 'Welcome to my beautiful country.' The words were like a caress on my tongue.

Usman was pretending that Afghanistan was at peace and we were on a pleasure tour. When he had shown us where to cross the Koksha, out of sight of the Taliban guns, and had warned us about the landmines on the bank, he said: 'Isn't it lovely?' And it was. The Koksha sparkled with spring sunlight, and was as clear as melted snow.

'This river is famous for its delicious fish,' said Usman, like a proper tour guide.

'Let's have some for lunch.'

'All right,' he agreed. 'If we have time, we'll go and pick up some grenades and throw them in to catch them.'

It was not just my knowledge that was fragmentary,

I thought. Despite its physical beauty, the structure of Afghanistan was crumbling under my feet.

We crossed the Koksha river on a raft of goatskins. On the far bank, the elders of Mawmaii were clustered, waiting for us. They were waving pieces of paper. In the painstaking handwriting of the barely literate, they had compiled lists of those who had died, and those who had disappeared. 'United Nations!' they cried, as we landed. 'At last you have come!'

We walked in a solemn procession up to the hill where their sons and fathers had lain, dotted like sheep on the soft grass. When they left Mawmaii, the Taliban had taken fifty-one men away in trucks as hostages. There was no space for the last seven, so they had shot them.

It was clear that when the villagers looked at the hill, they still saw the bodies lying there. A man with expressive eyes took off his turban to show us how they had found them. His friend, an ugly man with a pockmarked face, used it to tie his hands behind his back. Standing, bound and weeping, in the field, he said: 'And I said "Spare me – for I have not yet lived my life." But the Taliban commander said: "No. I do not understand your language." Then he shot me.' He rolled over on to his side, into the exact place where his brother's body had lain. The other men gathered him in a *puttu* and began to carry him away. 'You can still see the blood,' they said.

Of course, I thought, the blood had been washed away: it belonged to the dead past, the past in which they were living. But as they told me their tale, I imagined that I, too, could see the places where the bodies had lain, curled up foetally upon the slope. And when I looked closely, sure enough, there were little mirrors and cigarette packets, fallen from pockets, and here a spent Kalashnikov round.

Then I discerned what they were trying to show me. In every depression there was an outline of darker, harder earth and greener grass, where blood had nourished the soil.

'It has snowed several times since then,' they said, 'but the blood has left a mark. Blood is very strong.'

As they escorted us down the hill, one of the men turned to me. 'The Taliban who did this cannot have been Afghans,' he said. 'They must have been Pakistanis.'

The elders led us to a house in the village. As we stepped into the courtyard, we knew that something bad had happened there. We all felt it. It had left a residue, as tangible as a smell that you can't get rid of – a kick of ammonia. It sent us reeling.

In the courtyard there was a girl. Her face was turned to the wall. She was rocking on her haunches, hunched and silent. In another spot, a second girl was frozen in the same posture of grief. They did not try to comfort each other. An old man was staring into space. His faded blue eyes gazed at some other world, as if the things he saw consumed him, sapping his dignity, his self-respect, his desire to live.

The old man said his daughters had been like this for weeks – ever since the Taliban had come to their home. 'I was not here when the men came,' he said, as if this was an explanation. 'They had taken me prisoner.'

A third girl, in a blue veil, came out of the house. She began to speak in Uzbek, a language I could not understand. Her voice was clear and full of cadences, like a flute. There was something indescribably pure about it.

Usman translated what she said: 'The Taliban came to our house, and said: "We are going to make this place our headquarters." They told my mother and us children to leave. It was snowing, and my mother said: "Where will I go in the snow with my children?" Without hesitating even for a moment, a Talib lifted his Kalashnikov and shot her, just there, in the courtyard.'

I was sure that something had happened to them after their mother was killed, but I couldn't bring myself to broach the subject. I asked the girl who had spoken for her name. It was Fairuza, which means turquoise, the colour of her veil. How old was she? She was twelve. Her elder sister, Amina, was fifteen and her younger sister, Fawzia, was nine.

Sitting in a row, hunched in their veils – pink, yellow and blue – the girls looked like broken birds. All I could see of them was their huge dark eyes. Slowly, from the corner of one eye a tear appeared and quivered for a moment before it burst and flowed. I could not even imagine from what deep well of suffering this single drop had escaped.

How long did the men stay in the house with them, while their mother's body lay in the yard? The old man turned away. No other Afghan father would have allowed me to ask such a question. But he was impotent: he had not been there when the soldiers came.

The men had stayed alone with the girls for two days.

What did the soldiers do to them during that time? At this point, the eldest girl, Amina, covered her face and began to weep.

Fairuza had an unquenchable spirit. She looked at her sister, then tilted her chin at me and said, in that clear voice: 'They asked for food and water. What could we do? Our mother was dead. We had to do whatever they told us.'

18

People have written to me from across the US. Heartbreaking letters. I have come to dread them. 'I want to adopt the three little girls in your film,' says one. 'Don't let it bother you that I live in a trailer. I know I can love them. Surely that's what counts.'

Who am I to mock such misguided philanthropy? I ought to have learned by now that the sea of human suffering is infinite. Yet here I am, still trying to save the people I saw waving from the window.

After 11 September, *Beneath the Veil* was shown again and again on CNN. Although we had made the film before the attack on the World Trade Center, Western politicians on all sides had used the faces of the three girls in Mawmaii to further their own ends. The girls' suffering was used both as an argument for bombing Afghanistan and for delivering aid to it. They, of course, were unaware that they had become icons. As far as we knew, they were still living on the front line.

James Miller and I arrived back in Islamabad a week before the US air strikes began. James was directing, and I was reporting a follow-up to *Beneath the Veil* called *Unholy War*.

We had decided to try to return to Mawmaii and find the three girls. I had convinced my editors that the fate of Amina, Fairuza and Fawzia was the perfect metaphor for the plight of Afghanistan. As usual, however, I had an agenda of my own. I had abandoned Eastern daydreams for Western practicality. I was determined to use the documentary as an instrument to rescue those three girls.

You could no longer accuse the world of not paying attention to Afghanistan. There were so many journalists in Islamabad that the Marriott Hotel had installed sleeping cubicles in the gym. Battle lines were being drawn up between East and West. Yet I couldn't rid myself of the feeling that, although nominally opposed, both sides were colluding in some gigantic game.

Islamabad's graceful avenues and wide boulevards were barricaded with burning tyres. Tear gas hung in the air. The crowd was chanting: 'Death to America! Long live the Taliban!' The countdown to US air strikes had begun.

A man was touting T-shirts with the slogan: 'Osama Bin Laden, World Hero'. They were too expensive for locals: they were for the press. The demonstrators were lined up on one side of the street, the media on the other. As the protestors surged forward, the press edged back. They didn't look like two conflicting sides; they looked like dancers, keeping step.

A burning crate flew through the air, missing us by an inch. The crowd charged, and suddenly we were running for our lives. They were throwing bricks at us, and these were real enough – smashing into the pavement behind me. In the midst of my flight, my handbag burst open: my passport, my money, everything scattered on to the dust behind me. I glanced back at my pursuers: they were about fifty metres away and getting closer. It was like one of those panicky dreams in which you are fleeing from some foe, yet a part of you knows that it is not real. I dived for my valuables. The men stopped throwing rocks, and helped me. When everything – even my broken comb – had been collected and handed back, someone gave me a shove. My helpers waited for me to get ahead, then started throwing bricks at me again.

One of the protestors was yelling anti-American slogans. He thrust his face into the camera and a long, pent-up, wounded-animal howl came out. It contorted his entire face and sent his fist driving through the air. Droplets of spittle flew from his mouth and landed on the lens. He was saying terrible things: 'We will slaughter our children in defence of Islam! We will attack America and the whole world!' The force of his hatred was mesmerizing; he was utterly consumed by it. But then he turned it off like a tap, and asked the camera: 'Was that enough?'

The border was sealed, but a few refugees had straggled into Peshawar. Their faces had the numb expressions of people who had lost everything. For some this was the fourth time. They had fled Soviet invasion, mujahidin rockets, Taliban atrocities, and now American bombs.

A family of five – father, mother and three children – was occupying a square of baked earth outside the house of some distant relatives. They had walked all the way from Kabul. It had taken them three days to cross the mountains. In exchange for sleeping on this patch of earth, the children had to work. Our conversation was punctuated by the insistent clacking of a carpet loom. The youngest child, a girl of six or seven, didn't yet have the calluses needed for this job: her cuticles were bleeding. She was very pretty, but now her rosebud mouth was pouting in concentration, her grey eyes were set in a frown, and her thick fair hair was tangled down her back. As I watched, a woman came out of the house and scolded her. Perhaps, at home, the girl was rather spoilt because she opened her mouth as if to answer back. Then she changed her mind and turned to her father. He looked away.

The girl's mother bustled around, apologizing. If we had only come to visit them in Kabul, they would have received us properly. They had furniture, and a proper house with pictures on the walls. They had carpets and crockery, everything. In Kabul, we would have been welcome – they would have made us dinner, and invited us to stay with them – but here there was nowhere to sit, except on the bare earth.

The woman reminded me of Halima, with whom I had stayed in Kabul six months ago, and whom I had been trying to put out of my mind for weeks: Halima and her family working at their sewing-machines in the middle of the night; sitting in the dark with me, pretending to eat; Halima's daughter, left deaf and dumb by the trauma of rocket attacks. When the air strikes began again, she would be so frightened. How would anyone be able to explain to her that these were the bombs of friends?

An expectant silence had fallen. The interview had begun and they were waiting for me to ask something. I blurted out the first thing that came into my head: Why had they come here? Why had they risked so much, and left their homes behind?

In the slow, clear voice reserved for the simple-minded, the father said: 'The Taliban are living among the civilians. We are afraid that, if the Americans drop bombs on the Taliban, it is we civilians who will be killed.'

His wife added: 'You see, we know what it is to be bombed.'

That night President Bush appeared on television and said there had been surgical strikes on Kabul, Kandahar, Mazar i Sharif and Jalalabad. He promised a 'sustained' campaign. I was filled with contradictory feelings. This would mean the end of the Taliban but – somewhere far from the eyes of the world – Halima and her family were being bombed.

The Crusades brought eight hundred years of conflict between East and West. This felt like more than just a few bombing raids against the Taliban: it felt like we were heading into something momentous. In Pakistan's tribal area an Afridi weapons dealer told us the market in Stingers had shot through the roof. He had bought his stock from the mujahidin after the Soviets withdrew; the CIA had tried to get them back, but the Afridis had been in the business for long enough to understand Afghanistan's cycle of war and market forces. Now he had sold them to the Taliban's allies. Next month he would send his son to private school in America with the profits.

Abdul Haq, the former mujahidin commander, who had mediated many years ago with the mujahid who wanted to kill me, was trying to convince the USA that the Taliban could be overthrown in the ancient Afghan manner – by horse-trade and negotiation. His garden in Peshawar was dotted with grave-faced Pushtuns, the former mujahidin commanders who were now the rank and file of the Taliban. There was a gentle murmur of conversation in the garden, like the drowsy humming of bees. Buying them all off would probably cost less than the price of one smart bomb. But Abdul Haq, the peacemaker, was swimming against the tide. America was prepared to be beneficent to the Afghan people only after blood had been let.

Over the years, Abdul Haq had paid dearly for his friendship with the USA. The Taliban leadership were trying to kill him. They had even sent assassins to his home in Peshawar. He was out, so they shot his wife and child.

He and I used to be nearly the same age. Now he had grown old. He had seen too many people die, it had made him tired. He said: 'Why can't America understand? Bombing will just drive al-Qaida underground. I could deliver al-Qaida to them intact, without a shot being fired.'

Our meeting was brief: he was vainly trying to stop an all-out war, and I was in a hurry to begin our journey across the border into Afghanistan's Kunar province, in opposition-held northern Afghanistan.

Pakistan's frontier region was closed to foreigners, but James and I paid locals to smuggle us in. Anti-

Western feeling was running high. Our guides made a rapid assessment: James would have to hide under the *burqa* for fear of being lynched, I was considered Eastern enough to get through with a simple head covering.

Despite myself, I felt a glow of pleasure that I had fallen on the Eastern side. I wondered why being an Afghan was still so important to me. To this day, I dreaded the question, 'Where are you from?' Why did it matter to me that I could never answer in just one word? I had always longed to belong to a single place: why couldn't that place be the West?

Now I made a pact with fate. If I could save those girls, it would redeem the loss of my mythical Afghanistan. I would have done my bit to impose order upon this chaos, and maybe – just maybe – it would be all right to become a Westerner after all.

On the road to Chitral, the locals had posted up a warning to America: 'We yearn for death more than you yearn for life,' it said.

It would have been far safer to fly to Tajikistan and enter Afghanistan from there. But there were no flights for days and I was impatient. A ground offensive might have started at any time and once it did, Mawmaii, the girls' village, would be overrun by troops. It would be impossible to get there.

These were the mountains I had crossed on my first trip to Afghanistan, with Zahir Shah. These days, there were no more mujahidin, only mercenaries. We had found a group of men who had agreed to take us along the smugglers' route, north of the Durra Pass. The journey was dangerous – we would be travelling at about seventeen thousand feet, the height of Everest base camp – and for this privilege, the smugglers demanded a huge fee. It seemed appropriate: I was tired of talk of nobility and honour. I was happy to do things the Western way, with hard cash.

It began well. We drove for about an hour. Then we walked round a Pakistani check post: picking our way through people's back gardens; disturbing sleepy chickens and goats; hushing each other because the post was near. We did not dare to turn on our torches, and we could not see the way. We rejoined the vehicle, and drove a little further. When we reached the next post, we climbed a hill. 'Hurry, hurry,' said Khalil, the smugglers' leader, who was acting as our guide. Dogs barked. 'That is the post.' I was boiling hot. My feet plunged into an icy stream, and I relished the cool water. At the top of the hill, we sat on a rock. There was not yet a moon, but the stars had come out. The whole of the Milky Way stretched above us, powdered sugar spilled in the sky. Headlights passed below. We crouched down and made a break for the road. It was like a Hollywood movie.

Back in the vehicle, James and I giggled, and said that this was the best job in the world. With my self-imposed mission to rescue the three girls to sustain me, my feeling of hopelessness faded away.

A few weeks later, Abdul Haq slipped quietly into Afghanistan, and walked straight into a Taliban trap. He was executed. He, too, must have been on a mission, but no one could tell whom he was trying to save.

12 October 2001
11 p.m.

A wall of water is coming up to meet me. Slowly, I understand that we are falling. Time slows down. For an age, we teeter. Water becomes my whole world. Somehow I make it ashore. Close to the bank, the surface of the river is frozen and underneath is jelly-ice.

On our journey across the mountains, things have begun to go seriously wrong. Our guides have lost their way, and we have been forced to ford a frozen river. Khalil was carrying me across when we fell in. Now James has taken off his boots, and is wading with the camera. He, too, loses his balance. In all our travels, I have never heard him express fear, but now he shouts: 'Someone help me!' There is desperation in his voice. We grab the camera and pull him to shore.

We are drenched to the skin. The chill wind bites through me – my down jacket is soaked and has lost its warmth. Neither of us has a change of clothes. I take off my boots and turn them upside down. Iced river water gushes out. James opens his camera bag and gives me his only spare pair of dry socks. The gesture is immensely touching. It makes me want to burst into tears.

We crawl up a steep bank of rock, with nothing to hold on to but thorns, which lacerate our gloveless hands. We arranged for horses to meet us there, loaded with our baggage, including our cold-weather gear. They never come. Our wet clothes freeze to our bodies like boards. I have stopped shivering.

1 a.m.

We meet up with another group of smugglers. For a fee, they allow us to ride. We are like asylum-seekers, fallen into the hands of an extortionate mafia.

My guide leads me rapidly. Perhaps he is abducting me.

'Let me stop for a minute.'

'There are too many border guards.'

'Where are the others?'

'They are close.'

'How far is it to the border?'

'Not far – about seven hours.'

Sitting motionless on the pack-horse, my body is losing warmth. The cold begins in my feet and creeps up through my calves to my knees. It winds its way sensuously through my body, and joins the cold in my hands. It is a serpent of cold, erasing me. As I drove towards the gardens at Paghman, I was suddenly gripped by fear: if the gardens were a lie, a part of me would not exist either. That's what this feels like now: I am being extinguished.

3 a.m.

I can still feel the pain, but it has moved outside me. I feel it in the mountains, and the moon, and the clear air. Gradually even this vanishes. I am giving in. I have begun to hallucinate: I wonder if there will be a roaring fire at the border, and of course there is. Then I snap to, with the wind searing through me and the cold moon mocking me, and my cotton *shilwar* stiff with ice and think: Seven hours, seven hours of this.

'There are too many Islamic extremists about,' says Professor Majrooh. 'I am having to put rum in my Coca-Cola and it is giving me a stomach ache.' The miniatures on the walls are moving: the huntsmen and *houris* are made of countless animals, leaping and biting each other's tails.

'I am going to find out the truth about Afghanistan,' I tell him.

The Professor waves his stick. 'What makes you think you will recognize truth?' he says. 'Don't you know yet it has a thousand shapes and forms?'

4.30 a.m.

I am going to fight back. If I don't get off this horse, I will lose a foot from frostbite. My guide refuses to stop, but I jump down anyway. My legs collapse beneath me. I cannot walk. The man puts his arm round me and half carries me as I hobble along. So strange to walk on numb feet. I stumble on rocks I cannot feel. I want to sit down, cuddle up to them and fall asleep. A phrase from Sa'adi's *Gulistan* rings in my head: 'The sanctuary is before you, the thief is behind. If you go you win, if you sleep you die.' My world is as basic as this. I must keep putting one numb foot in front of the other.

There is an endless and exhausting climb. The altitude is very high: it makes you sob to catch your breath. At these heights, temperatures plunge. Fast-moving streams are frozen solid, and there is an icy wind.

Fool of me to forget the treachery of these mountains. Strange how your body remembers what your mind does not. How every movement tires you. How

273

you keep yourself going by taking three paces, then stopping for two beats. How even a moment's rest is a cure, but the second you move, the dizziness, nausea and thirst begin again.

Nowadays I know more about the risks of walking at this altitude without acclimatization. Cerebral oedema – swelling of the brain – can kill you in no time. But my theoretical knowledge has been of no use to me: I have ignored it.

The Afghan ruler Ibrahim ben Adhem gave up the throne of Balkh to search for knowledge. One day he saw a stone on the ground. It had written on it, 'Turn me over and read,' so he picked it up. On the other side it said: 'Why do you seek more knowledge when you pay no heed to what you know already?'

I have torn up my map of tales and – as if I have upset some delicate inner organ – my sense of balance is teetering: I can no longer tell dreams from reality.

At this altitude, we are close to the stars. I bow my head, for fear of grazing them.

19

When dawn broke, we stopped to rest on a rock. Like shipwreck survivors unexpectedly washed to shore, we took stock. Talking was difficult; our cheeks and lips had frozen. James had freeze burns on his fingers – last night, when he tried to film, the camera metal stuck to them. I had frostbite in my right foot. Two of my toes were immovable and dead, the nails grey. I wondered if they would fall off. In my dazed state, it didn't seem important.

We were both as weak as invalids. I limped ten metres, and this pathetic exertion gave me an immense sense of achievement.

During the night we had bribed another group of smugglers to let us use their horses. Now the horses that had been supposed to meet us at the beginning of our journey suddenly appeared with our baggage and warm clothing. We had waited for them in the wrong place. The horsemen demanded thousands of rupees, saying with great charm: 'You people are foreigners. We are poor Afghans – we must take all the money from you we can.'

I paid them without a fight. I thought they were probably right on both counts: they were poor, and I was a foreigner.

Now that it was no longer possible to die of cold, it

was pleasant to ride through the mountains. Our horses' hoofs slipped on the ice, but they never lost their footing. When we arrived at a vast deserted lake, of startling cobalt blue, I knew we must be inside Afghanistan. Nowhere else could a lake be so uncompromising.

We passed an outpost of the opposition Northern Alliance. Last time we were here, it had seemed only a matter of time before their forces were wiped out. Now the US was supporting their battle against the Taliban. The commander at the post sent his men to fetch a vehicle for us. He offered us refreshments and I realized that we hadn't drunk anything for more than eighteen hours.

We gulped green tea, our mouths crammed with boiled sweets. The sun was shining quite warmly, yet both James and I had pulled our woollen *puttus* tightly round us like blankets. Now that we had learned what it means to be really cold, neither of us could bear the lightest breeze. We had become fragile, as if our night in the hills had stuck to us, freeze-burning our insides.

I didn't feel like talking. I just sat, staring past the inevitable heavy machine-gun post, across the intense blueness of the lake to the dried-out slope of a hill beyond. I was thinking of another river, and another hillside, in the girls' village, Mawmaii.

Our driver, Noor, was indescribably filthy – his *shilwar kamis*, turban and waistcoat had all merged into a single shade of greasy brown. You could barely see his eyebrows against his grimy skin. Only his eyes were bright with alertness, like some creature of the forest that had learned how to fend for itself.

As we approached Faizabad, the capital of Badakhshan province, the mountains became less ferociously ugly and more majestic. A man on a chestnut horse galloped out of a field in front of us, and James and I said simultaneously: 'I've remembered why I like this country.'

From Faizabad, we set off for Khwaja Bahauddin, in the far north-east, down the dustiest road I have ever travelled. There must have been three or four inches lying like fine white snow on the surface. Dust spewed like smoke through the Datsun's ventilation ducts and in through the seams of the doors. For some reason, Noor seemed to prefer driving off-road, where it was even dustier.

After we had travelled for five hours or so, we were stopped at a Northern Alliance checkpoint. I asked the soldiers whether this was the right road.

'No, you'll have to go all the way back to Faizabad – Khwaja Bahauddin is in the other direction.'

When I enquired of Noor why he had brought us the wrong way, he said seamlessly: 'Because the road to Khwaja Bahauddin is very dusty.'

All of this dust was the country's precious topsoil blowing away. There was drought in Afghanistan. The Taliban leadership had insisted it was a punishment from God. Whatever the cause, it had not rained properly for three whole years, and now it was too late for a single good rainfall to put things right. A deluge would be too much for the eroded soil to bear.

On the road into town we passed a long convoy of journalists – all the people whose equipment had broken because of the dust – trying to leave the country. A container-truck full of water had heeled over, turning the dust into mud, and they were all stuck in a cloying bog.

Last time we were here, Khwaja Bahauddin was an abandoned backwater. Now it was over-saturated with world attention, as if the West, like Mother Nature, couldn't manage a gentle, sustaining rain: it had to bring either drought or deluge.

Journalists had settled in drifts on every aid worker's house, every government office, every nook and cranny. They lay in sleeping-bags on the floor of a local commander's guesthouse. Flurries of them swirled around the streets in four-wheel-drive vehicles. One American network had even settled in the villa where the key Northern Alliance figure, Ahmad Shah Massoud, had been assassinated by Osama bin Laden's men just before 11 September. Its ceilings were still blackened and cracked from the blast.

Khwaja Bahauddin was just behind the Northern Alliance lines, and the press pack was abuzz with rumours: 'Did you hear the B-52s passing overhead last night? There'll be a ground offensive any day now. They're about to push across the front line.'

In their impatience for a ground war, a few of the pack had resorted to fakery: crouching in the trenches, wearing flak jackets and pretending they were under fire. One European television team told us they had been to the front to expose this shameless practice but while they were there a real artillery battle had broken out. 'It was crazy,' said the reporter. 'The Northern

Alliance started firing their rockets, and the Taliban fired back. The shells landed close by. I was scared.' She looked at me in puzzled indignation. 'Why did they do it? I hadn't even asked them to shoot at me.'

There were thriving urban legends about exactly what was in the yellow humanitarian aid packages that the US was airdropping as part of its hastily orchestrated relief effort. The journalists maintained that some contained peanut butter and Pop-tarts. The local people were said to be puzzled by this strange fare, but at least the press pack claimed to be eating well.

We decided to head straight for Nawabad, which was only half an hour away from the girls' village, Mawmaii. Last time we were there, we had met an aid worker called John Weaver, who would let us stay with him. John was from North Carolina, but you wouldn't guess it to look at him. His staff said that, in the eight months he had been here, he had become an Afghan. There was something indefinably local about the dirty rag draped around his neck, the slope of his shoulders, the way he wore his *pukkal* tilted down over his gold-blond hair. He had acquired the easy stride of a man who had spent his life marching across the mountains and, somehow, along with all this other cultural baggage, he had picked up Persian. He was young – probably in his late twenties – his eyes were very blue and often crinkled with laughter.

John's guestroom was empty, except for a small tin trunk containing his possessions – a laptop computer, a change of clothes, a toothbrush and a couple of Dari textbooks. When James asked jokingly if these were all the belongings he had in the world, he looked embarrassed, as though we had caught him out in some profligacy. 'Oh, no – I have a fine collection of base-ball cards back home in America, but I don't really need it.'

John's apparent lack of needs made me slightly uncomfortable. When pressed, he admitted to being a devout Christian, but he didn't usually speak of it. A couple of his staff told us they knew that, in his heart, John was really a Muslim.

In the camps at Nawabad, the greens of spring had been replaced by the browns of autumn, the spongy mountain grass had long since frazzled away and the threat of winter hung in the air. There was a new energy, a nervous excitement among the refugees. There was talk of strange happenings: packages of American aid had been dropping down from the sky. Last night, the refugees had rushed to the site of an airdrop, but when they got there, Northern Alliance soldiers had already arrived. A fight broke out, the soldiers fired on them and now, they said, the rations were on sale in the bazaar.

A few families were digging trenches before the ground became too hard – last winter they had had no proper shelter and many children froze – but most people were saying, 'Why bother to make such prep-arations?' The Americans were coming to save them. In a week or two they would all be going home. It didn't matter that the Taliban had burned their houses: the Americans would build new ones; and roads and schools and clinics.

In one of the rag tents, a little girl was squatting on the ground, vomiting. A thin stream of yellow bile trickled out of her mouth. Her mother sat holding her head. All of the children were sick. They had not had enough to eat for over a year and the refugees knew that, as the weather got colder, they would begin to die.

Only a miracle could save them. It was not surprising that the people here wanted to believe a miracle was on its way.

Since we had seen him last, Usman had become a man. In April, he had taken part in his first battle. Before he took us back to Mawmaii, he insisted on showing us the scene of his heroic exploits. 'It is only five hundred metres from a Taliban post,' he wheedled. 'There is much rocketing. No journalists dare to go there.'

A few enterprising locals had set up war tours for journalists. For twenty dollars a horse and a guide would take you to the front line. Usman hired a couple of nags for James and me, and a gorgeously turned-out stallion for himself. Its coat was the colour of honey; its mane and tail flowed like milk. While our horses had pieces of string for reins, its saddle and bridle were of the finest workmanship. 'This is a *buzkashi* horse,' said Usman proudly. The pair pranced about, showing off.

We rode through parched, dusty villages and fields of drought-stunted crops. Rose-cheeked Uzbek children in tattered silk *chapans* and wellington boots stared at us, open-mouthed. Usman took the lead. He galloped along in a tornado of dust, with all the local dogs snarling at his heels. In one village he fired his sniper rifle into the writhing pack of them. He missed.

As we entered a wide, flat plain, the noise of artillery got louder. Then there was the unmistakable whoosh of shells. My eyes were automatically checking for cover. James said, 'I hate that noise.' It took a couple of goes before we realized that we were walking between the lines and that these were Northern Alliance shells, passing over our heads.

'That is the *jawab i hukmat* – the Alliance answer,' said Usman.

I asked: 'What was the question?' but he didn't get it.

Then the Taliban returned fire. There was a seemingly endless whine of shells through the air as their rockets passed parallel to us, slightly to our right. It was an extraordinary angle from which to be hearing them: for almost their whole trajectory there came the distinctive whistling rush that usually you hear very briefly, and only if they are going to land close by. About forty seconds later, they crashed with a dull explosion into the Northern Alliance post at Ai Khanom, about five kilometres behind us.

I couldn't work out where I had heard this strange combination before – the long whine without a proper detonation. Then it struck me: this was the sound I had heard when the ammunition dump exploded in Islamabad all those years ago.

We reached a wide river, waist deep and fast-moving. Undaunted, our horses marched straight ahead into the water. At once the choking dust was replaced with a cool breeze, the light was full of watery reflections and the roaring current blotted out the sounds of the shore. We passed a man driving a donkey, and a group of fishermen laughing as they cast their nets – a secret world of its own right there in the river.

When I looked down, I saw that the water flowing past had formed a dizzying *trompe l'oeil*. It seemed that my horse was walking on the spot, that the current was rushing past twice as fast and that instead of ever arriving upon the shore we would be borne downstream for ever in this fast-moving world.

As we began to climb up the mountainside, two fat flowers of artillery smoke appeared next to a group of Alliance soldiers down on the road we had just left. The men danced and cheered. 'They are showing that they are not afraid to die,' said Usman.

A middle-aged man climbed down the hill to meet us. Usman introduced us: 'This is my commander. Commander, take these people's bags and carry them up the hill. How is the battle?'

'Things are quiet,' said the commander. 'The Taliban are firing at us and we are firing back.'

We walked along the front-line trenches. 'If you put your head up here, they snipe at you,' said Usman, but none of the men ducked.

The post that Usman wanted to show us was just a few hundred metres away, across the valley. Four or five stick people – Taliban – stared back at us. I thought that the men on these two enemy positions must lead similar lives: hunkered down in their trenches, firing and being fired upon. In Usman's first battle last April, the Northern Alliance had taken the post opposite, killing (said Usman) a hundred and fifty Taliban and capturing a good deal of weaponry. It cost the lives of many of their own men. Unfortunately, a few days later, the Taliban counter-attacked, and now the front line was back to where it started. When I asked what the point of all this was, the soldiers looked at me as if I was mad. They said: 'It is war. This is Afghanistan.'

The youngest soldier to take part in the battle didn't look older than twelve, but he had already learned to be macho: 'I've seen tanks firing, shells landing, people being killed, people without hands, without eyes, without heads – so what?' he said.

I asked what he would do when the war ended and he said, in the singsong voice of a child reciting a lesson, that when peace came each person would go back to *kar i khud* – his own work. What was his work? He didn't know. Had he been to school? No. Could he read? No. Did he remember how to farm? No, and his family's farm was destroyed anyway.

Usman led us out of his commander's earshot and said: 'This country is full of men who know nothing except how to fight. They have no other way to earn a living. They have plenty of weapons and they will try to keep on fighting in any way they can.'

When we returned, the men were all clustered round their two-way radio, listening intently, with entranced expressions on their faces. A Talib on the post opposite was singing for them – a beautiful song from the next mountain. James tried to film this peaceful scene, but as soon as they saw the camera, the men threw down the radio and scurried through the trenches. They peered theatrically from side to side, and ferociously aimed their weapons at the enemy to whose songs they had been listening just moments ago.

20

The next day, Usman took us back to Mawmaii to look for the girls. This time, no one was waiting to meet us on the banks of the Koksha. Mawmaii's streets were empty, and shrouded in dust, like a book that has not been opened for a long time. It was oppressively silent; we could hear the dull thud of our feet as we walked along. The mud houses had been looted – their walls had crumbled, their roofs had fallen, even their wooden doors had been taken away. Had we come too late? None of us voiced our fears, but we dragged our feet more and more slowly through the soft dust, towards the girls' house.

I found myself thinking of the leafy lanes of the village in Kent where I grew up. When I was the age that these girls were now, I too had known no other world than my own small village. I wondered if, like me, they had ever dreamed of finding a way to escape.

Trudging towards us came a group of men with donkeys, heavily laden. The heads of both animals and men were bowed with weariness. We stopped, as travellers in Afghanistan do, to exchange greetings and news of the war. One was the man who had stood on the hill, bound with his own turban, explaining how he had found the body of his brother.

People were leaving Mawmaii, he said. It wasn't

286

because of the war, or even the massacre by the Taliban. It was because, once again this year, their crops had failed. There was no hope left in the village. Just the other day, a man had drowned himself in the Koksha, because he couldn't bear to see the hunger in his children's eyes.

These men had crept across the front line to Taliban-held Taloqan. They had walked on foot, by night over the mountains, braving the landmines and the Taliban. Now, in their donkeys' panniers was cooking oil and Pepsi Cola to sell at the market in Nawabad. It was no way to make a living, but what could they do? 'Everybody who can scrape together their money or their courage has left Mawmaii,' he said.

We asked them if the girls were still there, but they didn't know. They had problems of their own. As we said goodbye, I was wondering whether the people we had come so far to find had already gone.

We found Fairuza, Amina and Fawzia exactly where we had left them. They were sitting in the yard where they had watched their mother die. They were afraid to leave it, in case there were soldiers lying in wait for them outside.

It was very hot. The sun glared off the mud floor, and rebounded from the high mud walls that rose protectively on three sides. The family's house sealed off the fourth side. This square of cracked, baked mud, this two-roomed house was their world.

The overpowering sense of suffering had gone. The yard seemed emptier. There were no longer chickens pecking in the earth, the goat that had been tethered to a post had disappeared, and even the tiny vegetable plot had withered and died. The house, too, seemed barer than I remembered. Last time there had been colourful cloths strewn over the floor; now there was nothing but the same tightly packed earth as the yard.

The family had become very poor because the girls were still frightened to be left alone. This meant that their father could not smuggle goods from Taloqan to earn money and so, little by little, they had sold everything they had. There were seven children to feed in all – as well as the three girls there were four younger brothers and sisters ranging in age from two to about seven.

The girls came silently into the house, and sat down in a huddle. They were shy with me. I looked at their faces, searching for some spark of connection. I thought that until we could find a way to communicate, I would not know how to set them free.

On the wall was a photograph. It must have been taken at some family celebration, back in the seventies – before the Soviets invaded, before Afghanistan's long calamity began. The men wore Western clothes and handlebar moustaches, the women were unveiled. They were all very young, and they looked light-hearted, in a way that I seldom saw any Afghans look today. I glanced from the girls shrouded in their scarves, to the hungry faces of the small children, to the mud yard with its empty post, and tried to fit them to the picture or the picture to them. But I could not.

Their father pointed at a woman in the photograph and said: 'That was my wife, the one who was killed, and this is me.' He caught my expression of surprise and added, 'I am not an old man, you know. I am only forty – the war has turned my beard white.'

The woman in the picture had a strong, even face, and she was looking the camera straight in the lens. Her gaze was cool and challenging. I could imagine her as the kind of person who might answer back to the Taliban.

When I looked at Fairuza, I thought I saw the same spirit burning inside her, subdued, but still alive. I asked her what she needed and, again, I heard that clear, melodic voice: 'We have lived through a war and a revolution. We just want our country to be at peace.' She looked sadly at her two sisters. 'Until then, we will continue to suffer in silence. We just suffer in silence.'

There was something remarkable about this child – something pure and strong. She hadn't given up fighting yet. If she had half a chance now, she could become anything – a teacher, an ambassador, anything. And then I knew how I could help them. I would find a way to get them into school.

Fairuza liked the idea. 'I know that people who go to school become learned and they do great things,' she said. Then she stopped and looked at me with the same cool directness I had glimpsed in her mother's photograph. 'But there isn't a school around here. Where could we go to study?'

John Weaver said that as long as Mawmaii was on the front line, which meant as long as Afghanistan was at war, no responsible aid agency would build a school there. But then he told us that, by extraordinary coincidence, he had just built a girls' school in Nawabad, only about forty minutes' drive from Mawmaii.

When we visited, the girls were arriving for class. They seethed through the gates in a colourful, shrieking flock. All of them were wearing the same bright scarves that Fairuza, Amina and Fawzia had pulled so brokenly around them — but these children were running and shouting and jostling each other, and their veils trailed behind them like dazzling plumes.

The senior teacher was a tall, middle-aged woman, who could never have been beautiful, but when she spoke about her girls, a fire lit up in her face. 'Most of the girls you see here are living in refugee camps,' she said. 'Their lives are very hard. For instance, when the weather is cold, they have to mix mud and water to protect their tents from the rain. They are just little girls, their hands are very small. They are too young for this work.'

She showed us how the girls sat on the concrete floor, four or five of them sharing a textbook. In one classroom, the text was Jalaluddin Rumi's *Masnavi*, and I stopped to listen to the beautiful Persian language of a fable I, too, had heard as a child.

A merchant kept a parrot in a cage. One day, he asked if he could bring it back a gift from India, its homeland. 'Please could you just visit my relatives in the jungle, and tell them that I am imprisoned here,' said the parrot. But when the man came back after his journey, he said: 'I'm afraid I have bad news. I stood in the jungle, and shouted to the parrots there that you were living in a cage. One of your relatives – the shock must have killed him – came tumbling down from his tree and fell at my feet.' As soon as he heard these words, the merchant's parrot fell, quite rigid, to the floor of his cage. Sorrowfully, the man picked up his dead pet, and placed it on the window-sill. As soon as it was free, the parrot recovered, and flew away.

My heart went out to Amina, Fairuza and Fawzia, prisoners in their own cage in Mawmaii. Then the head teacher began to talk in a way I had never heard any woman in Afghanistan speak before: 'The girls in my class dream of becoming doctors or engineers or even journalists. I teach them that when they grow up they must try to bring about change in this under-developed country of ours where women have no role. Afghan women are courageous – they cannot be beaten, whatever the odds. We are optimistic and hopeful for the future.'

The school was built around a central courtyard, and from here the air was filled with the cacophony of the lessons that the girls were bellowing out from every classroom. I stood there for a long time, with my eyes closed. The dusty courtyard faded away and I imagined that I was standing in a cool, dark jungle, where thousands and thousands of coloured birds were swooping, singing and chattering for joy.

21

Years ago, during the eighties, I travelled with a group of German aid workers who had heard about an out-break of cholera in some inaccessible part of northern Afghanistan.

They loaded the life-saving vaccines on to camels, and we rode on horseback all the way so that we would get there faster. Even though we were on a mission of life or death, the journey was idyllic. My mare had a foal who was too young to be left behind, so it trotted beside us all the way. It was springtime, and streams gushed from the side of every mountain, while newly born kids played on the slopes. I thought that, if there could only be peace, this would be a perfect country for tourism. I wanted to stop and rest by a waterfall – it was so beautiful, and the foal was exhausted with trying to keep up – but the Germans reminded me sternly that every second was precious. Once the infec-tion spread, it would devastate whole communities. There was no time to linger beside waterfalls.

The aid workers were not enjoying the journey. They kept themselves going on slices of *wurst* they had brought, and complained about the vagueness of our guides. We had been told that our destination was a week's ride away but, as usual, that information was hopelessly misleading. It was at least ten days before we limped into the village where the outbreak had been reported.

The villagers greeted us with rapturous surprise. Everyone was fine. There had never been an epidemic – it was just one of those Afghan rumours. The Germans didn't want to stay the night so we packed up our vaccines, got on to our horses and went home.

Now, more than a decade later, the US and its allies wanted to sort out Afghanistan. They had defined a problem, and now they were setting out to solve it, on their own terms. Every day, American jets roared overhead, ready to seek out Osama bin Laden and get rid of the Taliban. Every night, their planes dropped humanitarian supplies to the Afghan people.

In a way, I was similar: I had given myself a personal mission and I wanted to finish it as quickly as possible.

Through all the excitement of the humanitarian air-drops and the build-up to a ground war, John Weaver had been stoically continuing his own relief efforts. I couldn't help suspecting that, had he been on the ill-fated cholera expedition with us, he would have taken time to linger by the odd waterfall – or at least to stay on in the village for a while.

However, when I woke up one morning, I found John in a fury, shouting into his radio in Dari. The day before, hundreds of bottles of cooking-oil had turned up, with urgent instructions to distribute four months' supply to the neediest families. But when John had looked at the bottles, he saw that the oil was due to expire in just a month's time.

The anonymous person at the other end of the line

must have been suggesting that he distribute it anyway – they were just refugees, after all – because John became incandescent with fury, and shouted: 'I can't do that. The expiry date has already been extended once. The oil is right at the end of its shelf life. What if – God forbid – someone should get sick? How could any of us live with that?' But when he put down the radio, I could see from his expression that he wasn't going to let that oil go to waste. For the poorest families, a drop of oil might make the difference between surviving or dying this winter.

So, he made a plan. He decided to give out just a month's supply of oil to a much larger number of families than he had originally intended. He knew that the very poorest families would use it at once because they had nothing else. His scheme was ambitious. The people had no ration cards, and he had to find a way of stopping families getting hold of extra bottles of oil and hoarding them.

At dawn the next day, heading towards the field where the oil was to be handed out, we saw a great white cloud – a moving sea – of dust. Widows in billowing *burqas* were gusting through it like sailing boats before the wind; old men were lashing their donkeys through it; barefoot small boys were racing through it; little girls were towing even smaller children through it. Hundreds – perhaps thousands – of people were already waiting for us, and more and more were arriving every second.

Overnight, John had sent messengers to the camps of displaced people and to selected villages. He had obtained lists of the poorest families, but everyone for miles around, without exception, had turned up.

Just looking at this immense crowd exhausted me. Surely John had set himself a hopeless task. We climbed up on to the back of the lorry loaded with oil. Even at this height the dust rose, engulfing us. John began to read names out from a list. Every name he called provoked a riot. Scuffles broke out as each of several candidates claimed to be the lucky person. All the while, others in the crowd hopefully shouted out their own names, while others still tried to guess the answers to John's security questions.

'What is your father's name?'

'Abdullah!'

'No.'

Then another man would step forward. 'Noor.'

'No,' and so on.

Through all of this, John had the patience of a saint. With his golden beard and blue eyes, he stood in the midst of the multitude, whipping up a commonplace miracle.

The refugees told us that last night there had been another US airdrop. The aid landed on the empty mountainside, where one lucky man was out hunting. He loaded more than two hundred packages on to his donkey, and now he had hidden them somewhere.

John tried to be diplomatic about the airdrops, but it was clear that he was frustrated to see all this bounty dropping straight into the arms of soldiers and entrepreneurs while he struggled to make sure that a few bottles of nearly out-of-date cooking-oil got to the people who needed it most. 'If they gave the aid to me, I'm sure I could distribute it better, and more cheaply,' he said.

In the midst of the mayhem, one of the refugees recognized me. I must have chatted to him when I was here six months ago, and he had remembered my name and my family background all this time. He told everyone about me, and soon the children were shouting, 'Saira! Saira!' and I had a huge crowd all of my own.

'Your father is from Paghman?' cried the refugees. 'But you are our compatriot! Where is your mother from? What is your father's name? But this is an Afghan name!'

At first I demurred – I explained that I was only half an Afghan, but they were quite adamant: 'No, no. Your father is from Paghman. That makes you a full Afghan. You are from our country.' They were genuinely over-joyed and proud to see an Afghan woman standing there on top of the lorry, handing out aid. My eyes blurred with tears. When at last they quietened down, James said mischievously: 'But she is from Paghman.'

'Paghman!' cried the refugees anew. 'But that is in Afghanistan! She is an Afghan!' And the whole thing started again.

We didn't stay long at John's food distribution because I wanted to arrive early in Mawmaii. I didn't know whether the girls would prefer to commute to school every day or move to Nawabad, but I was sure that if necessary we could pack up the family's few belongings, and get them on the raft over the Koksha that same day.

We strode confidently through the dust of Mawmaii. The girls' father had told me he wanted his daughters to attend school, but he had not believed that we would be able to make it happen. We smiled covertly at each other when we thought of the dramatic trans- formation we were about to bring about in the lives of this one family.

I couldn't contain my excitement as I told the girls' father about the school in Nawabad. But instead of being overjoyed, he looked confused and worried. 'I have been to Nawabad once before,' he said. 'It is another country.'

All at once, I began to see that a town which was a mere half-hour away to me was for him a strange and frightening world. He could not be expected to make the journey every day. He did not have access to a vehicle and, even if we gave him one, the soldiers would take it. Besides, he could not drive. There were all sorts of other difficulties I hadn't even considered. 'The girls are in *purdah* – how will they be able to go on the raft with men?' he asked.

I told him that the television company we worked for would pay transport, living costs and rental of a second house in Nawabad. He could come back to Mawmaii whenever he liked. The old man shook his head. If they left their house, even for a few days, they risked losing it. It would be looted or destroyed, like the other abandoned houses in the village. At the thought of that, he looked lost again, as he had been when I first saw him.

'I cannot leave my *qom* – my people. They are all

here in the village. In the winter, if we need firewood, we can always rely on someone to help us. In Nawabad, we will be strangers for the rest of our lives.'

He looked around the mud-walled house, trying to find a way to explain it to me. 'We built this house with our own hands,' he said. 'We brought water in buckets, all the way from the river. This is where we belong.'

I didn't know what to say to him because, for all his lack of education, the father of these girls at least knew the dangers of leaving the place where you belong.

Back in England, my own father had spent fruitless hours trying to pick up Kabul on his shortwave radio. Sometimes the faint melody of Dari Persian floated across uncharted miles. These were occasions for great rejoicing. We children were summoned: 'Listen well! This is your language!'

And we would all cluster reverently around the oversized radio, straining our ears to catch the ethereal murmurings of a language we could not speak.

I felt as if I was listening to coded messages of huge importance, but somebody had forgotten to give me the key.

After a while I despaired of getting the old man to leave Mawmaii, so I concentrated on extricating his daughters. Soon I had come up with a new plan: I suggested that we find a respectable woman to take care of them – perhaps the senior teacher. They could stay in Nawabad during the school week, and return to their father at the weekends.

The more I enthused, the more bewilderment and

suspicion I read in his eyes. We began a circular discussion, with the old man thwarting my logic at every turn. Perhaps he thought it was odd that I was taking so much interest in his daughters. Whatever his motives, he found an objection to every proposal I put forward, until it gradually became clear that he was not prepared to let the girls go to school at all.

Usman said: 'The problem is that he himself is not educated – it may be that he is making difficulties because he does not want his girls to receive more schooling than him.'

Finally, the old man said that, with his wife dead, he needed his girls to do the housework and to look after the younger children. What he really wanted, he said, was a wife to replace the one he had lost. If we gave him the money to buy a wife, then maybe – just maybe – he would consider letting the girls go to school.

We telephoned our production company. It wasn't the money they cared about – we had *carte blanche* to rehouse the family, hire a teacher or to build a school – but they told us that it was out of the question to go around buying wives.

Two people live inside me, and at that moment I realized that possibly they never will be reconciled. I admire my ancestor, Jan Fishan Khan, for taking the Red Fort, but I still quibble about the loss of his sons. I love the secret radio voices, but I never understand what they are saying. I had failed. Afghanistan had confounded me, just as it has always confounded the West.

We walked slowly back to the Koksha river. In our path, a small girl, no older than three or four, was clutching a yellow plastic sack, labelled: 'Humanitarian Rations – gift of the people of the USA'. It had obviously been dropped from a plane. I was consumed with curiosity to know whether the stories about the Americans dropping Pop-tarts and peanut butter were true. Suddenly – more than anything else in the world – I had to find out what was inside that bag. But when I put my hand out to take a peek inside, the child clung to her trophy with all her puny might.

I was in no mood to be thwarted. It would be easy enough, I thought, to take the bag by force. For a moment, the pair of us stood locked in an unequal tug-of-war. It must have looked ridiculous – an adult, dressed in the Western uniform of cold-weather fleece, Gore-Tex boots and specialized mountain gear – pitted against a tiny child clad in rags. Neither of us would give way. Laughing, a couple of soldiers passing by prised off her little fingers.

When I opened the bag, I saw that the rations had long since disappeared – her parents had bought the empty container in the market, and she was using it to collect fuel. It was full of goats' dung.

By the riverbank a tall lunatic cavorted and mocked us as we got back on to the raft. It seemed a fitting farewell from the people of Mawmaii.

When we reached Nawabad, John had just returned from his oil distribution. He was covered in dust and grime, and he looked exhausted. But I could see from the glow in his eyes that he had done it – he had made sure that every bottle of oil had got safely into the right pair of hands.

I told him how the old man had refused our help – how he had turned down a house, insisted he needed the girls to do the housework, and had even demanded that we buy him a wife. I expected him to be as indignant as I. But he just said, in his slow way: 'If their father remarried, I guess those children would have a mom. It seems to me that what that old man probably needs is a wife.'

It was our last evening. Usman invited us to a proper Western dinner party. He wanted everything to be perfect. To underline his sophistication, he told us not to arrive until half past six in the evening – just as we would in the West.

Noor, our driver, was appalled. 'I cannot drive so late at night – my doctor forbids it,' he said.

But we didn't want to let Usman down. Noor drove with reckless temper; the Datsun's wheels threw up great cascades of dust. In the headlights, it looked like flurries of snow.

A soldier at a roadblock stopped us. 'But it is already dark,' he said incredulously. 'It is the time for sleeping. Your friend will be in bed.'

When we arrived, Usman's house was indeed locked up. An old man wiped the sleep from his eyes as he opened the gate. There had been an emergency: Usman had rushed out to fetch a doctor for a sick relative. We should wait in his guest room. With a sideways look of triumph, Noor followed us inside, lay down on a pile of cushions, and fell asleep.

We waited for an hour. Just as we were leaving,

Usman arrived home, exhausted. He was surprised but overjoyed to find us still there. After some scrabbling in a tin trunk, he produced a pirated cassette tape of Western music. To create just the right atmosphere, he fiddled with the hurricane lamp. For some moments he turned it up and down, experimenting. His eyes met mine, and I saw a brief flicker of uncertainty; then, with the air of a man not prepared to spoil the ship for a ha'porth of tar, he turned down the lamp as low as it would go.

For the next half-hour, we sat in darkness, listening to Pakistani renderings of Ibiza house music. Conversation was stilted: James and I were wondering how soon we could decently leave; Usman looked like a man watching his dreams ebb away.

His wife brought us supper. She stood shyly outside the door and handed Usman the dishes without being seen. He leaped up and went outside. I got the impression that, to salvage the evening, he was asking her to break the rules of *purdah* and join us. Five minutes later, he came back in alone.

Then, almost as if he was justifying something, he began to tell us how he fell in love: 'My wife's father opposed the match. We weren't allowed to speak to each other, so we secretly wrote letters. Her little sister delivered them. For two whole years, we had an entire relationship in letters. We did everything that normal couples do. We had no secrets. We discussed all sorts of things. Sometimes we even had fights. After we had argued, we would make up and send each other kisses.

'One day my mother said to me: "You must understand that her father will never let you marry her." I was so unhappy, I wept for a week. My parents sent me away to Tajikistan, but I became ill from thinking about her, wondering if she would get engaged to somebody else. I knew that if I couldn't marry her, I would die.

'When I returned home, I persuaded her to see me in secret. We went for a picnic in the meadow. But this is Afghanistan. A shepherd saw us alone together and assumed that I was abducting her. He went home and fetched his gun, and then he pointed it at me, saying: "Who are you and who is this woman?"

'I pointed my gun back at him and I said: "This is my girlfriend."

'"Your girlfriend? Are you a Communist? I'll shoot you for that."

'So there we stood, in the middle of the field, pointing our guns at each other. Neither of us wanted to be the first to put his weapon down.

'Then suddenly it felt as though a lamp had been lighted in my head. I threw down my gun, and said: "Shoot me if you like – you will be doing me a favour, because if I cannot marry this woman then I prefer to die. Love is not just something to speak about: it is something that changes you for ever. I am a lover, and so I am willing to sacrifice everything."'

I had never heard Usman speak like this before, and now I saw that just talking about love had transformed him. In the minuscule light of the hurricane lamp, his face had lost its brash expression: it was animated and soft. I glanced across at the still-sleeping Noor. In

303

repose, all his toughness, too, had melted away. Curled up peacefully on the floor, he looked like a Summer of Love hippie. I had been so focused on saving the three girls, I hadn't spared a thought for these macho men. Now I wondered who really lay under their tough exteriors; what lives they might have chosen for themselves, if they had had the chance to live without war.

Usman seemed to feel that the evening was recovering. He fumbled in his trunk and produced a precious treasure: a bottle of whisky, smuggled from Tajikistan. Then, while his mind was still on love, he told me a story.

Once upon a time there was a woman who had three suitors. Before she could choose between them, she fell ill and died. One of the young men wandered the world, vowing to find a way to bring her back to life. The second spent his time comforting her aged father. The last threw himself on her grave and refused to budge.

It so happened that the wandering suitor rescued a wise man who had fallen down a well. The sage knew how to make an ointment that could bring the dead to life. However, he required the root of a particular tree, which was guarded by a ferocious monster. The young man vanquished the monster and got hold of the root; the ointment was prepared. When it was rubbed on to the woman's corpse, she was restored to life.

All the suitors began to pester the lady for her hand.

'I was a comfort to your father in his sorrow,' said the first young man.

'I lay by your grave, pining away with love,' said the second.

'But it was I who found the ointment that saved you,' said the third.

The woman said: 'The suitor who looked after my father was a son for him. The one who found the ointment is a humanitarian. But the man who lay weeping upon my grave after all hope had died, he is the one who behaved like a lover and I shall marry none but him.'

Early the next morning, we left Afghanistan. Usman came to see us off. Neither James nor I spoke on the brief, dusty journey to the northern border: we felt as choked and defeated as the broken road that lay ahead.

At the ramshackle border post, the officer glanced at my passport, then looked at it again, and said: 'But that is an Afghan name. Are you from Afghanistan?' I told him that my father came from Paghman, and then, to stop him launching into the usual rapturous cascade of greetings, I added severely: 'But *I* am from Britain. *I* am from the West.'

James, Usman and I stood awkwardly together beside the river Oxus. James was watching the metal pontoon make its leisurely way towards us; Usman was gazing yearningly across the water at the bright lights of Tajikistan on the other side.

My own thoughts were bitter. I remembered how, all through my childhood, a flag hung on my bedroom wall. Not the current Afghan one, but the old royalist standard, the emblem of a state that no longer exists. It was drenched in symbolism: black, for the family of the Prophet; red, for the blood of our martyrs; green, for

Islam. If only I had stopped to ask myself where *my* Afghanistan – the place I had crossed two continents to find – really was, I could have saved a lot of bother by pointing at that flag.

As for the real Afghanistan, I had assumed that I could give to and take from it on my own terms, that I could choose whom to save and how best to do it. I hadn't even managed to get three girls into school. Love, Usman had said, means continuing to care after hope has gone. I had failed as a humanitarian. Was I strong enough to learn how to be a lover?

I stepped on to the pontoon, guiltily glad to be leaving Afghanistan. A stretch of muddy brown water opened up between me and the shore.

Then, as I watched the distance between me and my homeland growing ever wider, the voice of the border official came wafting confidently from the bank I had just left: 'She may look like a *feranghee*, a foreigner, but her father is from Paghman and her mother is from . . . Indonesia. *Az khude ma hast*. She is one of us. She is an Afghan.'

Epilogue: The Tree of Knowledge

I am the slave of whoever will not at each stage imagine
   his journey is ended.
Many a caravanserai must be left behind before the
   traveller reaches his destination.

Masnavi, Jalaluddin Rumi

The other day, I went to visit my aunt Amina in London. She is over eighty now and still in fine form. We watched the celebrations in Kabul, where the Taliban had finally been ousted. The television commentator was saying triumphantly: 'It is over. Afghanistan's nightmare is finally over . . .' And, once again, the streets of the capital were full of joyful people. Through all the false endings and bitter disappointments, hope had survived deep in their hearts to burst forth again like the miracle of spring. Now they needed a miracle from the West in return. To repair the irreparable would take more than humanitarian goodwill: it would require the patience of a lover.

Amina and I hardly dared to hope that Afghanistan's misery might be drawing to a close so, instead, we began to talk about the old days. Soon we were roaring with laughter as we remembered how she had routed

Auntie Soraya, and had saved me from marrying my distant cousin, Jimmy, all those years ago. Of course, said Amina, her own experience of escaping arranged marriages had helped. As usual, before long, she had begun telling even older stories, delving into the vast storehouse of thoughts and experiences collected over thousands of years by many generations of my family.

Once upon a time there was a powerful king, who had a beautiful wife, a peaceful kingdom and riches beyond compare. He thought he had everything, until he heard that in faraway India there was a tree of such wonderful virtue that anyone who ate of its fruit would live for ever. The king became obsessed with this fruit. He sent his most trusted courtier on a quest to find it.

This faithful servant searched high and low for the magical fruit. Some people said they had never heard of it, others mocked him, yet others sent him in the wrong direction.

After twenty years, the man no longer believed that there was any such tree. He decided that it was his duty to go and tell this to the king and face his wrath. Before he returned home, he visited an ancient sage, to ask for a blessing.

When the old man heard the courtier's story, he began to laugh. He laughed, and he laughed and he laughed, until tears streamed down his wrinkled cheeks. When he could speak, he said: 'Oh, my poor friend! You will never find the fruit of a literal tree. What you seek is sometimes called a tree, sometimes a sun, sometimes a lake and sometimes a cloud. It is one — although it has thousands of forms. Pass over form and look for qualities. The tree you have been seeking is the tree of knowledge, its fruit is wisdom – and the least of its forms is eternal life.'

This story is from Jalaluddin Rumi's *Masnavi* and, when my father first told it to me many years ago, he added: 'Stories are like a tree growing on the horizon. March towards the tree, and it will keep you in a straight line. But the tree itself is not your goal. When you reach it, you have to let it go, and pick another point further on.'

I never found the mythical Afghanistan I spent so many years chasing, but the journey has taken me to places I could never have imagined when I started out. And, at last, I have learned the true value of my father's bequest. I carry his stories in my heart; if I listen for them, they are with me wherever I go.